Advanced Criminal Litigation in Practice

Advanced Criminal Litigation in Practice

Inns of Court School of Law

Institute of Law, City University, London

OXFORD

UNIVERSITY PRESS

OXFORD
UNIVERSITY PRESS

Great Clarendon Street, Oxford OX2 6DP

Oxford University Press is a department of the University of Oxford.
It furthers the University's objective of excellence in research, scholarship,
and education by publishing worldwide in

Oxford New York

Auckland Cape Town Dar es Salaam Hong Kong Karachi
Kuala Lumpur Madrid Melbourne Mexico City Nairobi
New Delhi Shanghai Taipei Toronto

With offices in

Argentina Austria Brazil Chile Czech Republic France Greece
Guatemala Hungary Italy Japan Poland Portugal Singapore
South Korea Switzerland Thailand Turkey Ukraine Vietnam

Oxford is a registered trade mark of Oxford University Press
in the UK and in certain other countries

Published in the United States
by Oxford University Press Inc., New York

British Library Cataloguing in Publication Data
Data available

Library of Congress Cataloging in Publication Data
Data available

Typeset by Newgen Imaging Systems (P) Ltd., Chennai, India
Printed in Great Britain
on acid-free paper by
Antony Rowe Ltd, Chippenham, Wiltshire

ISBN 0-19-928486-5 978-0-19-928486-3

1 3 5 7 9 10 8 6 4 2

6230731

FOREWORD

It is a privilege to write this Foreword, following the tradition set by my predecessor, the Hon. Mr Justice Elias.

The Bar Vocational Course (BVC) bridges the gap between completion of a university degree and the start of a professional working life, whether by way of pupillage preliminary to a career at the Bar, or otherwise. These Manuals are geared to the practical and professional approach that is central to the BVC. Updated and revised, the Manuals form an integral part of the student's vocational training; as such, they are an important ingredient in the constant drive to raise standards in the public interest.

The Manuals are written by staff at the Inns of Court School of Law (ICSL). The range and coverage of the Manuals have grown steadily. They are intended to provide a useful resource for all concerned in the training of legal skills, hopefully at whichever validated institution such training takes place.

Legal vocational training does not stand still; the ICSL and authors would welcome feedback from any source, which may assist to improve the Manuals in the future. Any such comments should be addressed to the BVC Course Director at the ICSL.

Finally a word of thanks is appropriate to the publishers for their enthusiasm and efficiency in arranging production and publication of the Manuals.

The Hon. Mr Justice Gross
Chairman, Advisory Board of the Institute of Law
City University, London
October 2005

OUTLINE CONTENTS

Foreword		v
Table of cases		xii
Table of statutes		xv

PART I	**Evidence and procedure**	**1**
	1 Introduction	3
	2 Sources for further study and preparation of cases	5
	3 Entry, search and seizure	8
	4 Abuse of process	21
	5 European Convention on Human Rights	27

PART II	**Substantive law**	**37**
	6 Dangerous drugs	39
	7 Public order offences	58
	8 Offensive weapons	78
	9 Road traffic offences: general	82
	10 Drink driving offences	92
	11 Road traffic offences: penalties	103

PART III	**A case to prepare**	**113**
	12 Introduction to the sample brief	115
	13 *R v Spring, Hanson and others*	119
	14 Sample advice in *R v Spring, Hanson and others*	164

Index		169

DETAILED CONTENTS

Foreword	v
Table of cases	xii
Table of statutes	xv

PART I	**Evidence and procedure**	**1**

1	**Introduction**	3

2	**Sources for further study and preparation of cases**	5
2.1	This Manual	5
2.2	Primary sources	5
2.3	Practitioner works	6
2.4	Periodicals	6

3	**Entry, search and seizure**	8
3.1	Introduction	8
3.2	Powers of search exercisable without a warrant	8
3.3	Powers of search with a warrant	10
3.4	Search warrants — general rules and restrictions	13
3.5	Seizure	18
3.6	Evidential consequences of breach of rules on search and seizure	20
3.7	Further reading	20

4	**Abuse of process**	21
4.1	Abuse of process	21
4.2	Procedural issues	25
4.3	Further reading	26

5	**European Convention on Human Rights**	27
5.1	The status of the ECHR in UK law	27
5.2	The rights contained in the ECHR	28
5.3	Procedure under the ECHR	32
5.4	The approach of the European Court of Human Rights	33
5.5	Reporting of ECHR cases	34
5.6	Further reading	34

PART II	**Substantive law**	**37**

6	**Dangerous drugs**	39
6.1	'Controlled drugs'	39
6.2	The offences	39
6.3	Statutory defences	44

6.4   Occupiers of premises   45
6.5   Permitted uses of controlled drugs   46
6.6   Enforcement   46
6.7   Confiscation orders under the Proceeds of Crime Act 2002   48
6.8   Further reading   57

7   **Public order offences**   **58**

7.1   Introduction   58
7.2   Riot   58
7.3   Violent disorder   59
7.4   Affray   59
7.5   Fear or provocation of violence   60
7.6   Harassment, alarm or distress   61
7.7   Racially or religiously aggravated public order offences   62
7.8   Offences of stirring up racial hatred   63
7.9   Football and sporting offences   66
7.10 Offences relating to public processions and assemblies   67
7.11 Bomb hoaxes   69
7.12 Offences in relation to collective trespass or nuisance on land   69
7.13 Harassment   74
7.14 Harassment alarm or distress of a person in a dwelling   75
7.15 Trespassing on a designated site   76
7.16 Demonstrating without authorisation in a designated area   77
7.17 Further reading   77

8   **Offensive weapons**   **78**

8.1   Introduction   78
8.2   Prevention of Crime Act 1953   78
8.3   Criminal Justice Act 1988   80
8.4   Other offences   81

9   **Road traffic offences: general**   **82**

9.1   Introduction   82
9.2   Dangerous driving   82
9.3   Careless driving   88
9.4   Failing to stop/failing to report   91

10   **Drink driving offences**   **92**

10.1 Introduction   92
10.2 Prescribed limits and specimen tests   92
10.3 Driving, attempting to drive or being in charge of a vehicle when unfit   93
10.4 Driving or being in charge above the prescribed limit   94
10.5 Failure to provide a specimen   96
10.6 Causing death by careless driving when under the influence of drink or drugs   101
10.7 Cycling when under the influence of drink or drugs   102
10.8 Procedure and sentence   102

11   **Road traffic offences: penalties**   **103**

11.1 Introduction   103
11.2 Endorsement   103
11.3 Disqualification   109
11.4 Special reasons   111

PART III   **A case to prepare**   **113**

12   **Introduction to the sample brief**   **115**

12.1 Advice on evidence   115

12.2 Preparing for conference   116
12.3 Preparing for trial   117
12.4 The papers in *R v Nicholas Spring, John Hanson and others*   118

13 *R v Spring, Hanson and others*   119

14 Sample advice in *R v Spring, Hanson and others*   164

Index   169

TABLE OF CASES

Afzal [1993] Crim LR 791 . . . 60
Afzal and Arshad *The Times*, 25 June 1991 . . . 47
Aitken v Lees 1994 SLT 182 . . . 83
Aldershot Youth Court, *ex p* A [1997] 3 Archbold News 2 . . . 25
Allamby [1974] 1 WLR 1494 . . . 79
Aramah (1982) 76 Cr App R 190 . . . 46
Aranguren and others (1994) 99 Cr App R 347 . . . 47
Arrowsmith v UK 3 EHRR 218 . . . 31
Artico v Italy [1980] 3 EHRR 1 . . . 34
Attorney-General's Reference (No 1 of 1975) [1975] QB 773 . . . 96
Attorney-General's Reference (No 1 of 1990) [1992] QB 630 . . . 21
Attorney-General's Reference (No 2 of 2001) [2001] 1 WLR 1869 . . . 22
Attorney-General's Reference (No 3 of 2000) [2002] 1 Cr App R 29 . . . 23

Badham [1987] Crim LR 202 . . . 9
Ball (1990) 90 Cr App R 378 . . . 62
Bates v Bulman [1979] 1 WLR 1190 . . . 78
Beckford [1996] 1 Cr App R 96 . . . 21
Benjafield [2002] 1 All ER 801 . . . 53
Bentley v Dickinson [1983] RTR 356 . . . 85
Best (1979) 70 Cr App R 21 . . . 39
Bett [1999] 1 All ER 600 . . . 45
Bilinski (1987) 86 Cr App R 146 . . . 46, 47
Blake (1978) 68 Cr App R 1 . . . 41
Bloomfield [1997] 1 Cr App R 135 . . . 22, 23
Boner v UK 19 EHRR 246 . . . 31
Bowers (1994) 15 Cr App R (S) 315 . . . 48
Bowman v Fels [2005] EWCA Civ 226 . . . 56
Boyesen [1982] 2 All ER 161 . . . 42
Bradford v Wilson [1993] Crim LR 482 . . . 92
Brannigan and McBride v UK, Series A, vol. 258-B . . . 29
Bristol Crown Court, *ex p* Jones [1986] RTR 259 . . . 90
Browne (1984) 6 Cr App R (S) 5 . . . 69
Butty v Davey [1972] RTR 75 . . . 90

Canterbury and St Augustine Justices, *ex p* Klisiak [1982] QB 398 . . . 24
Chamberlain, *The Independent*, 19 May 1997 . . . 47
Chambers and Edwards v DPP [1995] Crim LR 896 . . . 62
Chappell v DPP (1989) 89 Cr App R 82 . . . 62
Charles (1989) 11 Cr App R (S) 125 . . . 60

Chatters v Burke [1986] 1 WLR 1321 . . . 111
Chatwood [1980] 1 WLR 874 . . . 39
Chief Constable of Avon and Somerset v Singh [1988] RTR 107 . . . 99
Chief Constable of Gwent v Dash [1986] RTR 41 . . . 97
Connelly [1992] Crim LR 296 . . . 41
Cooksley [2004] 1 Cr App R (S) 1 . . . 87
Copus v DPP [1989] Crim LR 577 . . . 79
Cosgrove v DPP *The Times*, 29 March 1996 . . . 99
Crown Court at Southwark, *ex p* Bowles [1998] 2 All ER 193 . . . 17
Crowther v UK (App No 53741/00) *The Times*, 11 February 2005 . . . 55
Cuthbertson [1980] 2 All ER 401 . . . 48

D [2000] 1 Archbold News 1 . . . 23
Daniels v DPP [1992] RTR 140 . . . 99
Davies [1962] 3 All ER 97 . . . 94
Davis [1998] Crim LR 564 . . . 80
Davison [1992] Crim LR 31 . . . 60
Deegan [1998] 2 Cr App R 121 . . . 80
DeFreitas v DPP [1993] RTR 98 . . . 99
Dempsey (1985) 82 Cr App R 291 . . . 40, 45
Densu [1998] 1 Cr App R 400 . . . 79
Dhillon [2000] Crim LR 760 . . . 41
Dixon [1993] Crim LR 579 . . . 60
DPP v Baillie [1995] Crim LR 426 . . . 68
DPP v Clarke (1992) 94 Cr App R 359 . . . 62
DPP v Cotcher [1993] COD 181 . . . 60
DPP v Coyle *The Times*, 20 July 1995 . . . 99
DPP v Fountain [1988] Crim LR 123 . . . 99
DPP v Godwin [1991] RTR 303 . . . 97
DPP v H [1998] RTR 200 . . . 95
DPP v Humphrys [1977] AC 1 . . . 21
DPP v Hynde [1998] 1 WLR 1222 . . . 79
DPP v Jackson; Stanley v DPP [1998] 3 All ER 769 . . . 98
DPP v Jones [1999] 2 WLR 625 . . . 72
DPP v Kay [1999] RTR 109 . . . 92
DPP v O'Connor [1992] RTR 66 . . . 111
DPP v Orum [1989] 1 WLR 88 . . . 62
DPP v Pidhajeckvj [1991] RTR 136 . . . 85
DPP v Ramos [2000] Crim LR 768 . . . 61
DPP v Spurrier [2000] RTR 60 . . . 93
DPP v Stoke-on-Trent Magistrates' Court [2003] 3 All ER 1096 . . . 66
DPP v Varley [1999] Crim LR 753 . . . 99
DPP v Warren [1993] RTR 58 . . . 98

DPP v Watkins [1989] QB 821 . . . 94
DPP v Williams [1989] Crim LR 382 . . . 95
Dunbar (1987) 9 Cr App R (S) 393 . . . 69

Edwards v UK (2003) 15 BHRC 189 . . . 30
Emmanuel [1998] Crim LR 347 . . . 80
Epping Justices, *ex p* Quy [1998] RTR 158 . . . 98
Evans v Hughes (1972) 56 Cr App R 813 . . . 80

Fleming (1989) 153 JP 517 . . . 59

Gay News and Lemon v UK 5 EHRR 123 . . . 31
Gibson v Dalton [1980] RTR 410 . . . 84
Gibson v Wales [1983] 1 WLR 393 . . . 79
Gill (1993) 97 Cr App R 215 . . . 41
Gleaves v Insall [1999] 2 Cr App R 466 . . . 24
Glidewell (1999) 163 JP 557 . . . 78
Gordon [1995] 2 Cr App R 61 . . . 43
Gough and Smith v Chief Constable of Derbyshire
    [2002] 2 All ER 985 . . . 67
Granger v UK 12 EHRR 451 . . . 31
Grant [1996] 1 Cr App R 73 . . . 43
Greenock Ltd v UK (1985) 42 D & R 33 . . . 33
Gregory v UK (1997) 25 EHRR 577 . . . 30
Groom v DPP [1991] Crim LR 713 . . . 62
Guilfoyle [1973] 2 All ER 844 . . . 111
Gumbley v Cunningham [1988] QB 170 . . . 95

Haggard v Mason [1976] 1 WLR 187 . . . 41
Harding [1974] RTR 325 . . . 99
Harris v DPP (1992) 96 Cr App R 235 . . . 80
Hill (1993) 96 Cr App R 456 . . . 39
Hodder v DPP [1989] Crim LR 261 . . . 39
Hodges [2003] 2 Cr App R 15 . . . 42
Horseferry Road Magistrates' Court, *ex p* Bennett
    [1994] 1 AC 42 . . . 25
Horseferry Road Magistrates' Court, *ex p* DPP [1999] COD
    441 . . . 23
Horseferry Road Metropolitan Stipendiary Magistrate,
    ex p Siadatan [1991] 1 QB 260 . . . 60
Houghton v Chief Constable of Greater Manchester
    (1986) 84 Cr App R 319 . . . 79
Howell [1982] QB 416 . . . 9
Howells [2003] 1 Cr App R (S) 61 . . . 88
Hughes (1985) 81 Cr App R 344 . . . 41
Hunt [1987] AC 352 . . . 39
Hurley [1998] 1 Cr App R (S) 299 . . . 47
Hussain *The Times*, 27 June 1990 . . . 47

I and others v DPP [2001] 2 WLR 765 . . . 60
Ireland v United Kingdom (Judgment of 18 January 1978,
    Series A, No 25, p90); (1978) 2 EHRR 25 . . . 33

Jefferson, Skerritt, Keogh and Readman [1994] 1 All
    ER 270 . . . 58
Jeffrey v Black [1978] QB 490 . . . 20

Jeffries [1997] Crim LR 819 . . . 44
Johnson v Finbow [1983] 1 WLR 879 . . . 104
Jura [1954] 1 QB 503 . . . 78

Kelly [2001] 2 Cr App R (S) 341 . . . 62
Kelly v UK (1985) 42 D & R 205 . . . 33
Kennedy v DPP [2002] All ER (D) 77 . . . 99
Khan, Sakkaravej and Pamarapa [1997] Crim LR 508 . . . 20
Kjeldsen, Busk, Madsen and Pedersen (Judgment of 7
    December 1976, Series A, No 23, p27) . . . 34
Kouadio *The Times*, 21 February 1991 . . . 47
Kwasi Poku v DPP [1993] Crim LR 705 . . . 62

L v DPP [2003] QB 137 . . . 80
Lambert [2002] 2 AC 545 . . . 41, 42, 45, 80
Laskey v UK (1997) 24 EHRR 39 . . . 31
Leeson [2000] 1 Cr App R 233 . . . 45
Leethams v DPP (1999) RTR 29 . . . 94
Loade v DPP [1990] 1 QB 1052 . . . 60
Lodge v DPP *The Times*, 26 October 1988 . . . 62
Lodwick v Jones [1983] RTR 273 . . . 90
Losseley: Attorney-General's Reference (No 3 of 2000)
    [2002] 1 Cr App R 29 . . . 23
Luke [1999] 1 Cr App R (S) 389 . . . 46

M *The Times*, 1 March 1994 . . . 47
McCalla (1988) 87 Cr App R 372 . . . 78
McDonagh [1974] QB 48 . . . 94
McGowan [1990] Crim LR 399 . . . 45
McGuigan [1991] Crim LR 719 . . . 59
McNamara (1988) 87 Cr App R 246 . . . 42
Maginnis [1987] 1 All ER 907 . . . 40
Mahroof (1989) 88 Cr App R 317 . . . 59
Malnik v DPP [1989] Crim LR 451 . . . 80
Manning [1998] Crim LR 198 . . . 80
Mark Anthony Mathews [2003] EWCA Crim 813 . . . 80
Matto v Wolverhampton Crown Court [1987]
    RTR 337 . . . 99
Maxwell v UK 15 EHRR CD 101 and 19 EHRR 97 . . . 31
Meese [1973] 1 WLR 675 . . . 109
Monnell and Morris v UK, Series A, vol. 115 . . . 29, 31
Morris [1995] 2 Cr App R 69 . . . 43
Morris [2001] 1 Cr App R 4 . . . 47
Morrow and others v DPP and others [1994]
    Crim LR 58 . . . 62
Murray v DPP [1993] Crim LR 968 . . . 98
Murray v UK 22 EHRR 29 . . . 31

Norwood v DPP [2003] Crim LR 888 . . . 62

O'Brien [1993] Crim LR 70 . . . 60
Observer and Guardian v UK 14 EHRR 153 . . . 31
Ohlson v Hylton [1975] 1 WLR 724 . . . 78

P v P (Divorce: Proceeds of Crime) (2003) EWHC 2260
    (Fam); [2004] Fam 1 . . . 56

Panton [2001] EWCA Crim 611 *The Times*,
    27 March 2001 . . . 40
Peacock [1973] Crim LR 639 . . . 80
Percy v DPP [2002] Crim LR 835 . . . 62
Phillips v UK [2001] 11 BHRC 280 . . . 53
Police Prosecutor v Humphreys [1970] Crim LR 234 . . . 111
Practice Direction (Criminal: Consolidated) [2002] 3
    All ER 904 . . . 25
Purcell [1996] 1 Cr App R (S) 190 . . . 47

R (Ebrahim) v Feltham Magistrates' Court [2001] 2 Cr
    App R 23 23m . . . 24
R v Ahmed; R v Qureshi [2004] EWCA Crim 2599; [2005]
    1 WLR 122 . . . 52
R v Sawoniuk [2000] 2 Cr App R 220, CA . . . 22
Rabjohns v Burgar [1971] RTR 234 . . . 90
Republic of Ireland v UK, Series A, vol. 25 . . . 28
Rezvi, Re [2002] UKHL 1; [2003] 1 AC 1099 . . . 53
Richardson *The Times*, 18 March 1994 . . . 46, 47
Richardson v DPP [2003] All ER (D) 282 . . . 98
Robinson [1993] Crim LR 581 . . . 60
Ronchetti [1998] Crim LR 227 . . . 47
Rotherham JJ, *ex p* Brough [1991] Crim LR 522 . . . 24
Rotherham Magistrates' Court, *ex p* Todd, unreported
    16 February 2000 . . . 20
Rothwell and Barton [1993] Crim LR 626 . . . 59
Rowe and Davis v UK (2000) 30 EHRR 1 . . . 30
Rukwira and others v DPP [1993] Crim LR 882 . . . 60
Russell (1991) 94 Cr App R 351 . . . 40

Saggar [2005] EWCA Civ 174; *The Times*
    14 March 2005 . . . 56
Sanchez (1996) 160 JP 321 . . . 60
Sander v UK (2001) 31 EHRR 44 . . . 30
Saunders [2000] 1 Cr App R 458 . . . 63
Searle [1971] Crim LR 592 . . . 42
Sheffield Justices, *ex p* DPP [1993] Crim LR 136 . . . 24
Sheldrake v DPP [2003] 2 All ER 497 . . . 80
Sheldrake v DPP [2005] 1 AC 264 . . . 95
Shoult [1996] RTR 298 . . . 102
Siddiqui v Swain [1979] RTR 454 . . . 97
Simpson (1983) 78 Cr App R 115 . . . 79

Simpson v Peat [1952] 2 QB 447 . . . 88
Singleton [1995] 1 Cr App R 431 . . . 17
Smyth v DPP [1996] RTR 59 . . . 99
Soering v UK, Series A, vol. 161 . . . 28, 33
Solesbury v Pugh [1969] 2 All ER 1171 . . . 99
Southwell v Chadwick (1986) 85 Cr App R 235 . . . 79
Standford v UK, Series A, vol. 282 . . . 30
Stanley and Knight [1993] Crim LR 618 . . . 60
Stanley v DPP [1998] 3 All ER 769 . . . 98
Stewart v DPP [2003] All ER (D) 164 . . . 93
Strong *The Times*, 26 January 1990 . . . 42
Swanston v DPP (1997) 161 JP 203 . . . 60
Sykes v White [1983] RTR 419 . . . 99

Temple v UK 8 EHRR 319 . . . 33
Thind [1999] Crim LR 842 . . . 60
Thomas v DPP [1991] RTR 292 . . . 99
Thomas v Sawkins [1935] 2 KB 249 . . . 9
Tyrer v UK, Series A, vol. 26 . . . 28, 34

V v UK 15 EHRR CD 108 . . . 30
Veasey [1999] Crim LR 158 . . . 78
Vigon v DPP (1998) 162 JP 115 . . . 62

Walsh (1990) 12 Cr App R (S) 243 . . . 60
Warner v Metropolitan Police Commissioner [1968]
    2 All ER 356 . . . 41–2
Warren & Beeley [1996] 1 Cr App R 120 . . . 47
Wealden DC, *ex p* Wales *The Times*, 22 September 1995 . . . 73
Whittal v Kirby [1947] KB 194 . . . 111
Wijs [1998] 2 Cr App R (S) 436 . . . 47
Wilburn (1992) 13 Cr App R (S) 309 . . . 69
Winn v DPP (1992) 156 JP 881 . . . 60
Woolman v Lenton [1985] Crim LR 516 . . . 99
Worton (1990) 154 JP 201 . . . 59

X v UK 15 EHRR CD 113 . . . 30
X v UK (1969) 12 Yearbook 298 . . . 32
X, Y and Z v UK App No 21830/93 unreported . . . 31

TABLE OF STATUTES

Access to Justice Act 1999
  Sch.3
    para.5(2) . . . 10.8
Anti-Terrorism, Crime and Security Act 2001
  s.39 . . . 7.7

Children and Young Persons Act 1968
  s.32(1)-(1A) . . . 3.2.1
Copyright, Designs and Patents Act 1988
  s.107(1)-(2) . . . 6.7.1
  s.109 . . . 3.3.5
  s.198(1) . . . 6.7.1
  s.297A . . . 6.7.1
Crime and Disorder Act 1998 . . . 7.1
  s.28 . . . 7.7
    (1)-(5) . . . 7.7
  ss.29-32 . . . 7.7
  s.51 . . . 14
    (5) . . . 14
Criminal Appeal Act 1968
  s.29(1) . . . 5.2
Criminal Attempts Act 1981
  s.1(1) . . . 13
Criminal Damage Act 1971
  s.6 . . . 3.3.4
Criminal Justice Act 1967 . . . 13
  s.10(2)(b) . . . 13
Criminal Justice Act 1987
  s.2 . . . 3.3.5
Criminal Justice Act 1988 . . . 6.7, 6.7.2,
  6.7.3, 8.3, 8.4
  s.40 . . . 13, 14
  s.139 . . . 8.3.1, 8.3.2
    (1)-(5) . . . 8.3.1
    (7) . . . 8.3.1
  ss.139A-B . . . 8.3.2
  ss.141-141A . . . 8.4
Criminal Justice Act 2003
  s.33(2) . . . 14
  s.281(5) . . . 7.14
Criminal Justice (International Co-operation) Act 1990
  s.12 . . . 6.7.1
  s.19 . . . 6.7.1
Criminal Justice and Police Act 2001 . . . 3.5.2, 7.1
  s.42A(1)-(7) . . . 7.14
  s.50 . . . 3.4.2.1, 3.5.1, 3.5.2
    (1)-(4) . . . 3.5.2
  s.51 . . . 3.4.2.1, 3.5.1
  ss.53-55 . . . 3.5.2
  s.59 . . . 3.5.2

s.62 . . . 3.5.2
Sch.1
  Part 1 . . . 3.5.2
Criminal Justice and Public Order Act 1994 . . . 7.1
  ss.34-35 . . . 5.2
  s.61
    (1)-(6) . . . 7.12.1
    (9) . . . 7.12.1
  s.63(1)-(10) . . . 7.12.2
  s.64 . . . 7.12.2
  s.65(1)-(5) . . . 7.12.2
  ss.66-67 . . . 7.12.2
  s.68(1)-(4) . . . 7.12.3
  s.69 . . . 7.12.3
    (1)-(5) . . . 7.12.3
  s.77 . . . 7.12.5
    (1)-(3) . . . 7.12.5
  s.78(1)-(5) . . . 7.12.5
  s.155 . . . 7.8.2
Criminal Law Act 1967
  s.6(3) . . . 9.2.3
Criminal Law Act 1977 . . . 3.2.1, 7.1
  ss.6-8 . . . 3.2.1
  s.10 . . . 3.2.1
  s.51
    (1)-(2) . . . 7.11
    (4) . . . 7.11
Criminal Procedure and Investigations Act 1996 . . . 4.1.4
  s.5 . . . 13
  s.6A . . . 14
Crossbows Act 1987 . . . 8.4
Customs and Excise Management Act 1979
  s.50 . . . 6.2.1
    (2) . . . 6.7.1
    (3) . . . 6.2.1, 6.7.1
  s.68(2) . . . 6.7.1
  s.170 . . . 6.7.1
    (2) . . . 6.2.1

Drug Trafficking Act 1994 . . . 6.7, 6.7.3
  ss.55-56 . . . 3.3.2
Drugs Act 2005 . . . 6.2.4.2, 6.6.2

Explosives Act 1875 . . . 3.2.5

Firearms Act 1968
  s.3(1) . . . 6.7.1
Football (Disorder) Act 2000 . . . 7.1, 7.9.3

Football (Offences) Act 1991 . . . 7.1
  s.2 . . . 7.9.1
  s.3 . . . 7.9.1
    (2)(b) . . . 7.9.1
  s.4 . . . 7.9.1
  s.5(2) . . . 7.9.1
Football Spectators Act 1989 . . . 7.1, 7.9.3
  Sch.1 . . . 7.9.3
Forgery and Counterfeiting Act 1981
  s.7 . . . 3.3.5
  ss.14–17 . . . 6.7.1
  s.24 . . . 3.3.5

Human Rights Act 1998 . . . 5.1
  s.2(1) . . . 5.1
  s.3 . . . 6.3
    (1)–(2) . . . 5.1

Immigration Act 1971
  s.25(1) . . . 6.7.1
Incitement to Disaffection Act 1934 . . . 5.2
Insolvency Act 1986
  s.386 . . . 6.7.2

Knives Act 1997 . . . 8.4

Misuse of Drugs Act 1971 . . . 3.3.2, 6.1, 6.2.4.1, 6.3,
  6.7.1, 8.3.1
  s.2 . . . 6.1
  s.3 . . . 6.2.1
  s.4 . . . 6.2.2
    (1) . . . 6.2.3.1
      (b) . . . 6.2.3.2
    (2) . . . 6.3, 6.7.1
      (a)–(b) . . . 6.2.2
    (3) . . . 6.3, 6.7.1
      (a) . . . 6.2.3
      (b)–(c) . . . 6.2.3.3
  s.4A . . . 6.6.2
  s.5
    (2) . . . 6.2.4, 6.3
    (3) . . . 6.2.3.1, 6.2.4, 6.3, 6.7.1
    (4) . . . 6.3
    (4A) . . . 6.2.4.2
    (4B) . . . 6.2.4.2
  s.6 . . . 6.2.2
  s.7 . . . 6.5
  s.8 . . . 6.4, 6.7.1
    (b) . . . 6.4
  s.20 . . . 6.7.1
  s.23 . . . 3.2.4
    (1) . . . 3.2.4
    (2) . . . 3.1, 3.2.4, 6.6.1
    (3) . . . 3.3.2, 6.6.1
    (4) . . . 3.2.4
  s.27 . . . 6.7.6
    (1) . . . 6.6.3
  s.28 . . . 6.3
    (2)–(3) . . . 6.3
  s.37
    (1) . . . 6.2.2
    (3) . . . 6.2.4.1

Sch.2 . . . 6.1, 6.5
  Part 1
    para.5 . . . 6.1
  Sch.4 . . . 6.6.2

Obscene Publications Act 1959
  s.3 . . . 3.3.5
Offences Against the Person Act 1861
  s.18 . . . 13
  s.65 . . . 3.3.5
Offensive Weapons Act 1996 . . . 8.4
Official Secrets Act 1911 . . . 3.2.5

Police and Criminal Evidence Act 1984 . . . 3.1, 3.4.1, 3.4.2,
  3.4.2.1, 3.5.1, 3.5.2, 3.6, 13
  ss.1–3 . . . 3.1
  s.8 . . . 3.3.1, 3.4.2.4
    (1) . . . 3.3.1
    (2) . . . 3.3.1, 3.5.2
  s.9(2) . . . 3.4.2.1
  ss.11–12 . . . 3.4.2.2
  s.14 . . . 3.4.2.3
  s.15 . . . 3.4.1
    (1)–(8) . . . 3.4.1
  s.16 . . . 3.4.1
    (1)–(12) . . . 3.4.1
    (3A) . . . 3.3.1
    (3B) . . . 3.3.1
  s.17 . . . 3.2.1
    (5)–(6) . . . 3.2.1
  s.18 . . . 3.2.2, 3.2.3
    (2)–(8) . . . 3.2.2
  s.19 . . . 3.5.1
    (6) . . . 3.5.1, 3.5.2
  s.21 . . . 3.5.1
    (4)–(8) . . . 3.5.1
  s.22 . . . 3.5.2
    (1) . . . 3.5.1
  s.24(2) . . . 7.8.2
  s.32 . . . 3.2.3
    (1) . . . 3.1
    (2)
      (a) . . . 3.1
      (b) . . . 3.2.3
    (3)–(7) . . . 3.2.3
  s.58 . . . 10.5.4
  s.76 . . . 14
  s.78 . . . 3.6, 10.5.1, 14
  s.107(2) . . . 3.2.2
  Sch.1 . . . 3.4.2.4
    paras.1–4 . . . 3.4.2.4
    paras.12–14 . . . 3.4.2.4
  Codes of Practice
    Code A . . . 3.1
    Code B . . . 3.1
      paras.3–6 . . . 3.4.1
      para.5 . . . 3.1
    Code D . . . 14
Powers of Criminal Courts (Sentencing) Act 2000
  s.3 . . . 6.7.1
  s.4 . . . 6.7.1
  s.6 . . . 6.7.1
  s.92 . . . 3.2.1
  s.130 . . . 6.7.6
  s.152 . . . 13

Prevention of Crime Act 1953 . . . 8.2, 8.4
  s.1 . . . 8.2, 8.3.1, 8.3.2
    (1)–(2) . . . 8.2
    (4) . . . 8.2.2, 8.2.3
Proceeds of Crime Act 2002 . . . 6.6.3, 6.7, 6.7.1, 6.7.2,
  6.7.11, 6.7.12
  s.6 . . . 6.7.1, 6.7.2, 6.7.4, 6.7.8, 6.7.9
    (7) . . . 6.7.1
  s.7
    (1)–(2) . . . 6.7.2
    (5) . . . 6.7.2
  s.8 . . . 6.7.2
  s.9 . . . 6.7.2, 6.7.4
    (2) . . . 6.7.2
  s.10 . . . 6.7.3, 6.7.4
    (6)–(8) . . . 6.7.3
  s.11 . . . 6.7.5
  s.13 . . . 6.7.6
    (4) . . . 6.7.6
  s.14 . . . 6.7.8
    (3) . . . 6.7.8
    (6) . . . 6.7.8
  s.15 . . . 6.7.8
    (4) . . . 6.7.8
  s.16 . . . 6.7.4
    (3)–(5) . . . 6.7.4
  s.17(1)–(2) . . . 6.7.4
  s.18 . . . 6.7.4
    (4) . . . 6.7.4
  ss.19–25 . . . 6.7.9
  s.31 . . . 6.7.10
  ss.34–37 . . . 6.7.7
  s.38 . . . 6.7.7
    (5) . . . 6.7.7
  s.39 . . . 6.7.7
  ss.40–69 . . . 6.7.7
  s.70 . . . 6.7.1
  s.75 . . . 6.7.1
    (2) . . . 6.7.1
     (a)–(c) . . . 6.7.1
    (3) . . . 6.7.1
     (a)–(b) . . . 6.7.1
    (5) . . . 6.7.1
  s.76 . . . 6.7.1
    (4)–(5) . . . 6.7.2
    (7) . . . 6.7.2
  s.77 . . . 6.7.2
  s.80 . . . 6.7.2
    (2)–(3) . . . 6.7.2
  s.82 . . . 6.7.2
  s.245A–D . . . 6.7.7
  s.327 . . . 6.7.1
  s.328 . . . 6.7.1, 6.7.12
  s.338 . . . 6.7.12
  s.352 . . . 3.4.2.4
  s.354 . . . 3.4.2.4
  Sch.2 . . . 6.7.1
Protection from Harassment Act 1997 . . . 7.1
  s.1 . . . 7.13
    (1) . . . 7.13
    (1A) . . . 7.13
    (2) . . . 7.13
    (3) . . . 7.13
  s.2 . . . 7.7, 7.13
    (1)–(2) . . . 7.13
  s.4 . . . 7.7, 7.13

    (1)–(6) . . . 7.13
Public Order Act 1936
  s.1 . . . 3.2.1
Public Order Act 1986 . . . 7.1
  Part 1 . . . 7.14
  s.1 . . . 7.2
    (1)–(6) . . . 7.2
  s.2
    (1) . . . 7.3, 13
    (2)–(5) . . . 7.3
  s.3(1)–(7) . . . 7.4
  s.4 . . . 3.2.1, 7.5, 7.7, 13
    (1)–(3) . . . 7.5
  s.4A . . . 7.5.1, 7.7
    (1)–(5) . . . 7.5.1
  s.5 . . . 7.6, 7.7
    (1) . . . 7.6
     (b) . . . 7.7
    (2)–(5) . . . 7.6
  s.6
    (1) . . . 7.2
    (5)–(7) . . . 7.2
  s.8 . . . 7.2, 7.4
  s.11 . . . 7.10.1
    (1)–(2) . . . 7.16
    (7)–(9) . . . 7.10.1
  s.12 . . . 7.10.2, 7.16
    (4)–(6) . . . 7.10.2
  s.13 . . . 7.10.3, 7.16
    (7)–(9) . . . 7.10.3
  s.14 . . . 7.10.3, 7.16
    (4)–(6) . . . 7.10.4
  s.14A . . . 7.12.4
  s.14B
    (1)–(3) . . . 7.12.4
    (5)–(7) . . . 7.12.4
  s.14C . . . 7.12.4
    (1)–(2) . . . 7.12.4
    (4)–(5) . . . 7.12.4
  s.17 . . . 7.8.1
  s.18 . . . 7.8
    (1)–(2) . . . 7.8.1
    (4)–(5) . . . 7.8.1
  s.19 . . . 7.8
    (1) . . . 7.8.2
  s.20 . . . 7.8
    (1)–(4) . . . 7.8.3
  s.21 . . . 7.8
    (1) . . . 7.8.4
    (3)–(4) . . . 7.8.4
  s.22 . . . 7.8
    (1)–(6) . . . 7.8.5
  s.23 . . . 7.8
    (1)–(3) . . . 7.8.6
  s.24 . . . 3.3.5
  s.27(3) . . . 7.8

Restriction of Offensive Weapons Act 1959 . . . 8.4
Road Traffic Act 1988 . . . 8.3.1, 9.2.3, 11.2.3
  s.1 . . . 9.2.3, 11.2.3
  s.2 . . . 9.2.2, 11.2.3
  s.2A . . . 9.2
    (1)–(4) . . . 9.2
  s.3 . . . 9.2.2, 9.2.3, 9.3, 10.6, 11.2.3
  s.3A . . . 9.2.3, 10.5.2, 10.6, 11.2.3

(1) . . . 9.2.3, 10.6
(2)–(3) . . . 10.6
s.4 . . . 3.2.1, 10.3, 10.5.2
  (1) . . . 9.2.3, 10.3, 10.6, 11.2.3, 13
  (2) . . . 9.2.3, 10.3, 11.2.3
  (3) . . . 10.3, 10.4.2
  (4)–(7) . . . 10.3
s.5 . . . 10.4.3, 10.5.2, 10.5.4
  (1) . . . 10.4, 10.5.2
    (a) . . . 9.2.3, 10.4.3, 10.6, 11.2.3
    (b) . . . 9.2.3, 10.4.3, 11.2.3
  (2) . . . 10.4, 10.4.2
  (3) . . . 10.4
s.6 . . . 11.2.3
  (1)–(6) . . . 10.5.1
s.7 . . . 10.5.2, 10.5.6, 11.2.3
  (1)–(3) . . . 10.5.2
  (4) . . . 10.2, 10.5.2
  (4A) . . . 10.5.2
  (5) . . . 10.5.2
  (6) . . . 9.2.3, 10.5.2, 10.6
  (7) . . . 10.5.2, 10.5.5
s.7A . . . 10.5.6, 11.2.3
  (1)–(7) . . . 10.5.6
s.8(2) . . . 10.5.2
s.9 . . . 10.5.1, 10.5.2, 10.5.5, 10.5.6
s.11(4) . . . 10.5.2
s.12 . . . 11.2.3
s.22 . . . 9.2.2, 11.2.3
s.22A . . . 11.2.3
s.23 . . . 11.2.3
ss.28–29 . . . 9.2.2, 9.2.3
s.30 . . . 10.7
ss.35–36 . . . 9.2.2, 11.2.3
s.38(7) . . . 9.1
s.40A . . . 11.2.3
s.41A . . . 11.2.3
s.87(1) . . . 11.2.3
s.92
  (3) . . . 11.2.3
  (10) . . . 11.2.3
s.93 . . . 11.2.3
s.94(3)–(3A) . . . 11.2.3
s.94A . . . 11.2.3
s.96 . . . 11.2.3
s.99(5) . . . 11.2.3
s.103(1)(a)–(b) . . . 11.2.3
s.143 . . . 11.2.3
s.163 . . . 3.2.1
s.165(2)(a) . . . 9.4
s.170 . . . 9.4
  (1)–(3) . . . 9.4
  (4) . . . 9.4, 11.2.3
  (5)–(6) . . . 9.4
  (7) . . . 9.4, 11.2.3
  (8) . . . 9.4
s.171 . . . 11.2.3
s.172 . . . 11.2.3
  (5) . . . 11.2.3
  (11) . . . 11.2.3
s.192 . . . 10.3
Road Traffic Act 1991 . . . 9.2
Road Traffic Acts . . . 10.1
Road Traffic (New Drivers) Act 1995 . . . 11.3.1.4
Road Traffic Offenders Act 1988
s.1 . . . 9.2.2

(1) . . . 9.2.2
  (c)(i) . . . 9.2.2
(1A) . . . 9.2.2
(2)–(4) . . . 9.2.2
s.2 . . . 9.2.2
  (1) . . . 9.2.2
  (3) . . . 9.2.2
  (4) . . . 9.2.2, 9.3.1
s.15(2) . . . 10.4.1
s.24 . . . 9.2.2, 9.2.3, 9.3.1, 10.6
  (1)–(4) . . . 9.2.3
  (6) . . . 9.2.2, 9.2.3
s.28(1)–(6) . . . 11.2.3
s.29 . . . 11.3.1.2
s.34(3) . . . 11.3.1.1
s.35 . . . 11.3.1.2
  (4) . . . 11.3.1.2
s.36 . . . 11.3.3
s.57(5) . . . 11.2.3
s.77(5) . . . 11.2.3
Sch.2 . . . 11.2.3
Road Traffic Regulation Act 1984 . . . 11.2.3
s.16(1) . . . 11.2.3
s.17(4) . . . 11.2.3
s.25(5) . . . 11.2.3
s.28(3) . . . 11.2.3
s.29(3) . . . 11.2.3
s.89(1) . . . 11.2.3

Serious Organised Crime and Police Act
  2005 . . . 6.7.7, 7.1
s.97 . . . 6.7.1
s.128(1)–(10) . . . 7.15
s.132(1)–(7) . . . 7.16
s.133 . . . 7.16
s.134 . . . 7.16
  (2) . . . 7.16
s.135 . . . 7.16
s.136 . . . 7.16
s.138 . . . 7.16
Sexual Offences Act 1956
s.2-s.3 . . . 6.7.1
s.9 . . . 6.7.1
s.22 . . . 6.7.1
s.24 . . . 6.7.1
ss.28–31 . . . 6.7.1
ss.33–34 . . . 6.7.1
Sexual Offences Act 1967
s.5 . . . 6.7.1
Sporting Events (Control of Alcohol etc) Act 1985 . . . 7.1
s.1 . . . 7.9.2
  (2)–(4) . . . 7.9.2
s.2 . . . 7.9.2
  (1)–(2) . . . 7.9.2

Terrorism Act 2000 . . . 3.2.5
s.56 . . . 6.7.1
Theft Act 1968
s.21 . . . 6.7.1
s.26 . . . 3.3.3
Trade Marks Act 1994
s.92(1)–(3) . . . 6.7.1
Trade Union and Labour Relations (Consolidation)
  Act 1992
s.220 . . . 7.16

International legislation
European Convention on Human Rights . . . 1, 5, 5.1, 5.2, 5.3,
    5.3.3, 5.3.5, 5.4, 6.3, 6.7.3, 7.9.3
    art.3 . . . 5.2, 5.4
    art.5 . . . 5.2
      (1) . . . 5.2
        (a)–(f) . . . 5.2
      (2)–(5) . . . 5.2
    art.6 . . . 4.1.1, 5.2, 6.3, 6.7.3, 8.3.1, 10.4.2
      (1) . . . 5.2, 6.7.7
      (2) . . . 5.2
      (3) . . . 5.2, 10.5.2
        (c)–(d) . . . 5.2
    art.8 . . . 6.7.2

art.10
    (1) . . . 5.2, 7.6
    (2) . . . 5.2
art.11 . . . 5.2
art.14 . . . 5.2
art.15 . . . 5.2
    (1)–(3) . . . 5.2
arts.16–18 . . . 5.2
art.35
    (1) . . . 5.3.3
    (2)(b) . . . 5.3.1
    (3) . . . 5.3.1
art.41 . . . 5.3.5

Evidence and procedure

Introduction

A significant number of barristers practise exclusively in the field of criminal law. An even greater number have a general common law practice which contains an element of criminal work. As far as those in pupillage and the early stages of practice are concerned, criminal defence work is (subject to temporary fluctuations) the most common type of work, even for those who regard themselves as civil lawyers. Further, among those who decide after pupillage to become employed barristers, the most popular destination is the Crown Prosecution Service.

Accordingly, the Advanced Criminal Law option is aimed at two groups of students:

- those intending in due course to go into specialist criminal practice; and
- those destined for a general common law practice with a significant element of crime.

Like other subjects offered as options on the Vocational Course, this option may seem similar to one of the core subjects which students must have taken before embarking upon the Vocational Course. But this option will differ radically from criminal law studied as a core subject.

First, the topics which this course covers are those which are not dealt with in any detail in the core study of criminal law, but which are of particular value in the early years of practice, such as public order offences and the law relating to the misuse of dangerous drugs.

Second, in line with the spirit of the Vocational Course generally, the methods employed on this option aim to provide a taste of criminal practice. We will be dealing with a practical training exercise, which will provide opportunities for the use of skills in the context of criminal law, and act as a vehicle for the acquisition of knowledge. Further, a number of questions of practice, procedure and tactics will be canvassed in the course.

The chapters which follow deal with a selection of topics which represent the areas of substantive law and practice upon which the course will concentrate. They build both upon your knowledge of core law, and upon what you have already learned on the Vocational Course, particularly in criminal litigation, evidence, and sentencing.

Part I of this Manual deals with certain areas of procedure which are of crucial practical importance to the criminal practitioner. **Chapter 3** deals with the issues relating to search and seizure. It looks at the question of powers to search for and seize evidence, and the consequences at trial if those powers are exceeded. **Chapter 4** covers the doctrine of abuse of process. It examines the circumstances in which the court may exercise its discretion to stay a prosecution which it considers to be an abuse of its own process. **Chapter 5** covers the European Convention on Human Rights. The Convention is being utilised with ever greater frequency by criminal practitioners, and this chapter attempts to summarise its relevant provisions, give an idea of the procedure which it adopts, and deal with some of the relevant cases.

Part II covers chosen areas of substantive law. **Chapter 6** is devoted to the offences connected with dangerous drugs, **Chapter 7** deals with a variety of offences against public order and **Chapter 8** covers offensive weapons. Road traffic is an area which is particularly required for the barrister in the first few years of practice, and it is covered in **Chapters 9, 10** and **11** which deal with some of the most common offences and the penalty system for driving offences.

Part III gives you an opportunity to practice some of the skills utilised by the criminal practitioner on a realistic set of papers for a trial in prospect. You are instructed for the defence in a Crown Court trial, the indictment containing counts of grievous bodily harm with intent, violent disorder, attempted robbery and driving while unfit through drink or drugs. The papers contain a number of the documents with which the criminal practitioner is constantly dealing, eg, the custody record, the plea and case management questionnaire. **Chapter 12** describes the way in which the papers might be used. To start with, they form the instructions to write an Advice on Evidence. Thereafter, they can form the basis for preparing a conference with the client. Finally, they can be used in order to plan the advocacy tasks necessary for a trial. The papers themselves appear in **Chapter 13**. In **Chapter 14**, there is a sample Advice on Evidence prepared in response to the instructions in the brief.

Sources for further study and preparation of cases

2.1 This Manual

This Manual is designed to introduce you to some of the main topics that the practitioner will meet from the early years of practice onwards. Subjects that are already covered in the main *Criminal Litigation* and *Evidence Manuals* are not covered here and a knowledge of those areas is assumed. This Manual does not provide you with all the materials you will need to undertake the case you will meet on the Advanced Criminal Litigation Option. You will find it necessary, in addition, to undertake further legal research which will require the use of practitioner texts and primary sources.

2.2 Primary sources

2.2.1 Statutory materials

You should be familiar with accessing statutory material through electronic and hard copy sources so that you are prepared for all circumstances.

2.2.1.1 Electronic sources

The commercial providers (Lawtel, LexisNexis, Butterworths and Westlaw) all provide statutes and statutory instruments online. Useful information is also available through government websites such as the Office of Public Sector Information (formerly HMSO) (http://www.opsi.gov.uk/), where both existing and draft legislation is available, and the Home Office (http://www.homeoffice.gov.uk/), where consultation on legislative proposals is available. Other commercial providers such as Crimeline (http://www.crimeline.info) provide a certain amount of free relevant news and updating. For further guidance on electronic sources see the *Case Preparation Manual*.

2.2.1.2 Paper sources

For proceedings in the Crown Court the two main practitioners' texts, *Archbold: Criminal Pleading, Evidence and Practice* and *Blackstone's Criminal Practice*, should include most of the provisions you will need. For proceedings in the magistrates' court you could additionally refer to either *Stone's Justices' Manual* or *Archbold Magistrates' Courts Criminal Practice*. For road traffic offences you should refer to *Wilkinson's Road Traffic Offences*.

Richardson, J., and Thomas QC, D. (ed.), *Archbold: Criminal Pleading, Evidence and Practice* (London: Sweet & Maxwell, annual).

Murphy, P., and Stockdale, E. (ed.), *Blackstone's Criminal Practice* (Oxford: Oxford University Press, annual).

Carr, P., and Turner, A. (ed.), *Stone's Justices' Manual* (London: LexisNexis UK, annual).

Padfield, N. (ed.), *Archbold Magistrates' Courts Criminal Practice* (Oxford: Oxford University Press, annual).

Swift, K., and McCormac, K. (ed.), *Wilkinson's Road Traffic Offences* (London: Sweet & Maxwell, updated).

2.2.2 Law Reports

Many criminal cases are reported in the ordinary reports with which you are acquainted (eg: AC, QB, WLR, All ER). However, you must develop familiarity with the specialist series which frequently report cases that are not reported elsewhere:

Criminal Appeal Reports (Cr App R)
Criminal Appeal Reports (Sentencing) (Cr App R (S))
Criminal Law Review (Crim LR)
Road Traffic Reports (RTR)

The *Criminal Appeal Reports* are published ten times per year, the *Criminal Appeal Reports (Sentencing)* six times per year, the *Criminal Law Review* is published monthly. They are usually quicker to report cases than the general series of law reports. The *Criminal Law Review* is often the quickest of the three, and case reports are frequently followed by a commentary providing useful analysis. Cases reported in any of the main or specialist series may easily be accessed through the main electronic services: Lawtel, LexisNexis, Casetrack and Westlaw.

2.3 Practitioner works

You will need to make regular use of practitioner texts. The two main texts are:

Richardson, J., and Thomas QC, D. (ed.), *Archbold: Criminal Pleading, Evidence and Practice* (London: Sweet & Maxwell, annual).

Murphy, P., and Stockdale, E. (ed.), *Blackstone's Criminal Practice* (Oxford: Oxford University Press, annual).

Archbold is regarded as the standard text by most practitioners in the Crown Court. However, *Blackstone's* is often preferred by the junior practitioner and those practising in the magistrates' courts, not least because it provides more extensive coverage of issues that concern those courts.

For road traffic offences you should refer to:

Swift, K., and McCormac, K. (ed.), *Wilkinson's Road Traffic Offences* (London: Sweet & Maxwell, updated).

2.4 Periodicals

You may also find reference to the specialist journals and periodicals useful for keeping up-to-date with current developments and as a source of insightful commentary. Also, articles on criminal law and evidence appear regularly in all the main general legal periodicals.

2.4.1   Specialist journals

The leading specialist journal is the *Criminal Law Review*, containing articles, comment, case notes, reports and reviews.

Other journals of particular interest include the *Journal of Criminal Law*, the *Modern Law Review* and the *Law Quarterly Review*.

2.4.2   Updating periodicals

Archbold News, published ten times per year, provides access to updated developments including cases, legislation and commentary in the field of criminal law. Significantly, it includes reports of cases that are not reported elsewhere.

Criminal Law Week, published weekly, is a comprehensive digest of developments in the criminal law. It is available as a printed version and online at http://www.criminal-law.co.uk.

The monthly and weekly publications, *Legal Action* and *New Law Journal*, are also useful for up-to-date information on recent cases, often before they have been reported, and articles surveying a particular topic, often from a highly practical perspective.

3

Entry, search and seizure

3.1 Introduction

This chapter is concerned with the legal powers:

- to enter premises for the purpose of searching for persons or things (search); and
- to seize such persons or things if found (seizure).

The powers range from the general to the very specific and emphasis will here be placed upon the main powers. By far the most important statutory provisions are to be found in the Police and Criminal Evidence Act (PACE) 1984 backed up by PACE Code of Practice B.

This chapter is not concerned with situations where one person enters and remains on another's premises with that other's consent (but see PACE Code of Practice B, para 5), nor with the powers of the police to stop and search an individual or vehicle without entering premises (for important examples of such powers see PACE 1984, ss 1–3 and s 32(1) and (2)(a), Misuse of Drugs Act 1971, s 23(2) — see generally PACE Code of Practice A).

Perhaps the main distinction to be drawn when considering the powers to enter premises is between:

- powers which can be exercised without a warrant; and
- those which can only be exercised with a warrant.

In this context the warrant referred to is an express authorisation given by 'the court' to enter premises. Such warrants are often called search warrants and are to be distinguished from arrest warrants. Further details about search warrants are given below at **3.4**.

For the evidential consequences of a failure to comply with the rules on search and seizure described in this chapter, see **3.6** below.

3.2 Powers of search exercisable without a warrant

3.2.1 Police and Criminal Evidence Act 1984, s 17

A constable may enter and search premises without a warrant for the purpose of:

(a) executing a warrant of arrest issued in connection with or arising out of criminal proceedings;

(b) arresting a person for an indictable offence;

(c) arresting a person for an offence under the Public Order Act 1936, s 1, the Public Order Act 1986, s 4, the Criminal Law Act 1977, ss 6, 7, 8 or 10, or the Road Traffic Act 1988, ss 4 or 163;

(d) arresting, in pursuance of the Children and Young Persons Act 1968, s 32(1A), any child or young person who has been remanded or committed to local authority accommodation under s 32(1) of that Act;

(e) recapturing a person unlawfully at large while liable to be detained in a prison, remand centre, young offenders institution, or secure training centre, or in pursuance of the Powers of Criminal Courts (Sentencing) Act 2000, s 92 in any other place;

(f) recapturing a person who is unlawfully at large and whom he is pursuing;

(g) saving life or limb or preventing serious damage to property.

Except for the purpose specified in (g) these powers are exercisable only if the constable has reasonable grounds for believing that the person whom he is seeking is on the premises. Also, the power of entry to arrest for the offences under the Criminal Law Act 1977 mentioned in (c) above, is exercisable only by a constable in uniform.

Section 17(5) provides that, subject to s 17(6), all the common law rules under which a constable has power to enter premises without a warrant are abolished. Section 17(6) preserves the common law power of entry to deal with or prevent a breach of the peace. The scope of this common law power was considered in *Thomas v Sawkins* [1935] 2 KB 249. Although it seems to be a wide power the police do not in practice appear to rely on it heavily. This may be due partly to the narrowness of the definition of 'breach of the peace' used by the Court of Appeal in *Howell* [1982] QB 416, *viz* 'an act done or threatened to be done which either actually harms a person or, in his presence, his property, or is likely to cause such harm, or which puts someone in fear of such harm'.

3.2.2 Police and Criminal Evidence Act 1984, s 18

A constable may (subject to s 18(3)–(8)) enter and search any premises occupied or controlled by a person who is under arrest for an indictable offence, if he has reasonable grounds for suspecting that there is on the premises evidence other than items subject to legal privilege (for which see below at **3.4.2**) that relates to that offence or to some other indictuble offence which is connected with or similar to that offence. The constable may seize and retain anything for which he may search (s 18(2)).

Section 18(3)–(8) provide that:

(a) the extent of the search is limited to that which is reasonably required for the purpose of discovering the type of evidence specified;

(b) the power is exercisable only if an officer of the rank of inspector or above has authorised it in writing (see *Badham* [1987] Crim LR 202), *unless* it is exercised before the arrested person is taken to a police station or released on 'street bail' under s 30A of the Act and that person's presence at a place other than a police station is necessary for the effective investigation of the offence (in such an exceptional case the constable in question must inform an officer of the rank of inspector or above that he has made the search as soon as practicable after he has made it). Note here the effect of s 107(2), permitting a sergeant to assume the powers of an inspector if he has been authorised by an officer of at least the rank of chief superintendent;

(c) the officer who authorises (or is informed of) the search must keep a written record of the grounds for the search and the nature of the evidence sought.

3.2.3   Police and Criminal Evidence Act 1984, s 32

By s 32(2)(b) (subject to s 32(3)–(7)), in any case where a person has been arrested for an indictable offence at a place other than a police station, a constable shall have the power to enter and search any premises, in which the arrested person was when arrested or immediately before he was arrested (whether or not he was the occupier or controller of such premises, *cf* s 18 above) for evidence relating to the offence for which he was arrested.

Section 32(3)–(7) provide that:

(a) the extent of the search is limited to that which is reasonably required for the purpose of discovering the type of evidence specified;

(b) a constable may not undertake a s 32(2)(b) search unless he has reasonable grounds for believing that there is evidence on those premises for which such search is permitted;

(c) insofar as the s 32(2)(b) search relates to premises consisting of two or more separate dwellings, it is limited to a search of the dwelling in which the arrest took place or in which the person arrested was immediately before his arrest and any parts of the premises which the occupier of such dwelling uses in common with the occupiers of any other dwellings comprised in the premises.

3.2.4   Misuse of Drugs Act 1971, s 23

By s 23(1), a constable (or other person authorised by a general or special order of the Secretary of State) shall, for the purposes of the execution of this Act, have power to enter the premises of a person carrying on business as a producer or supplier of any controlled drugs and to demand the production of, and to inspect, any books or documents relating to dealings in any such drugs and to inspect any stocks of any such drugs. Section 23(2) further provides that a constable who has reasonable grounds to suspect that a person is in possession of a controlled drug in contravention of the Act may search that person (or any vehicle or vessel in which it is suspected the drug may be found) and seize and detain anything which appears to him to be evidence of an offence under the Act. Section 23(4) creates a range of offences relating to the obstruction of a person exercising the powers contained in s 23(1).

3.2.5   Other statutory powers

The main powers of entry without a warrant have now been dealt with. However, there are several specific statutory powers which, in very limited circumstances, permit a search of premises to be authorised by a senior police officer (usually a superintendent). See, for example, the Terrorism Act 2000, the Explosives Act 1875, the Official Secrets Act 1911.

3.3   Powers of search with a warrant

3.3.1   Police and Criminal Evidence Act 1984, s 8

By s 8(1), on an application made by a constable, a justice of the peace may issue either:

(a) A *Specific Premises Warrant*. This is a warrant which authorises a constable to enter and search one or more sets of premises specified in the application; or

(b) An *All Premises Warrant*. This is a warrant which authorises a constable to enter and search any premises occupied or controlled by a person specified in the application, including such sets of premises as are so specified.

A justice of the peace may only issue a Specific Premises Warrant if satisfied that there are reasonable grounds for believing:

(a) that an indictable offence has been committed; *and*

(b) that there is material on such premises which is likely to be of substantial value (whether by itself or together with other material) to the investigation of the offence; *and*

(c) that the material is likely to be relevant and admissible in evidence at a trial; *and*

(d) that it does not consist of or include items subject to legal privilege, excluded material or special procedure material; *and*

(e) that in relation to each set of premises specified in the application it is not practicable to communicate with any person entitled to grant entry to the premises, or although it is practicable to communicate with such person it is not practicable to communicate with any person entitled to grant access to the evidence, or that entry to the premises will not be granted unless a warrant is produced, or that the purpose of a search may be frustrated or seriously prejudiced unless a constable arriving at the premises can secure immediate entry to them.

(For the definition of 'excluded material' and 'special procedure material' and the special procedures relating to such material, see **3.4.2** below.)

A justice of the peace may only issue an All Premises Warrant if additionally satisfied:

(a) that because of the particulars of the offence, there are reasonable grounds for believing that it is necessary to search premises occupied or controlled by the person in question which are not specified in the application in order to find the material sought; and

(b) that it is not reasonably practicable to specify in the application all the premises which he occupies or controls and which might need to be searched.

However, where an All Premises Warrant has been issued, premises other than those specified in the warrant may only be searched if a police officer of at least the rank of inspector has given written authorisation (s 16(3A)).

In either case it is unnecessary to have already tried other methods of entry and failed, nor is it necessary to demonstrate that other methods would be bound to fail, when applying for a warrant.

By s 8(2), a constable may seize and retain anything for which a search has been authorised under s 8(1).

Either type of warrant may authorise entry to and search of premises on more than one occasion, if the justice of the peace is satisfied that it is necessary to authorise multiple entries in order to achieve the purpose for which he issues the warrant. If it authorises multiple entries, the number of entries authorised may be unlimited, or limited to a maximum. However, no premises may be searched for the second or subsequent time under a warrant authorising multiple entries unless an officer of at least the rank of inspector has given written authorisation (s 16(3B)).

The most significant point about s 8 is that it is not limited to particular offences (unlike all previous statutory provisions allowing the issue of search warrants). However, under s 8 the offence must be an indictable offence. It thus may sometimes be necessary to have regard to the *specific* statutory powers to issue search warrants which are still in force.

Once the police have a search warrant, the date and time of its execution are a matter for them to decide. However, the warrant will cease to be valid three months after the date of its issue; also, execution should occur at a reasonable hour (unless this would frustrate the purpose of the search).

3.3.2   Misuse of Drugs Act 1971, s 23(3)

If a justice of the peace is satisfied by information on oath that there is reasonable ground for suspecting:

- that any controlled drugs are, in contravention of this Act, in the possession of a person on any premises; or
- that a document relating to a transaction or dealing which was (or would if carried out be) an offence under this Act is in the possession of a person on any premises,

he may grant a warrant authorising any constable acting for the police area in which the premises are situated to enter, if need be by force, the premises named in the warrant and to search the premises and any persons found therein, and if there is reasonable ground for suspecting that an offence under this Act has been committed in relation to any drugs or document found, to seize and detain those drugs or that document. See also the Drug Trafficking Act 1994, ss 55 and 56.

3.3.3   Theft Act 1968, s 26

If it is made to appear by information or order before a justice of the peace that there is reasonable cause to believe that any person has in his custody or possession or on his premises any stolen goods, the justice may grant a warrant to search for and seize the same. The warrant must be addressed to a constable (unless a particular enactment expressly provides otherwise).

3.3.4   Criminal Damage Act 1971, s 6

If it is made to appear by information on oath before a justice of the peace that there is reasonable cause to believe that a person has in his custody, his control or on his premises something which there is reasonable cause to believe has been used or is intended for use without lawful excuse, to destroy or damage either property belonging to another or his own property (if damage to it would endanger the life of another), the justice may grant a warrant to search for and seize the same.

3.3.5   Other statutory powers

The powers of entry with a warrant which are of most general application have now been dealt with. However, there are numerous specific statutory powers of entry with a warrant. For important examples see the Offences Against the Person Act 1861, s 65, the Obscene Publications Act 1959 s 3, the Forgery and Counterfeiting Act 1981, ss 7 and 24, the Criminal Justice Act 1987, s 2, the Copyright, Designs and Patents Act 1988, s 109, the Public Order Act 1986, s 24.

3.4   Search warrants — general rules and restrictions

3.4.1   Procedure

Although PACE 1984 left intact many specific statutory powers to search *with a warrant*, the Act, in ss 15 and 16, laid down rules and restrictions of general application to search warrants issued to a constable under *any enactment* (the rules and restrictions also apply to Customs and Excise Officers and Environmental Protection Officers).

Since these sections contain relatively straightforward procedural rules they are set out in full below. The procedure is augmented by Code of Practice B, paras 3–6.

15.—*(1)*   *This section and section 16 below have effect in relation to the issue to constables under any enactment, including an enactment contained in an Act passed after this Act, of warrants to enter and search premises; and an entry on or search of premises under a warrant is unlawful unless it complies with this section and section 16 below.*

(2)   *Where a constable applies for any such warrant, it shall be his duty—*

    (a)   *to state—*

        (i)   *the ground on which he makes the application; and*

        (ii)   *the enactment under which the warrant would be issued; and*

        (iii)   *if the application is for a warrant authorising entry and search on more than one occasion, the ground on which he applies for such a warrant, and whether he seeks a warrant authorising an unlimited number of entries, or (if not) the maximum number of entries desired;*

    (b)   *to specify the matters set out in subsection (2A) below; and*

    (c)   *to identify, so far as is practicable, the articles or persons to be sought.*

(2A)   *The matters which must be specified pursuant to subsection (2)(b) above are—*

    (a)   *if the application is for a specific premises warrant made by virtue of section 8(1A)(a) above or paragraph 12 of Schedule 1 below, each set of premises which it is desired to enter and search;*

    (b)   *if the application is for an all premises warrant made by virtue of section 8(1A)(b) above or paragraph 12 of Schedule 1 below—*

        (i)   *as many sets of premises which it is desired to enter and search as it is reasonably practicable to specify;*

        (ii)   *the person who is in occupation or control of those premises and any others which it is desired to enter and search;*

        (iii)   *why it is necessary to search more premises than those specified under sub-paragraph (i); and*

        (iv)   *why it is not reasonably practicable to specify all the premises which it is desired to enter and search.*

(3)   *An application for such a warrant shall be made ex parte and supported by an information in writing.*

(4)   *The constable shall answer on oath any question that the justice of the peace or judge hearing the application asks him.*

(5)   *A warrant shall authorise an entry on one occasion only unless it specifies that it authorises multiple entries.*

(5A)   *If it specifies that it authorises multiple entries, it must also specify whether the number of entries authorised is unlimited, or limited to a specified maximum.*

(6)   *A warrant—*

    (a)   *shall specify—*

        (i)   *the name of the person who applies for it;*

        (ii)   *the date on which it is issued;*

        (iii)   *the enactment under which it is issued; and*

(iv)   each set of premises to be searched, or (in the case of an all premises warrant) the person who is in occupation or control of premises to be searched, together with any premises under his occupation or control which can be specified and which are to be searched; and

(b)   shall identify, so far as is practicable, the articles or persons to be sought.

(7)   Two copies shall be made of a specific premises warrant (see section 8(1A)(a) above) which specifies only one set of premises and does not authorise multiple entries; and as many copies as are reasonably required may be made of any other kind of warrant.

(8)   The copies shall be clearly certified as copies.

16.—(1)   A warrant to enter and search premises may be executed by any constable.

(2)   Such a warrant may authorise persons to accompany any constable who is executing it.

(2A)   A person so authorised has the same powers as the constable whom he accompanies in respect of—

(a)   the execution of the warrant, and

(b)   the seizure of anything to which the warrant relates.

(2B)   But he may exercise those powers only in the company, and under the supervision, of a constable.

(3)   Entry and search under a warrant must be within three months from the date of its issue.

(3A)   If the warrant is an all premises warrant, no premises which are not specified in it may be entered or searched unless a police officer of at least the rank of inspector has in writing authorised them to be entered.

(3B)   No premises may be entered or searched for the second or any subsequent time under a warrant which authorises multiple entries unless a police officer of at least the rank of inspector has in writing authorised that entry to those premises.

(4)   Entry and search under a warrant must be at a reasonable hour unless it appears to the constable executing it that the purpose of a search may be frustrated on an entry at a reasonable hour.

(5)   Where the occupier of premises which are to be entered and searched is present at the time when a constable seeks to execute a warrant to enter and search them, the constable—

(a)   shall identify himself to the occupier and, if not in uniform, shall produce to him documentary evidence that he is a constable;

(b)   shall produce the warrant to him; and

(c)   shall supply him with a copy of it.

(6)   Where—

(a)   the occupier of such premises is not present at the time when a constable seeks to execute such a warrant; but

(b)   some other person who appears to the constable to be in charge of the premises is present,

subsection (5) above shall have effect as if any reference to the occupier were a reference to that other person.

(7)   If there is no person present who appears to the constable to be in charge of the premises, he shall leave a copy of the warrant in a prominent place on the premises.

(8)   A search under a warrant may only be a search to the extent required for the purpose for which the warrant was issued.

(9)   A constable executing a warrant shall make an endorsement on it stating—

(a)   whether the articles or persons sought were found; and

(b)   whether any articles were seized, other than articles which were sought and,

unless the warrant is a specific premises warrant specifying one set of premises only, he shall do so separately in respect of each set of premises entered and searched, which he shall in each case state in the endorsement.

(10)   A warrant shall be returned to the appropriate person mentioned in subsection (10A) below—

(a)   when it has been executed; or

(b)   in the case of a specific premises warrant which has not been executed, or an all premises warrant, or any warrant authorising multiple entries, upon the expiry of the period of three months referred to in subsection (3) above or sooner.

(10A) *The appropriate person is—*

    (a)   *if the warrant was issued by a justice of the peace, the designated officer for the local justice area in which the justice was acting when he issued the warrant;*

    (b)   *if it was issued by a judge, the appropriate officer of the court from which he issued it.*

(11)   *A warrant which is returned under subsection (10) above shall be retained for 12 months from its return—*

    (a)   *by the designated officer for the local justice area, if it was returned under paragraph (i) of that subsection; and*

    (b)   *by the appropriate officer, if it was returned under paragraph (ii).*

(12)   *If during the period for which a warrant is to be retained the occupier of premises to which it relates asks to inspect it, he shall be allowed to do so.*

3.4.2 Protected material: special procedures

Although PACE 1984 creates a general power to issue search warrants in cases where there are reasonable grounds for believing that an indictable offence has been committed (see **3.3.1**), three categories of material are to a greater or lesser extent protected from being the object of search. These categories are:

- items subject to legal privilege;
- excluded material; and
- special procedure material.

3.4.2.1 Items subject to legal privilege

This category should require no introduction — see *Evidence Manual* at **17.2.2**. Since:

- PACE 1984 provides no power to search for legally privileged items; and
- the Act states, in s 9(2), that any Act preceding PACE 1984 shall cease to have effect in so far as it authorises a search for *any* of the three protected categories; and
- no subsequent Act provides a power to grant a warrant to search for legally privileged items,

they may be treated as being fully protected (at least until a subsequent Act alters the position).

However, while there may be no power to issue a warrant to search for legally privileged material, a constable may nevertheless seize such material during the course of a search in certain circumstances (see the Criminal Justice and Police Act 2001, ss 50 and 51, and **3.5.2** below).

3.4.2.2 Excluded material

Excluded material consists of:

- personal records acquired, or created, in the course of any trade, business, profession or other occupation or for the purposes of any paid or unpaid office, and which are held in confidence;
- human tissue or tissue fluid taken for the purposes of diagnosis or medical treatment and held in confidence;
- journalistic material held in confidence (s 11).

Personal records include medical records and spiritual and welfare counselling records about an individual (whether living or dead) who can be identified from them (s 12).

A special warrant to search for such material may be obtained by leave of a circuit judge (for the procedure, see **3.4.2.4**).

3.4.2.3 Special procedure material

Special procedure material consists of any material (falling outside the first two categories) which a person acquired, or created, in the course of any trade, business, profession or other occupation or for the purpose of any paid or unpaid office, and which he holds subject to an express or implied undertaking to keep it confidential, and journalistic material (even if not held in confidence) (s 14). A special warrant to search for such material may be obtained by leave of a circuit judge (for the procedure, see **3.4.2.4**).

3.4.2.4 Special warrants

As noted above (at **3.3.1**) an ordinary search warrant (under s 8 of PACE 1984) cannot be issued in relation to items subject to legal privilege, excluded material or special procedure material. However, as regards excluded or special procedure material, if the procedure laid down in Sch 1 of PACE 1984 is followed (see below), a circuit judge may order that such material should be produced or that access to it should be given. If the person to whom the order is addressed fails to comply with the order the judge may then issue a special warrant (pursuant to Sch 1, para 12).

Schedule 1 of PACE 1984 states:

1. *If on an application made by a constable a judge is satisfied that one or other of the sets of access conditions is fulfilled, he may make an order under paragraph 4 below.*

2. *The first set of access conditions is fulfilled if—*
    (a) *there are reasonable grounds for believing—*
        (i) *that an indictable offence has been committed;*
        (ii) *that there is material which consists of special procedure material or also includes special procedure material and does not also include excluded material on premises specified in the application, or on premises occupied or controlled by a person specified in the application (including all such premises on which there are reasonable grounds for believing that there is such material as it is reasonably practicable so to specify);*
        (iii) *that the material is likely to be of substantial value (whether by itself or together with other material) to the investigation in connection with which the application is made; and*
        (iv) *that the material is likely to be relevant evidence;*
    (b) *other methods of obtaining the material—*
        (i) *have been tried without success; or*
        (ii) *have not been tried because it appeared that they were bound to fail; and*
    (c) *it is in the public interest, having regard—*
        (i) *to the benefit likely to accrue to the investigation if the material is obtained; and*
        (ii) *to the circumstances under which the person in possession of the material holds it,*
    that the material should be produced or that access to it should be given.

3. *The second set of access conditions is fulfilled if—*
    (a) *there are reasonable grounds for believing that there is material which consists of or includes excluded material or special procedure material on premises specified in the application, or on premises occupied or controlled by a person specified in the application (including all such premises on which there are reasonable grounds for believing that there is such material as it is reasonably practicable so to specify);*
    (b) *but for section 9(2) above a search of such premises for that material could have been authorised by the issue of a warrant to a constable under an enactment other than this Schedule; and*
    (c) *the issue of such a warrant would have been appropriate.*

4. An order under this paragraph is an order that the person who appears to the judge to be in possession of the material to which the application relates shall—

    (a) produce it to a constable for him to take away; or

    (b) give a constable access to it,

    not later than the end of the period of seven days from the date of the order or the end of such longer period as the order may specify.

. . .

12. If on an application made by a constable a judge—

    (a) is satisfied—

        (i)   that either set of access conditions is fulfilled; and

        (ii) that any of the further conditions set out in paragraph 14 below is also fulfilled in relation to each set of premises specified in the application; or

    (b) is satisfied—

        (i)   that the second set of access conditions is fulfilled; and

        (ii) that an order under paragraph 4 above relating to the material has not been complied with,

    he may issue a warrant authorising a constable to enter and search the premises or (as the case may be) all premises occupied or controlled by the person referred to in paragraph 2(a)(ii) or 3(a), including such sets of premises as are specified in the application (an 'all premises warrant').

12A. The judge may not issue an all premises warrant unless he is satisfied—

    (a) that there are reasonable grounds for believing that it is necessary to search premises occupied or controlled by the person in question which are not specified in the application, as well as those which are, in order to find the material in question; and

    (b) that it is not reasonably practicable to specify all the premises which he occupies or controls which might need to be searched.

13. A constable may seize and retain anything for which a search has been authorised under paragraph 12 above.

14. The further conditions mentioned in paragraph 12(a)(ii) above are—

    (a) that it is not practicable to communicate with any person entitled to grant entry to the premises to which the application relates;

    (b) that it is practicable to communicate with a person entitled to grant entry to the premises but it is not practicable to communicate with any person entitled to grant access to the material;

    (c) that the material contains information which—

        (i)   is subject to a restriction or obligation such as is mentioned in section 11(2)(b) above; and

        (ii) is likely to be disclosed in breach of it if a warrant is not issued;

    (d) that service of notice of an application for an order under paragraph 4 above may seriously prejudice the investigation.

It is permissible for the police to seek voluntary disclosure even if there would be no chance of an application under Sch 1 succeeding (see *Singleton* [1995] 1 Cr App R 431).

Note: There is a distinction between (i) cases where protected material is sought in an investigation into whether a criminal offence has been committed and (ii) cases where such material is sought for the purposes of an investigation (as part of confiscation proceedings) into whether any person has benefited from any criminal conduct. In the latter situation, an order may be granted under the Proceeds of Crime Act 2002, s 352 (these are not dealt with here as confiscation is a specialist area). Section 354 expressly provides that a warrant issued for this purpose does not confer a right to seize privileged or excluded material. However, as the section is silent on special procedure material, it is submitted that such material may be seized under this type of warrant. The fact that an incidental effect of confiscation proceedings (and orders under s 352) might be to reveal the commission of an offence will not be a bar to the making of such an order (see *Crown Court at Southwark, ex p Bowles* [1998] AC 641).

3.5 Seizure

3.5.1 Pace 1984

Section 19 of PACE 1984 made general provisions with regard to the seizure of things in circumstances where a constable is lawfully on any premises. A constable may seize anything which is on the premises if he has reasonable grounds for believing:

(a) that it has been obtained in consequence of the commission of an offence; and that it is necessary to seize it in order to prevent it being concealed, lost, damaged, altered or destroyed; or

(b) that it is evidence in relation to an offence which he is investigating or any other offence; and that it is necessary to seize it in order to prevent the evidence being concealed, lost, altered or destroyed.

The constable may require any information which is stored in any electronic form and is accessible from the premises to be produced in a form in which it can be taken away and in which it is visible and legible or from which it can readily be produced in a visible and legible form if he has grounds for believing:

(a) that

  (i) it is evidence in relation to an offence which he is investigating or any other offence; or

  (ii) it has been obtained in consequence of the commission of an offence; and

(b) that it is necessary to do so in order to prevent it being concealed, lost, tampered with or destroyed.

It will be noted that these are very wide powers. They are restricted by the operation of s 19(6) which provides that no power of seizure conferred on a constable under *any* enactment (including an Act passed after the 1984 Act) is to be taken to authorise the seizure of an item which the constable exercising the power has reasonable grounds for believing to be subject to legal privilege. This provision does not to apply to the powers of seizure exercisable under ss 50 and 51 of the Criminal Justice and Police Act 2001 (see **3.5.2** below).

Under s 21, the officer in charge of an investigation is required to allow access to or provide copies or photographs of things seized unless allowing such access would prejudice the investigation in which the thing was seized (or related investigations) (s 21(4)–(8)). However, things seized may be retained by the police for as long as is necessary in all the circumstances (s 22(1)). Retention will, for example, be necessary if a photograph or copy is insufficient for police purposes, or because the thing is stolen or might be used to cause damage or injury.

3.5.2 Criminal Justice and Police Act 2001

The powers of seizure under PACE 1984 (and other statutory powers of seizure — see Sch 1, pt 1 of the 2001 Act) have been considerably widened by the new 'search and seize' provisions in the Criminal Justice and Police Act (CJPA) 2001.

CJPA 2001, s 50 is designed to address two problematic areas, namely:

(a) where it cannot be determined during the course of the search whether an item, or its contents, are subject to a power of seizure; and

(b) where material is discovered during a search which *is* subject to a power of seizure but it is inextricably linked to other material, including legally privileged, excluded or special procedure material, for which there is no power of seizure.

Under s 50(1) of the Act, where a person who is lawfully on any premises finds something that he has reasonable grounds for believing may be, or may contain, something for which he is authorised to search and which he is entitled to seize but, in the circumstances, it is not practicable to determine whether he is in fact entitled to seize it, then he may seize so much of what he has found as is necessary to enable that to be determined.

Under s 50(2), where a person is lawfully on any premises and finds something which he would be entitled to seize but for its being comprised in other material that he has no power to seize and, in all the circumstances, it is not reasonably practicable for the seizable property to be separated on the premises, then that person may seize both the seizable and the other property. This power is particularly relevant to information held on computer media. Significantly, PACE 1984, s 19(6) does not apply to this provision (s 50(4)) and so a person conducting a search would be entitled to seize legally privileged material.

When considering whether a determination (s 50(1)) or a separation (s 50(2)) would be reasonably practicable regard must be had to the list of criteria in s 50(3) which includes the length of time that it would take, the number of persons that would be involved, the nature of any equipment required and whether the process would be likely to involve damage to property.

Section 53 provides that any property seized must be examined as soon as is reasonably practicable after its seizure and that property must be returned unless it falls into one of the following categories:

(a) it is property for which the person seizing it had power to search but which does not have to be returned on the grounds:

    (i)   that it is legally privileged material (see the reference to s 54 below), or

    (ii)   that it is excluded or special procedure material;

(b) it is property that was seized on any premises by a constable who was lawfully on the premises and there are reasonable grounds for believing that:

    (i)   it is property obtained in consequence of the commission of an offence and it is necessary for it to be retained in order to prevent its being concealed, lost, damaged, altered or destroyed; or

    (ii)   there are reasonable grounds for believing that it is evidence in relation to any offence and that it is necessary for it to be retained in order to prevent its being concealed, lost, damaged, altered or destroyed;

(c) it is something which, in all the circumstances, it will not be reasonably practicable, following the examination, to separate from property falling within category (a) or (b) above without prejudicing the use of the rest of that property.

By s 54, there is an obligation to return any legally privileged material as soon as is reasonably practicable after its seizure unless it falls into category (c).

By s 55, where the seizure is made under PACE 1984, s 8(2) there is a similar obligation to return any excluded or special procedure material unless it comes within category (b) or (c).

Where legally privileged, excluded or special procedure material has been seized or retained it may only be examined, copied or put to any other use where to do so is necessary to facilitate the use of the material in which it is comprised in any investigation or proceedings (s 62).

The retention of any property that has been seized under s 50 is additionally subject to PACE 1984 s 22 (see **3.5.1**).

The Act makes provision for anyone with an interest in the seized property to apply to a judge of the Crown Court for its return on the grounds that its seizure or retention is unlawful (s 59).

3.6 Evidential consequences of breach of rules on search and seizure

At common law, evidence obtained by illegal search or seizure is admissible (*Jeffrey v Black* [1978] QB 490). However, a court may exclude such evidence by virtue of the discretion under PACE 1984, s 78. In order to do so it must be satisfied that the admission of the evidence would adversely effect the fairness of the proceedings. In *Rotherham Magistrates' Court, ex p Todd*, unreported, 16 February 2000, DC, Lord Justice Simon Brown said:

Absent bad faith or a flagrant and deliberate breach of one of the codes of practice issued pursuant to the 1984 Act, or some other matter affecting the quality of the evidence, the mere fact that evidence is discovered in the course of an unlawful search is unlikely to render the admission of the evidence unfair.

Thus, an accused will ordinarily have to point to some prejudice over and above the unlawfulness of the search before a court will exclude evidence obtained during an illegal search. See also *Khan, Sakkaravej and Pamarapa* [1997] Crim LR 508.

3.7 Further reading

Clark, D., *Bevan and Lidstone's The Investigation of Crime: a Guide to the Law of Criminal Investigation*, 3rd edn., London: LexisNexis UK, 2004.

Stone, R., *The Law of Entry, Search, and Seizure*, 4th edn., Oxford: Oxford University Press, 2005.

Zander, M., *The Police and Criminal Evidence Act 1984*, 5th edn., London: Sweet & Maxwell, 2005.

Abuse of process

4.1 Abuse of process

The criminal courts have the power to prevent the prosecution from proceeding against a defendant in certain situations. One of these situations is where the court finds that there has been an abuse of process.

Lord Salmon stated in the case of *DPP v Humphrys* [1977] AC 1, HL:

It is only if the prosecution amounts to an abuse of the process of the court and is oppressive and vexatious that the judge has the power to intervene. Fortunately, such prosecutions are hardly ever brought but the power of the court to prevent them is, in my view, of great constitutional import-ance and should be jealously preserved. For a man to be harassed and be put to the expense of perhaps a long trial and then given an absolute discharge is hardly from any point of view an effective substitute for the exercise by the court of the power to which I have referred.

If established, the court can stay the proceedings and as you will see, there are a number of situations in which an abuse of process argument can be advanced. Although not an exhaustive list, the most commonly encountered grounds for mounting an argument to stay proceedings include:

(a) where there has been a substantial delay in bringing the prosecution;

(b) where the prosecution has failed to honour an undertaking given to the defendant;

(c) where the police/investigating agency have contributed to the commission of the offence itself;

(d) where the prosecution has failed to retain, secure or has lost or destroyed relevant evidential material;

(e) where the prosecution has manipulated certain procedures so as to deprive the defendant of some right.

In *Beckford* [1996] 1 Cr App R 96, the Court of Appeal identified two principles upon which proceedings could be stayed for abuse of process. It is for the defendant (as he is the one who is asserting the abuse) to prove either:

(a) that the defendant could not receive a fair trial; and/or

(b) that it would be unfair to try the defendant.

Accordingly, in considering the following most commonly encountered grounds for mounting an argument, bear in mind which of these two limbs you are aiming to establish.

4.1.1 Delay

The *Attorney-General's Reference (No 1 of 1990)* [1992] QB 630 states that stays imposed on the ground of even an unjustifiable delay should only be granted in exceptional circumstances. This despite Article 6 of the European Convention on Human Rights, which entitles a person who is charged with a criminal offence to a 'fair and public hearing within a reasonable time by an independent and impartial tribunal'. What constitutes a 'reasonable time' does not in itself determine whether the overriding right to a 'fair trial' has been compromised. In order for a defendant to argue successfully for a stay in proceedings on the grounds of delay, he must show that (a) a fair trial is no longer possible or (b) that it would be unfair to try him.

Accordingly, notwithstanding that a trial may not have been reached within a 'reasonable time', a judge will first consider the admissibility of the evidence and his control of it; the trial process itself which will involve putting the relevant factual issues arising from the delay before the jury to weigh up in their deliberations; together with his power to give appropriate directions to the jury during his summing up. In *R v Sawoniuk* [2000] 2 Cr App R 220, CA, a delay of 56 years did not constitute an abuse of process. The trial judge was able to adequately safeguard the interests of a fair trial by his careful direction to the jury on this issue of delay, alerting them to the impact of the delay on the direction and conduct of the defence, and the prosecution burden and standard of proof.

Certain types of case will always entail some degree of delay, for example, cases of childhood sexual abuse where the victim does not complain until many years later; and complex fraud cases. Again, the deciding issue will be whether the defendant can show, on the balance of probabilities, that a fair trial would be impossible: *Attorney-General's Reference (No 2 of 2001)* [2001] 1 WLR 1869.

In determining whether a defendant has been so prejudiced by the delay that a fair trial would be impossible, the court will look at the nature of the defence proposed; whether any admissions were made; whether independent witnesses present at the time may be traced or even if they were traced, their ability to recall the events; contamination of evidence between prosecution witnesses, inconsistencies in prosecution evidence and the ability of the defence, given the delay, to adequately test those inconsistencies, for example, by calling other witnesses; the reason for the delay (eg was the defendant responsible for the delay?) and any other factors that are relevant to the particular issues in the case. Where the reason for the delay is attributable, even in part, to inefficiency on the part of the prosecution, or worse, bad faith, then, if the delay is substantial and the court considers the defendant has been prejudiced as a result, an abuse of process argument is more likely to succeed. Each case will turn on its facts, however, and the above list is not exhaustive.

4.1.2 Prosecution failure to honour an undertaking given to the defendant

Where the prosecution go back on a promise not to prosecute an individual, in exchange for his cooperation for example, or on the basis that his plea of guilty to some, but not all, counts on an indictment was acceptable, then this may amount to an abuse of process. However, breach of a promise does not necessarily amount to an abuse of process. The defendant will have to show prejudice. Two of the key factors that the court will take into account in making its decision will be the length of time that an individual is left to believe he will not be prosecuted, and the existence of any prejudice that may have resulted from any cooperation he has given to the police.

In *Bloomfleld* [1997] 1 Cr App R 135, CA, prosecution counsel took the view that it would be wrong to proceed against the defendant because he agreed with the defence contention that the police had 'set-up' the offence. At the plea and directions hearing (now the plea and case management hearing), prosecution counsel informally advised defence counsel of his intention and told the judge the same in chambers. Prosecution counsel successfully applied for the matter to be adjourned to another day so that no evidence could be offered. The Crown Prosecution Service did not agree with the course taken by counsel and sought to proceed with the case. It was held that to allow the prosecution to go ahead would be an abuse of process as it would bring the administration of justice into disrepute. It was irrelevant whether prosecution counsel had the authority to drop the case, the defence were entitled to assume that counsel had such authority and rely upon the promise.

In *Horseferry Road Magistrates' Court, ex p DPP* [1999] COD 441, DC, a stipendiary magistrate (now district judge) stayed a prosecution where an earlier assurance that no action would be taken had been given to the defendant's solicitor. The Divisional Court quashed the stay, stating that breach of an earlier promise would not, on its own, justify staying the proceedings. There would have to be some particular prejudice or special circumstances. For example, in *Bloomfleld*, above, no evidence would have been offered but for the prosecution's request for an adjournment which they made for their convenience.

In *D* [2000] 1 Archbold News 1, CA, it was held to be an abuse of process to reinstate proceedings some years after the defendant had received a letter informing him that a final decision had been taken not to prosecute him in relation to an allegation of indecent assault against a 10-year-old boy. In the interim period the law had changed so that the boy's allegation no longer required corroboration. The prejudice pointed to was that exculpatory evidence was no longer available.

4.1.3   Entrapment

The House of Lords in *Looseley; Attorney-General's Reference (No 3 of 2000)* [2002] 1 Cr App R 29, HL made clear that the appropriate course of action, where it is alleged that there has been entrapment, would be to apply for a stay on the grounds of abuse of process.

In such cases, the defendant need not necessarily show that he has been prejudiced or that he would not have a fair trial. The overriding principle in such applications is that the rule of law must be maintained and that the integrity of the executive agents of the state, responsible for law enforcement, is maintained. Luring citizens into criminal conduct and then prosecuting them for it would be entrapment, a misuse of state power and would certainly undermine the integrity of the court.

It is not always clear, however, where the line should be drawn. It is quite common, for example, for police to engage in undercover operations in cases of suspected drug dealing. Arranging test purchases would not *per se* amount to entrapment; badgering a vulnerable drug addict to supply drugs in return for vast sums of money would.

4.1.4   Failing to secure evidence/destroying or losing evidence

Where that evidence may have exonerated the defendant, the guidelines laid out in the case of *R (Ebrahim) v Feltham Magistrates Court* [2001] 2 Cr App R 23, DC set out the approach that should be taken by the courts. The case concerned CCTV tapes but the principles apply to all types of evidence. Certainly, with the prevalence of CCTV in the UK, the seizure and retention of such evidence is vital.

The first question to be asked was the extent to which the investigator was under a duty to obtain and/or retain the material in question. In answering this question consideration should be given to the code of practice issued under the Criminal Procedure and Investigations Act 1996 and the *Attorney-General's Guidelines: Disclosure of Information in*

Criminal Proceedings. If there was no duty to obtain and/or retain the material before the defence first sought it then there could be no grounds to stay the proceedings. If there was a breach of the duty to obtain and/or retain the material, the defence must establish, on the balance of probabilities, that as a result of the breach the defendant is seriously prejudiced. By 'seriously prejudiced' the court in *Ebrahim* meant 'could not have a fair trial'. It was stressed that the normal forum for challenges to the prosecution case was the trial process itself, which was well equipped to deal with most complaints about how the investigators or the prosecution have behaved.

Where the prosecution have acted in bad faith or at least with a serious degree of fault, it can be argued, alternatively, that it would not be fair to try the defendant — the second limb of the '*Beckford* test'.

Consider the following scenario. Police officers arrest a defendant on a public order offence. Whilst he is taken into the cells in the custody suite, two police officers allege that he further assaulted them whilst trying to resist being placed in his cell. They state they had to use some force to restrain him, which is why he has sustained some injury in the form of bruising to his arms and back. They themselves sustained minor injury but sought no medical attention. The defendant states that nothing of the sort happened and that it was whilst he was being arrested for the public order offence that he was assaulted by the police en route to the police van. The officers, he says, are trying to account for his injuries by making up this story about his behaviour in the cells.

The custody suite is constantly under video surveillance. The street on which the public order offence was alledgedly committed is also under CCTV surveillance. The CCTV from the public area did not capture the arrest and is of no evidential value. However, the custody suites' tape was not seized at the time and have now been misplaced. How would you argue that proceedings should be stayed on the grounds that there has been an abuse of process?

4.1.5   Manipulation of procedure

An application to stay the proceedings may be an appropriate remedy where the defence contend that the prosecution has wrongfully manipulated a particular procedure. Is the prosecution, for example, entitled to proceed on purely summary only offences, thus depriving the defendant of a right to jury trial, where triable either way offences would ordinarily be appropriate?

In *Canterbury and St Augustine Justices, ex p Klisiak* [1982] QB 398, it was held that the court should only interfere with the prosecution's decision as to what offences to proceed upon 'in the most obvious circumstances which disclose blatant injustice'. In *Sheffleld Justices, ex p DPP* [1993] Crim LR 136, it was said that it would only be appropriate for the court to interfere where it concluded that the prosecution was acting in bad faith, ie deliberately manipulating the system to deprive a defendant of his rights. In *Rotherham JJ, ex p Brough* [1991] Crim LR 522, DC, the prosecution deliberately delayed proceedings so that the defendant could not be tried in the youth court and had to be tried in the Crown Court. This was held not to be an abuse of process as the court perceived the behaviour of the prosecution as amounting to an error of judgement rather than bad faith. The court was also of the view that the defendant faced no prejudice as the sentencing judge in the Crown Court would, in giving the defendant credit for his youth, focus on the age he was when he committed the offence and not his age at the sentencing hearing. In *Gleaves v Insall* [1999] 2 Cr App R 466, DC, the prosecution was refused a summons in one magistrates' court so renewed its application in another. Unsurprisingly, perhaps, this was held to be an abuse of process.

4.2 Procedural issues

4.2.1 The magistrates' court

The magistrates' court has the power to stay criminal proceedings for abuse of process. However, in *Horseferry Road Magistrates' Court, ex p Bennett* [1994] 1 AC 42, it was stated that the jurisdiction existed only in matters relating to the fairness of a defendant's trial, eg matters of delay and manipulation of procedure. The supervisory jurisdiction such as the upholding of the rule of law (sometimes described as 'process values') was a matter for the High Court. The magistrates' court may decline jurisdiction because of complexity or novelty and allow the matter to be dealt with by the High Court by way of judicial review.

4.2.2 The burden and standard of proof

As intimated earlier in the chapter, it is for the party who asserts the abuse of process to prove it. The burden is on the defence to establish the abuse and if necessary the prejudice to the defendant. The standard is the balance of probabilities.

4.2.3 The time of an application for a stay

Typically the time to apply to stay proceedings will be before plea although there is no reason why the application cannot be made at a later stage (*Aldershot Youth Court, ex p A* [1997] 3 Archbold News 2, DC (CO/1911/96)).

4.2.4 *Practice Direction (Criminal: Consolidated)*

Practice Direction (Criminal: Consolidated) [2002] 3 All ER 904, para 36 lays down the procedure to be followed where an abuse of process application is made in the Crown Court:

36.1   In all cases where a defendant in the Crown Court proposes to make an application to stay an indictment on the grounds of abuse of process, written notice of such application must be given to the prosecuting authority and to any co-defendant not later than 14 days before the date fixed or warned for trial (the relevant date). Such notice must: (a) give the name of the case and the indictment number; (b) state the fixed date or the warned date as appropriate; (c) specify the nature of the application; (d) set out in numbered sub-paragraphs the grounds upon which the application is to be made; (e) be copied to the Chief Listing Officer at the court centre where the case is due to be heard.

36.2   Any co-defendant who wishes to make a like application must give a like notice not later than 7 days before the relevant date, setting out any additional grounds relied upon.

36.3   In relation to such applications, the following automatic directions shall apply:

(a) the advocate for the applicant(s) must lodge with the Court and serve on all other parties a skeleton argument in support of the application at least 5 clear working days before the relevant date. If reference is to be made to any document not in the existing trial documents, a paginated and indexed bundle of such documents is to be provided with the skeleton argument;

(b) the advocate for the prosecution must lodge with the Court and serve on all other parties a responsive skeleton argument at least 2 clear working days before the relevant date, together with a supplementary bundle if appropriate.

36.4   All skeleton arguments must specify any propositions of law to be advanced (together with the authorities relied upon in support, with page references to passages relied upon), and where appropriate, include a chronology of events and a list of dramatis personae. In all instances where reference is made to a document, the reference in the trial documents or supplementary bundle is to be given.

36.5   The above time limits are minimum time limits. In appropriate cases the Court will order longer lead times. To this end in all cases where defence advocates are, at the time of the Plea and Directions hearing, considering the possibility of an abuse application, this must be raised with the Judge dealing with the matter who will order a different timetable if appropriate, and may wish in any event to give additional directions about the conduct of the application.

This practice direction only applies to proceedings before the Crown Court. In magistrates' court proceedings there is no set procedure. However, the standard practice is for the defence to flag up any potential abuse of process argument at the pre-trial review stage and to lodge and serve a skeleton argument in support of their application in advance of the abuse of process hearing. The prosecution will be required to lodge and serve a skeleton argument in reply.

4.3   Further reading

Choo, A. L.-T., *Abuse of Process and Judicial Stays of Criminal Proceedings*, Oxford: Clarendon Press, 1993.

Corker, D., *Abuse of Process and Fairness in Criminal Proceedings*, 2nd edn., London: Butterworths, 2003.

Jackson, J., and Johnstone, J., 'The Reasonable Time Requirement: An Independent and Meaningful Right' [2005] Crim LR, 3–23.

Webster, A., 'Delay and Article 6(1): An End to the Requirement of Prejudice?' [2001] Crim LR 786–794.

5

European Convention on Human Rights

The European Convention on Human Rights (ECHR) was signed in 1950, and came into force in 1953. It was produced by the Council of Europe, of which the United Kingdom was one of the original ten members (now considerably expanded), in the aftermath of the Second World War and the Nuremberg Trials. There is of course no direct connection between the Council of Europe and the European Union (EU). By now, however, the Convention has been signed and ratified by all the member States of the EU, as well as a number of countries which are outside the EU and including a number of former communist States.

The Council of Europe has a Commission and a Court. These institutions are based in Strasbourg. The European Court of Justice has at times relied on the ECHR as an influence on the general principles of EU law, but the Convention has no formal role in determining EU law.

5.1 The status of the ECHR in UK law

The ECHR is an international treaty to which the United Kingdom is a signatory, and it is binding on all its signatories in international law. In some member countries of the Council of Europe, the ECHR has been made a directly enforceable part of the domestic legal system. That was not the case, however, as far as the United Kingdom is concerned until recently. When the Convention was ratified, it was not considered necessary to enact legislation to give it effect in UK law, perhaps because it was assumed that the rights which it contained were already protected in this country. In virtually all the member countries of the Council of Europe, the ECHR has been made a directly enforceable part of the domestic legal system, and the question whether this should also be done by the United Kingdom has figured high on the political agenda for some years. As a result of the provisions of the Human Rights Act 1998, the ECHR was incorporated into the domestic law of the United Kingdom in October 2000. Section 2(1) of the Act provides that a court or tribunal determining a question in connection with a Convention right must take into account any judgment, decision, declaration or opinion made or given by the European Court of Human Rights, the Commission, or the Committee of Ministers of the Council of Europe. Even more significantly, s 3 states:

3.—(1) So far as it is possible to do so, primary legislation and subordinate legislation must be read and given effect in a way which is compatible with the Convention rights.

(2) This section—

(a) applies to primary legislation and subordinate legislation whenever enacted;

(b)   *does not affect the validity, continuing operation or enforcement of any incompatible primary legislation; and*

(c)   *does not affect the validity, continuing operation or enforcement of any incompatible sub-ordinate legislation if (disregarding any possibility of revocation) primary legislation prevents removal of the incompatibility.*

The provisions of the ECHR are therefore applicable at all levels, including the magistrates' courts. Moreover, as a result of s 3(1), the courts are required to interpret legislation so as to uphold Convention rights unless the legislation is so clearly incompatible with the ECHR that it is impossible. In doing so, they will have to have regard to the substantial body of case law which has evolved as a result of the decisions of the various bodies set up under the auspices of the ECHR.

It is now possible for an individual to complain of a breach of the ECHR before an English court. In the event of such a breach, the person aggrieved also has the right of individual petition. This right was recognised by the United Kingdom in 1966. The machinery to enforce the right is supplied by the European Court of Human Rights.

5.2   The rights contained in the ECHR

A number of the provisions of the Convention have relevance to criminal practice in this country. Extracts from the most important Articles in the Convention for our purposes are set out below, together with a commentary, where appropriate.

Article 3
No one shall be subjected to torture or to inhuman or degrading treatment or punishment.

Cases in which the UK has been involved where this Article has formed the basis of the petition have included:

- the use of corporal punishment as a criminal sanction (*Tyrer v UK*, Series A, vol. 26);

- extradition to face a possible death penalty in the United States of America (*Soering v UK*, Series A, vol. 161);

- the treatment of terrorist suspects (*Republic of Ireland v UK*, Series A, vol. 25).

Article 5
1.   *Everyone has the right to liberty and security of person. No one shall be deprived of his liberty save in the following cases and in accordance with a procedure prescribed by law:*

(a)   *the lawful detention of a person after conviction by a competent court;*

(b)   *the lawful arrest or detention of a person for non-compliance with the lawful order of a court or in order to secure the fulfilment of any obligation prescribed by law;*

(c)   *the lawful arrest or detention of a person effected for the purpose of bringing him before the competent legal authority on a reasonable suspicion of having committed an offence or when it is reasonably considered necessary to prevent his committing an offence or fleeing after having done so;*

(d)   *the detention of a minor by lawful order for the purpose of educational supervision or his lawful detention for the purpose of bringing him before the competent legal authority;*

(e)   *the lawful detention of persons for the prevention of the spreading of infectious diseases, of persons of unsound mind, alcoholics or drug addicts or vagrants;*

(f)   *the lawful arrest or detention of a person to prevent his effecting an unauthorised entry into the country or of a person against whom action is being taken with a view to deportation or extradition.*

2.   *Everyone who is arrested shall be informed promptly, in a language which he understands, of the reasons for his arrest and of any charge against him.*

3. Everyone arrested or detained in accordance with the provisions of paragraph 1(c) of this Article shall be brought promptly before a judge or other officer authorized by law to exercise judicial power and shall be entitled to trial within a reasonable time or to release pending trial. Release may be conditioned by guarantees to appear for trial.

4. Everyone who is deprived of his liberty by arrest or detention shall be entitled to take proceedings by which the lawfulness of his detention shall be decided speedily by a court and his release ordered if the detention is not lawful.

5. Everyone who has been the victim of arrest or detention in contravention of the provisions of this Article shall have an enforceable right to compensation.

There have been a number of cases brought against the UK, based upon this Article which involve the detention of suspected terrorists in the context of the situation in Northern Ireland (see, for example, *Brannigan and McBride v UK*, Series A, vol. 258-B).

In *Monnell and Morris v UK*, Series A, vol. 115, the applicants had been convicted of criminal offences, and applied for leave to appeal despite advice not to do so. The appeal was unsuccessful, and the Court of Appeal made a direction for loss of time (see **Criminal Litigation and Sentencing Manual, 19.8.1**). The applicants claimed that those loss of time orders resulted in a deprivation of liberty contrary to Article 5. They argued that the loss of time was in effect a further period of imprisonment imposed not for an offence, but for seeking leave to appeal. The practice was alleged to be discriminatory, because people who were not detained at the time of applying for leave to appeal did not suffer from the danger of a direction for loss of time. The Court held that, despite the fact that persons who were at liberty did not run the same risk, the difference in treatment had an objective and reasonable justification because:

... Whilst the loss of time ordered by the Court of Appeal is not treated under domestic law as part of the applicants' sentences as such, it does form part of the period of detention which results from the overall sentencing procedure that follows conviction. As a matter of English law, a sentence of imprisonment passed by a Crown Court is to be served subject to any order which the Court of Appeal may, in the event of an unsuccessful application for leave to appeal, make as to loss of time. Section 29(1) of the [Criminal Appeal Act 1968] is couched in rather wide and flexible terms. However, the power of the Court of Appeal to order loss of time, as it is actually exercised, is a component of the machinery existing under English law to ensure that criminal appeals are considered within a reasonable time and, in particular, to reduce the time spent in custody by those with meritorious grounds waiting for their appeal to be heard.

As a result:

... there was a sufficient and legitimate connection, for the purposes of the deprivation of liberty permitted under sub-paragraph (a) of Article 5(1), between the conviction of each applicant and the additional period of imprisonment undergone as a result of the loss-of-time order made by the Court of Appeal. The time spent in custody by each applicant under this head is accordingly to be regarded as detention of a person after conviction by a competent court, within the meaning of sub-paragraph (a) of Article 5(1).

Article 6

1. In the determination of his civil rights and obligations or of any criminal charge against him, everyone is entitled to a fair and public hearing within a reasonable time by an independent and impartial tribunal established by law. Judgment shall be pronounced publicly but the press and public may be excluded from all or part of the trial in the interests of morals, public order or national security in a democratic society, where the interests of juveniles or the protection of the private life of the parties so require, or to the extent strictly necessary in the opinion of the court in special circumstances where publicity would prejudice the interests of justice.

2. Everyone charged with a criminal offence shall be presumed innocent until proved guilty according to law.

3. *Everyone charged with a criminal offence has the following minimum rights:*

    (a) *to be informed promptly, in a language which he understands and in detail, of the nature and cause of the accusation against him;*

    (b) *to have adequate time and facilities for the preparation of his defence;*

    (c) *to defend himself in person or through legal assistance of his own choosing or, if he has not sufficient means to pay for legal assistance, to be given it free when the interests of justice so require;*

    (d) *to examine or have examined witnesses against him and to obtain the attendance and examination of witnesses on his behalf under the same conditions as witnesses against him;*

    (e) *to have the free assistance of an interpreter if he cannot understand or speak the language used in court.*

This article is of particular importance to criminal practice, and there have been a number of cases against the United Kingdom, based upon different issues which arise from it.

For example, in *X v UK* 15 EHRR CD 113, the decision of an English court to screen witnesses from the petitioner was held not to be an infringement of his rights under Article 6(1) or 6(3)(d). The accused must, however, in adversarial proceedings such as those in this country, have the right to participate fully. This includes the right to be present, to hear and to follow proceedings (*Standford v UK*, Series A, vol. 282). The right of participation also implies that the applicant should be able to understand the proceedings and conduct a defence (*V v UK* 15 EHRR CD 108). It is under the provisions of this Article that the effects of prejudicial press coverage may be considered, for example, if the campaign was so extreme that it deprived the accused of a fair trial.

A central principle contained in Article 6 is that of 'equality of arms'. The underlying notion is that the accused should be equal to the prosecution in procedural terms. This means that there should be defence access to the evidence gathered by the prosecution, given the superior resources available to the State in terms of investigation and interrogation. This has implications for the way in which the prosecution duty to disclose unused material is defined (see the article on 'Disclosure, Appeals and Procedural Traditions' by Field and Young, referred to in **5.6**, the case of *Edwards v UK* (2003) 15 BHRC 189 and the case of *Rowe and Davis v UK* (2000) 30 EHRR 1). 'Equality of arms' also means that both parties to an action in an adversarial system must generally have the right to challenge and confront each other's witnesses, with the power to cross-examine.

Another aspect of trial which has been scrutinised for compliance with Article 6 is the investigation of allegations of bias in the jury room. In *Gregory v UK* (1997) 25 EHRR 577, one of the jury made an allegation of racial bias in the deliberations of the jury after retirement. The judge recalled the jury and gave them a clear direction on their duty to return a verdict on the basis of the evidence alone. The defendant was convicted, and claimed before the European Court of Human Rights that he had been denied a fair trial before an impartial tribunal in accordance with Article 6. The European Court of Human Rights rejected his argument and concluded that the judge had done sufficient to dismiss any legitimate doubts as to the impartiality of the jury. In *Sander v UK* (2001) 31 EHRR 44, the European Court of Human Rights was again faced with an allegation of racism among the jurors. However, they distinguished *Gregory* on the basis that in that case the complaint had been vague, imprecise and unsubstantiated. In the case of *Sander*, by contrast, they found that the trial judge's direction to disregard any bias was not sufficient to dismiss legitimate doubts about the impartiality of the jury.

Article 6(3)(c) has relevance to the availability of legal aid. In limiting the right to those without the means to pay for it, and to cases where the interests of justice require it, the provision is based upon premises similar to those of our own legal aid. However, the United Kingdom's provision of legal aid for appellants making oral representations to the High Court of Justiciary in Scotland has been successfully challenged in a series of cases before the Court (*Granger v UK* 12 EHRR 451; *Maxwell v UK* 15 EHRR CD 101 and 19 EHRR 97; *Boner v UK* 19 EHRR 246).

In *Murray v UK* 22 EHRR 29, the UK was alleged to have violated the Convention in two respects:

(a) by denying the applicant access to legal advice for the first 48 hours of detention;

(b) by allowing inferences to be drawn from the applicant's silence (under the Northern Ireland predecessor of the provisions in ss 34 and 35 of the Criminal Justice and Public Order Act 1994).

The Court upheld the complaint as far as (a) was concerned, but not with regard to (b).

Article 10

1.   Everyone has the right to freedom of expression. This right shall include freedom to hold opinions and to receive and impart information and ideas without interference by public authority and regardless of frontiers. This Article shall not prevent States from requiring the licensing of broadcasting, television or cinema enterprises.

2.   The exercise of these freedoms, since it carries with it duties and responsibilities, may be subject to such formalities, conditions, restrictions or penalties as are prescribed by law and are necessary in a democratic society, in the interests of national security, territorial integrity or public safety, for the prevention of disorder or crime, for the protection of health or morals, for the protection of the reputation or rights of others, for preventing the disclosure of information received in confidence, or for maintaining the authority and impartiality of the judiciary.

Cases have been brought against the United Kingdom alleging violations of this Article, eg in respect of:

(a) blasphemous libel (*Gay News and Lemon v UK* 5 EHRR 123);

(b) contempt of court (eg, the 'Spycatcher' case (*Observer and Guardian v UK* 14 EHRR 153));

(c) the Incitement to Disaffection Act 1934 (*Arrowsmith v UK* 3 EHRR 218).

Article 14

The enjoyment of the rights and freedoms set forth in this Convention shall be secured without discrimination on any ground such as sex, race, colour, language, religion, political or other opinion, national or social origin, association with a national minority, property, birth or other status.

Article 14 prohibits discrimination only with respect to the enjoyment of the rights set out in the Convention. It follows that complaint about the violation of Article 14 can only be brought where some other Article of the Convention has allegedly been breached.

This Article has been invoked against the UK, eg, in respect of:

(a) exclusion of a solicitor from interviews with terrorist suspects in Northern Ireland (*Murray v UK* 22 EHRR 29);

(b) the legal treatment of transsexuals (*X, Y and Z v UK* App No 21830/93 unreported);

(c) directions for loss of time for appellants in custody (*Monnell and Morris v UK*, dealt with under Article 5 above);

(d) the treatment of sado-masochistic acts between consenting males compared to boxing (*Laskey v UK* 24 EHRR 39).

Article 15

1.   In time of war or other public emergency threatening the life of the nation any High Contracting Party may take measures derogating from its obligations under this Convention to the extent strictly required by the exigencies of the situation, provided that such measures are not inconsistent with its other obligations under international law.

2.   No derogation from Article 2, except in respect of deaths resulting from lawful acts of war, or from Articles 3, 4 (paragraph 1) and 7 shall be made under this provision.

3.   Any High Contracting Party availing itself of this right of derogation shall keep the Secretary General of the Council of Europe fully informed of the measures which it has taken and the reasons therefor. It shall also inform the Secretary General of the Council of Europe when such measures have ceased to operate and provisions of the Convention are again being fully executed.

Article 16
Nothing in Articles 10, 11 and 14 shall be regarded as preventing the High Contracting Parties from imposing restrictions on the political activity of aliens.

These Articles (together with Articles 17 and 18, which are less frequently invoked) set out the restrictions on the scope of the Convention. The UK has made use of the right to derogate under Article 15, informing the Secretary General of derogations relating to the situation in Northern Ireland. The Commission and the Court are responsible for ensuring that the requirements of Article 15(1) are met, but the tendency has been to allow the contracting State a wide 'margin of appreciation' (see **5.4**) in judging, eg, whether there is a public emergency threatening the life of the nation. There can in any event, by virtue of Article 15(2), be no derogation from certain of the Articles, eg, Article 3.

5.3   Procedure under the ECHR

The procedure commences with a petition to the Secretary General of the Council of Europe, who forwards it to the Court. There is provision for public funding to applicants in the Court's Rules of Procedure, although such funding is in fact only granted in a small proportion of cases.

5.3.1   Requirements for admissibility

When determining admissibility, the Court must be satisfied that the applicant has exhausted all domestic remedies, and has presented the petition within six months of the final decision reached through the pursuit of those remedies. In addition, the petition must raise a matter which is not substantially the same as one already ruled on by the Court, and has not been submitted to 'another procedure of international investigation or settlement' (art. 35(2)(b)). Further, the Court will rule inadmissible any application 'incompatible with the provision' of the ECHR, 'manifestly ill-founded', or 'an abuse of the right of petition' (art. 35(3)).

5.3.2   Exhausting domestic remedies

As far as the requirement that the applicant exhaust domestic remedies is concerned, certain remedies may not be regarded as normal, eg, an application for *habeus corpus* is not considered as part of the normal appeal procedure (*X v UK* (1969) 12 *Yearbook* 298). Further, there is no obligation to pursue remedies which clearly offer no chance of success. Where an appeal would clearly fail because there is a binding domestic precedent which stands in the way of the applicant, then the case does not have to be pursued all the way to the House of Lords.

5.3.3   The time limit

The six month period within which the petition must be brought to the Court begins with the date when the final decision is taken (art. 35(1)). This has been defined as 'the date of a "final decision" taken in the exhaustion of an effective and sufficient domestic remedy, or from the date of the act or decision complained of where such an act or decision finally determines the applicant's position on the domestic level' (*Greenock Ltd v UK* (1985) 42 D & R 33 at 41). Time will usually cease to run on the date of the first letter to the Court indicating an intention to lodge an application, and the nature of the complaint (*Kelly v UK* (1985) 42 D & R 205), but the Court may look at the circumstances of the case to decide on the relevant date eg, where pursuit of the case has been unreasonably delayed. Where the breach of the ECHR is a continuing one, then time will not begin to run until the continuing state of affairs ceases to exist (*Temple v UK* 8 EHRR 319).

5.3.4 Settlement

If the Court decides that the application is admissible, it proceeds to the next stage. It usually receives further evidence and submissions. At the same time, it will try to reach a 'friendly settlement' or negotiated agreement between the parties. Such a settlement may involve, for example, payment of compensation, or a change in the law or administrative practice which is the subject of the complaint.

If there is no settlement, the government and the applicant may make further written and oral submissions.

5.3.5 The hearing

The oral hearings are short, typically lasting a couple of hours. Speeches have to be written in advance to aid simultaneous translation.

The Court has a number of judges equivalent to the members of the Council of Europe, but it usually sits in chambers of nine judges. The procedure is in the main written, affidavits and other documents being filed with the Court in compliance with time limits. A date is fixed for a public oral hearing, in which the applicant, although not strictly a party to the proceedings, is in practice allowed to participate, represented by an advocate. The final judgment of the Court is by a majority, and dissenting judgments are common. It has the power to order a State which is in breach of the ECHR to make just compensation (art. 41). In addition, a judgment finding that a State's laws are in breach of the ECHR imposes a duty on the State in question to rectify the law.

5.4 The approach of the European Court of Human Rights

The approach of the judges in Strasbourg is determined by the fact that they are engaged in interpreting what is in effect a Code containing a limited number of general provisions. Frequently, they are required to fill in the details to what is a very broad statement of rights and freedoms. In doing so, the approach which they adopt may be said to have the following characteristics:

(a) It is purposive, ie, the Court searches for the purposes underlying the broad statement contained in the Convention. For example, in *Soering v UK*, Series A, vol. 161 at paragraph 87, the Court stated:

> In interpreting the Convention regard must be had to its special character as a treaty for the collective enforcement of human rights and fundamental freedoms (see the *Ireland v United Kingdom* judgment of 18 January 1978, Series A, No 25, p 90 §239). Thus, the object and

purpose of the Convention as an instrument for the protection of individual human beings require that its provisions be interpreted and applied so as to make its safeguards practical and effective (see, *inter alia*, the *Artico* judgment of 13 May 1980, Series A, No 37, p 16 §33). In addition, any interpretation of rights and freedoms guaranteed has to be consistent with 'the general spirit of the Convention, an instrument designed to maintain and promote the ideals and values of a democratic society' (see the *Kjeldsen, Busk, Madsen and Pedersen* judgment of 7 December 1976, Series A, No 23, p 27 §53).

(b) It is evolutionary, interpreting the Convention in the light of current thinking and the social climate (eg in *Tyrer v UK*, Series A, vol. 26, where the practice of corporal punishment as part of the criminal justice system on the Isle of Man was examined and held to be a breach of Article 3, the Court stated that 'the Convention is a living instrument which . . . must be interpreted in the light of present-day conditions').

(c) It produces decisions which are based on the specific set of facts which it is considering, rather than laying down propositions of general application, eg, often the Court will emphasise that it is interpreting the Convention specifically in relation to the facts before it.

(d) It recognises the principle of proportionality: that restrictions on human rights or penalties imposed for infringement of the law should be proportional to their aims.

(e) It has based itself on the principle of the margin of appreciation. This principle derives from a recognition of the legal and social diversity existing within the States which are signatories to the ECHR. It leaves individual States a measure of discretion in the way in which they implement the principles of the Convention. In interpreting an article, the Court will concentrate on the broad picture and the limits of acceptable conduct, rather than prescribing exactly how a State should comply with its treaty obligations.

5.5   Reporting of ECHR cases

The edited *European Human Rights Reports* are published by Sweet & Maxwell (cited as EHRR).

The Publications of the European Court of Human Rights include the following:

- Series A is the Judgments of the Court.
- Series B is the Reports of the Commission.
- Decisions and Reports of the Commission (cited as D & R).

5.6   Further reading

The following books and articles may prove helpful in exploring the growing impact of the Convention's provisions on our criminal justice system:

Ashworth, A., 'Article 6 and the Fairness of Trials' [1999] Crim LR 261.

Brandon, B., 'Terrorism, Human Rights and the Rule of Law: 120 years of the UK's Legal Response to Terrorism' [2004] Crim LR 981.

Farran, S., *The UK Before the European Court of Human Rights: Case Law and Commentary* (Blackstone Press, 1996).

Field and Young, 'Disclosure, Appeals and Procedural Traditions: *Edwards v United Kingdom*' [1994] Crim LR 264.

Manchester, Salter, Moodie and Lynch, *Exploring the Law* (Sweet & Maxwell, 1996) (see ch. 3).

Munday, 'Inferences from Silence and European Human Rights Law' [1996] Crim LR 370.

Nash and Furse, 'Self Incrimination, Corporate Misconduct and the Convention on Human Rights' [1995] Crim LR 855.

Nicholson and Reid, 'Arrest for Breach of the Peace and the European Convention on Human Rights' [1996] Crim LR 764.

Quinn, K., 'Jury Bias and the European Convention on Human Rights: a Well-kept Secret?' [2004] Crim LR 998.

Sharpe, S., 'Article 6 and the Disclosure of Evidence in Criminal Trials' [1999] Crim LR 273.

Stone, R., *Textbook on Civil Liberties and Human Rights*, 4th edn (Oxford University Press 2002).

Uglow, S., 'Covert Surveillance and the European Convention on Human Rights' [1999] Crim LR 287.

Wadham, J. and Mountfield, H., *Blackstone's guide to the Human Rights Act 1998*, 3rd edn (Oxford University Press, 2000).

Substantive law

Dangerous drugs

6.1 'Controlled drugs'

The Misuse of Drugs Act 1971 applies to 'controlled drugs'. Section 2 of the Act defines this term as the substances listed in Sch 2 to the Act. Schedule 2 divides controlled drugs into three classes: A (eg cocaine, lysergide (LSD), morphine and diamorphine (heroin)), B (eg amphetamine and codeine), and C (eg diazepam, temazepam and cannabis). The relevance of this distinction is that offences involving class A drugs attract a more severe sentence than offences involving class B drugs, and class B drug offences are more serious than class C drug offences. This distinction is based on the degree of harm a particular drug can do.

To be controlled, the substance must be listed in Sch 2. So the coco-leaf (from which cocaine may be extracted) is specifically listed. The 'magic mushroom' is not listed per se and so in its natural state is not a controlled drug. However, when it is 'prepared' (Sch 2, Pt 1, para 5) so as to produce psilocin (which is listed in Sch 2) it does become a controlled drug (*Hodder v DPP* [1989] Crim LR 261).

Whether or not the particular substance in question is a controlled drug has to be proved by chemical analysis (*Hunt* [1987] AC 352; *Hill* (1993) 96 Cr App R 456). However, it was said in *Chatwood* [1980] 1 WLR 874, that an admission by the defendant that the substance is a controlled drug is prima facie evidence as to the nature of the substance, and so such an admission can found a case to answer.

Note that cannabis and cannabis resin are listed separately, and so the prosecution must specify which is alleged (*Best* (1979) 70 Cr App R 21).

For full details on offences relating to drugs, see *Blackstone's Criminal Practice*, 2005, B20.

6.2 The offences

6.2.1 Import/export

Section 3 of the Misuse of Drugs Act 1971 prohibits the export and import of controlled drugs. However, the section by itself does not create an offence. The offence is committed under s 50(3) of the Customs and Excise Management Act 1979, which creates the offence of importing or being concerned with the importing of any goods contrary to any prohibition with intent to evade that prohibition or s 170(2) of the same Act which creates the offence of being knowingly concerned in the fraudulent evasion (or attempted evasion) of any prohibition. The latter offence covers both import and (unlike s 50) export of prohibited goods.

6.2.2 Production

Section 4 of the Misuse of Drugs Act 1971 creates these offences:

(a) producing a controlled drug (s 4(2)(a)). Section 37(1) defines 'producing' as including manufacture or cultivation. Growing cannabis can be charged under this section or under s 6 which deals specifically with cannabis;

(b) being concerned in the production of a controlled drug by another person (s 4(2)(b)) (this is a sort of statutory conspiracy).

Converting one controlled drug into another controlled drug amounts to production (eg, converting cocaine hydrochloride into freebase cocaine, ie, 'crack') (*Russell* (1991) 94 Cr App R 351).

6.2.3 Supply/offer to supply

Under s 4(3)(a) of the Misuse of Drugs Act 1971, it is an offence to supply or offer to supply a controlled drug to another person (ie drug dealing).

6.2.3.1 Supply

The meaning of 'supply' was considered by the House of Lords in *Maginnis* [1987] 1 All ER 907. The defendant in that case was found to be in possession of some cannabis. He said that he was looking after it for a friend who was going to retrieve it later. It was held that a person who was in unlawful possession of a controlled drug which had been deposited with him by another person for safekeeping had the necessary intent to supply it to another if it was the defendant's intention to return it to the person who had given it to him for that other person's purposes. The handing over must be for the recipient to use the thing handed over for his or her own purposes, but it was not necessary that the supply be made out of the defendant's own personal resources. It follows that a person who hands another a drug for temporary safekeeping and intending to reclaim it does not commit an offence, since the person looking after it cannot use it for his own purposes. In *Dempsey* (1985) 82 Cr App R 291, a registered drug addict who was in lawful possession of a controlled drug, asked someone to hold some of the drug for him while he went into the toilet to inject himself with the rest of it. The police then arrested both of them. The Court of Appeal held that, on the facts of the particular case, there was no act of supply. The addict had not transferred the drugs to his friend so that she could use them herself or pass them on to someone else (and her return of the drugs to him was not an unlawful supply, since he was lawfully entitled to possession of the drugs).

In *Panton* [2001] EWCA Crim 611 The Times, 27 March 2001, the defendant was charged with possession of controlled drugs with intent to supply. He relied on the defence of duress, claiming that he had been an involuntary custodian of the drugs for unnamed depositors, following threats made to himself and his family after he had failed to settle drug-related debts. The jury rejected the defence of duress. It was held, following *Maginnis*, that the ordinary and natural meaning of the word 'supply' is to furnish or provide a person with something which that person wants or requires for that person's purposes. It follows that a return of goods to a depositor by a custodian, who had held those goods for safekeeping, constitutes a supply. For the purposes of ss 4(1) and 5(3) of the Misuse of Drugs Act 1971, it is irrelevant whether the custodian was a voluntary or involuntary custodian of the drugs.

6.2.3.2 Offering to supply

If the defendant offers to supply one controlled drug, thinking mistakenly that it is another controlled drug, the offence is still made out. If the defendant offers to supply what he or she believes to be a controlled drug but which in fact is not a controlled drug, the offence is nonetheless committed (*Haggard v Mason* [1976] 1 WLR 187). Further, an offence is committed even if the defendant did not in fact intend to supply the drug he was offering to supply (*Gill* (1993) 97 Cr App R 215).

In *Dhillon* [2000] Crim LR 760, the defendant was charged with offering to supply a controlled drug (s 4(1)(b)). He argued that by the date specified in the charge the offer had been accepted and so it could no longer be treated as an offer. The Court of Appeal rejected this argument, holding that it would be wrong to introduce the principles of the law of contract into the trial of a person charged with this offence.

6.2.3.3 Being concerned in supply

Under s 4(3)(b), it is an offence to be concerned in the supplying of a controlled drug to another person. Under s 4(3)(c), it is an offence to be concerned in the making of an offer to supply a controlled drug to another person.

The last two offences require the prosecution to prove:

- supply/offer to supply (by someone other than the defendant);
- that the defendant is a participant in the supply/offer;
- that the defendant knows the nature of the enterprise.

See *Hughes* (1985) 81 Cr App R 344.

'Another person' in this context cannot be someone who is charged in the same count, though it may be someone who is charged under a different count in the same indictment (*Connelly* [1992] Crim LR 296 (CA)).

A person may be concerned by being involved at a distance in the making of an offer to supply a controlled drug (*Blake* (1978) 68 Cr App R 1) (one person introducing another to someone who could supply a controlled drug).

6.2.4 Possession/possession with intent to supply

Section 5(2) of the Misuse of Drugs Act 1971 creates the offence of being in possession of a controlled drug. Section 5(3) creates the offence of being in possession of a controlled drug with intent to supply it to another person.

6.2.4.1 Possession

The only definition of 'possession' given by the 1971 Act is that contained in s 37(3). This says that a person is in possession of something even if it is in the custody of someone else provided that it is subject to the control of the possessor. However, this section is dealing with the fairly unusual situation where custody and control are separated.

In *Lambert* [2002] 2 AC 545, it was held by the House of Lords that there are two elements to possession: the physical element and the mental element. The House confirmed the approach taken by the House in the earlier cases of *Warner v Metropolitan*

Police Commissioner [1968] 2 All ER 356 and *Boyesen* [1982] 2 All ER 161, and by the Court of Appeal in *McNamara* (1988) 87 Cr App R 246.

So far as the physical element is concerned, this requires proof that the thing is in the custody of the defendant or subject to his or her control. So far as the mental element is concerned, the essential point is that a person must know that he or she is in possession of something which is, in fact, a controlled drug. To satisfy this element, the defendant need not know the true nature of the thing: so long as the defendant knows that the thing, whatever it is, is under his or her control, then it is in his or her possession. It follows, therefore, that a person does not possess something of which he or she is completely unaware, and so if drugs are put into someone's pocket without their knowledge, that person is not in possession of those drugs.

It also follows that ignorance of (or mistake as to) the nature of the substance in question does not prevent the accused being in possession of it, provided that the substance turns out to be a controlled drug. Thus, if the substance turns out to be heroin, it is irrelevant (so far as the meaning of possession is concerned) that the accused believed the substance to be aspirin.

Where a controlled drug is in a container, it was held in *Lambert* that, if the defendant is in possession of the container and knows that there is something in it, he or she will be taken to be in possession of the contents of the container. It follows that where the drugs are in a container, it is sufficient for the prosecution to prove that the defendant had control of the container, that he or she knew of its existence and knew that there was something in it, and that the something was in fact the controlled drug which the prosecution alleges it to be. The prosecution does not have to prove that the accused knew that the thing was a controlled drug.

The exception to this is where the accused had no right to open the container and ascertain its contents. In such a case, it is probable that the accused is not in possession of the contents (according to dicta in *Warner* and *McNamara*).

Even if the accused is, as a matter of law, in possession of drugs according to the case law set out above, he or she may nonetheless have a statutory defence (see **6.3** below).

Where more than one person has the right to draw on drugs which form a common pool, all those having such control may be charged with possession (*Searle* [1971] Crim LR 592). Everyone who has the right to say what is done with the drugs possesses them (*Strong* The Times, 26 January 1990).

The issue in *Boyesen* (mentioned above) was whether one can be said to be in possession of a quantity of a controlled drug which is so minute that it is not 'usable'. The answer given by the House of Lords was yes, provided that the prosecution are able to prove possession and provided that the drug is 'visible, tangible, measureable and capable of manipulation' (per Lord Scarman, at p 166).

6.2.4.2   Proving intent to supply

The greater the quantity of drugs, the less likely it is that they were for the accused's personal use, making a charge of possession with intent to supply more likely.

If the accused is seen to be supplying a substance to other people, and that substance turns out to be an illegal drug, it can be inferred that any of the drug still in his or her possession was held with the intent to supply it to other people.

Intent to supply can also be inferred from the 'paraphernalia' of drug dealing — for example, scales and packaging materials.

Experienced police officers are entitled to give expert evidence on some matters. For example, in *Hodges* [2003] 2 Cr App R 15, the prosecution case, that the defendants were commercial drug dealers, relied on the evidence of a police officer who stated that the drugs found were in too great a quantity for personal use. The officer had 16 or 17 years' experience; he obtained his information through training, observation and speaking to other officers, people arrested and informers. The Court of Appeal upheld the trial judge's decision to allow this evidence to be adduced. The defence argued that the officer's evidence should not be admitted if the people who supplied the information on which he based his opinion were not also called as witnesses. The Court rejected this argument, holding that it is not necessary for the various people to whom the witness had spoken to be called before the witness could give expert evidence based upon what they had said. The Court added that it is relevant that the defence can challenge the officer's evidence through cross-examination.

In *Morris* [1995] 2 Cr App R 69, it was held that evidence of large amounts of money in the possession of a defendant, or of an extravagant life style, prima facie explicable only if derived from drug dealing, can be admissible as part of the proof of intent to supply. An explanation by the defendant for the possession of the money does not render the evidence inadmissible, since the Crown may have evidence to rebut that explanation. If the judge decides that such evidence is admissible as a matter of law, he or she must then decide, as a matter of discretion, whether or not to admit it (having regard to both its probative value and its prejudicial effect). If the evidence is admitted, the judge must direct the jury as to the possible probative significance of the evidence, making it clear that the jury must decide whether or not it in fact has that probative significance. The judge must also warn the jury that, if they conclude that the defendant is a drug dealer, this is not of itself either evidence of possession of drugs on a particular occasion or a basis for disbelieving the defendant.

In *Gordon* [1995] 2 Cr App R 61, the Court of Appeal noted that where a defendant is charged with possession with intent to supply, the intention to supply has to relate to the drugs found in the possession of the defendant. In order to be admissible, evidence of cash or other property found in the possession of the defendant, or of financial dealings by the defendant, must therefore be relevant to the intention to supply the particular drugs in order to be admissible.

Grant [1996] 1 Cr App R 73 confirms that the finding of money either in the home or the possession of the accused (in conjunction with a substantial quantity of drugs) is capable of being relevant to the issue of whether there was an intent to supply. It is a matter for the jury to decide whether the presence of money is in fact indicative of an ongoing trade in the drugs, so that the presence of the drugs at the time of the arrest is capable of being construed as possession with intent to supply. However, where such evidence is admitted, the jury should be directed that any innocent explanation put forward by the accused must first be rejected before they can regard the finding of the money as relevant to the offence. If they conclude that the presence of the money indicates not merely past dealing but an ongoing dealing in drugs, then finding the money (together with the drugs in question) is a matter that they can take into account in considering whether the necessary intent has been proved.

The Drugs Act 2005 adds subsections 5(4A) and (4B) to the 1971 Act. These provide that if it is proved that the defendant had an amount of a controlled drug in his possession which is not less than the 'prescribed amount' (ie an amount prescribed in regulations under the Act), the court must assume that the defendant intended to supply those drugs unless evidence is adduced which is sufficient to raise an issue that he or she may not have had the drug in his possession with that intent. It should be noted that the burden on the defendant is an evidential, not legal, burden.

The relevant JSB Specimen Direction (see http://www.jsboard.co.uk/criminal_law/ index.htm) is as follows:

36. Drugs — Allegation of Supply — Money Found in Possession of Defendant/ Evidence of Extravagant Lifestyle etc.

The prosecution has called evidence that the defendant [eg was found to be in possession of £ . . . and/or to the effect that he was living to a standard which they suggest was much higher than that which might be expected of a man of his means].

By itself this evidence does not prove anything against the defendant, and certainly not that he was in possession of drugs. But it is evidence which you may be entitled to take into account, if you think it right to do so, when deciding whether he was [unlawfully in possession of drugs/in possession with intent to supply/supplying these drugs to another].

You would only be entitled to take this evidence into account in this way in circumstances which I will now explain. First, of course, you would have to be sure that the defendant was indeed [in possession of this money and/or living to a standard much higher than that which might be expected]. Then you would have to be sure that his explanation for his possession of the money/standard of living is untrue, and that his possession of the money/standard of living can only be explained by his connection with drugs as alleged in this case (adding, in a supply or intent to supply case) and indicates not merely past dealing but continuing dealing in drugs/an intention to supply drugs in the future.

6.2.5   Expert evidence

As well as expert evidence proving that the substance in question is indeed a controlled drug (see **6.1**), a police officer in the drugs squad is entitled to give expert evidence on the street value of drugs and on the use of paraphernalia by drug dealers (eg giving evidence that certain equipment is commonly used by drug dealers to produce crack cocaine). However, in *Jeffries* [1997] Crim LR 819 it was held that a police officer was not entitled to say that, in her opinion, a list containing dates, names and figures related to the sale of drugs: to do so would amount to her giving as her opinion the fact that the defendant is guilty as charged.

6.3   Statutory defences

The dicta on the meaning of possession set out in **6.2.4.1** must be related to the defences contained in the Misuse of Drugs Act 1971, s 28. Section 28(2), which applies, *inter alia* to s 4(2) and (3) and s 5(2) and (3), creates the defence that the defendant 'neither knew of nor suspected nor had any reason to suspect the existence of some fact alleged by the prosecution which it is necessary for the prosecution to prove if he is to be convicted of the offence charged'.

Section 28(3) further provides that where the prosecution have to prove that a particular substance was a controlled drug, it is *not* a defence for the defendant to show that he did not realise that it was the particular controlled drug alleged by the prosecution; however, it *is* a defence that the defendant did not realise (and could not reasonably have realised) that the substance was a controlled drug at all. So, it is a statutory defence to a charge of possession of cocaine to say 'I reasonably believed the substance to be aspirin' but it is not a defence to say 'I thought it was cannabis'.

In *Leeson* [2000] 1 Cr App R 233, the defendant was charged with unlawful possession of a controlled drug, namely cocaine, with intent to supply (contrary to s 5(3) of the 1971 Act). The defendant said that he believed that the drug was 'speed' (amphetamine). It was held that, under s 5(3), all that the prosecution has to establish is that the defendant had in his possession 'a' controlled drug with intent to supply the substance which was in his possession to another. It was not necessary to prove an intention to supply the specified drug. Therefore, the possibility of mistake by the defendant as to the nature of the drug in his possession does not afford him any defence under s 28 of the Act.

It had been thought that the burden of proof under s 28 rested on the defendant (to prove the defence on the balance of probabilities). However, in *Lambert* [2002] 2 AC 545 the House of Lords said that such a burden would amount to a violation of the presumption of innocence enshrined in Article 6 of the European Convention on Human Rights. However, by invoking s 3 of the Human Rights Act 1998, s 28 could be read in a way that is compatible with the Convention. This requires s 28 to be construed as imposing no more than an evidential burden on the accused (ie a burden to raise the issue). If sufficient evidence is adduced by the defence to raise the issue, it will then be for the prosecution to show, beyond reasonable doubt, that the s 28 defence is not made out.

The s 28 defence is only available in respect of offences under the 1971 Act. It is not therefore available in a case where common law conspiracy is charged instead (*McGowan* [1990] Crim LR 399).

As well as the general defence in s 28, s 5(4) makes it a defence to a charge of being in possession of a controlled drug that the defendant was in possession of the drug in order to deliver it to someone who could lawfully take custody of it. The defendant bears the burden of proving this defence (on the balance of probabilities). The defence will only succeed if it is shown that the defendant's purpose was to act in accordance with s 5(4) (*Dempsey* (1985) 82 Cr App R 291 (CA)).

6.4 Occupiers of premises

Section 8 of the Misuse of Drugs Act 1971 applies to a person who is the occupier of premises or concerned in the management of the premises. The occupier is the person who has a legal right to exercise sufficient control over the premises as to be able to prevent the forbidden activities from taking place.

Such a person commits an offence if he or she knowingly permits or allows specified activities to take place on the premises including:

- producing a controlled drug;
- supplying/offering to supply a controlled drug;
- smoking cannabis, cannabis resin or opium.

In *Bett* [1999] 1 All ER 600 the defendant was charged with permitting premises to be used for supplying a controlled drug (contrary to s 8(b) of the Misuse of Drugs Act 1971). The trial judge directed the jury that it had to be proved that the defendant knowingly permitted the premises to be used for supplying *a* controlled drug but that it was not necessary to prove that he knew the particular identity or class of the drug that was in fact being supplied. The Court of Appeal upheld this direction.

6.5 Permitted uses of controlled drugs

Many of the controlled drugs have legitimate medical uses (eg morphine, a class A drug, is a painkiller and drugs such as Lorazepam, Diazepam and Temazepam, all class C drugs, are very commonly prescribed sleeping tablets). So s 7 of the 1971 Act requires the making of regulations to permit doctors, dentists, pharmacists and veterinary surgeons to produce and supply controlled drugs. The regulations in question are the Misuse of Drugs Regulations 2001 (SI 2001 No 3998) and the Misuse of Drugs (Designation) Regulations 2001 (SI 2001 No 3997). Effectively, these regulations permit the appropriate use of drugs for medicinal purposes or which are contained in a medicinal product.

Accordingly, one must first check Sch 2 to the Misuse of Drugs Act 1971 to see if the drug in question is a controlled drug and then check the 2001 Regulations to see if the particular use of the particular drug in question is authorised.

6.6 Enforcement

6.6.1 Search and seizure

The Misuse of Drugs Act 1971, s 23(2) says that a constable who has reasonable grounds to suspect that a person is in possession of a controlled drug may detain and search that person, stop and search a vehicle in which the constable suspects that drugs may be found, and seize and detain anything found in the course of the search which appears to be evidence of an offence under the Act. See also **Chapter 3**.

Section 23(3) empowers a justice of the peace to grant a search warrant if satisfied by information given on oath that there are reasonable grounds for suspecting that controlled drugs are on any premises, or that there is on the premises a document relating to unlawful dealing in controlled drugs.

6.6.2 Penalties: sentencing guidelines

The maximum sentences are set out in the Misuse of Drugs Act 1971, Sch 4.

Cases involving class A drugs attract more severe sentences than those involving class B drugs, which in turn attract more severe sentences than cases involving class C drugs. Importation and production are generally regarded as the most serious offences, followed by supply and possession with intent to supply, followed by possession for personal use. A custodial sentence is usually appropriate for all drugs offences except those involving possession for personal use. All acts of supply are seen as serious. For example in *Luke* [1999] 1 Cr App R (S) 389, the defendant was a university student. He supplied cannabis to some friends. He made no profit from the transaction and the cannabis was intended for personal use by the recipients. The Court of Appeal held that a sentence of immediate custody was appropriate.

Factors relevant to determining the sentence include the following:

(a) First and foremost, the type and quantity of the drug. The severest sentences are reserved for cases involving class A drugs (see *Richardson* The Times, 18 March 1994, where the Lord Chief Justice speaks of the harm done by hard drugs). Guidelines in cases of importing drugs were laid down by the Court of Appeal in *Aramah* (1982) 76 Cr App R 190 and *Bilinski* (1987) 86 Cr App R 146. Those guidelines are based on the street value of the drug in question. However, in *Aranguren and others* (1994) 99 Cr App R 347 the Court of Appeal issued fresh guidelines for class A drugs, such as heroin and cocaine, to the effect that the sentence should be based on the weight of the drugs seized rather than their street value. The purity of the drug is to be taken into account in determining its weight. Guidelines for sentencing in cases involving Ecstasy were given in *Warren & Beeley* [1996] 1 Cr App R 120, for cases involving LSD in *Hurley* [1998] 1 Cr App R (S) 299, for cases involving importation of cannabis in *Ronchetti* [1998] Crim LR 227, and for cases involving importation of amphetamine in *Wijs* [1998] 2 Cr App R (S) 436. In *Chamberlain, The Independent*, 19 May 1997, the Court of Appeal said that being concerned in the management of premises used for the production of a controlled drug should, for sentencing purposes, be considered analogous to importing controlled drugs, thus attracting sentences at the higher end of the scale.

(b) If the defendant has provided information to the authorities, this will result in a lower sentence (partly because it shows remorse). However, regard will be had to the actual value of the assistance and to the risk of possible reprisals faced by the offender or his family (*Richardson*, supra); the information must actually be useful to the authorities, assisting in the speedy arrest of other offenders and the prevention of further distribution of drugs (*M* The Times, 1 March 1994).

(c) The court must consider not only what the defendant in fact did, but also what he thought he was doing. If the defendant thinks he is importing cannabis when in fact it is heroin, the sentence should be reduced (*Bilinski*, supra). Similarly, if the defendant thinks he is importing high-quality heroin when in fact its purity is only 1%, the sentence will take account of the low purity of the heroin (*Afzal and Arshad* The Times, 25 June 1991). In *Purcell* [1996] 1 Cr App R (S) 190 the appellant believed that he was carrying 'speed' (amphetamine sulphate, a class B drug). Later analysis showed that the substance was not, in fact, a controlled drug. He was convicted of attempting to import a controlled drug. In light of this (and the fact that he confessed at the earliest opportunity, and that, as a courier, he would have received very little profit) the Court of Appeal reduced his sentence from three years to two years.

(d) The degree of organisation and planning, and any steps taken to avoid detection will be relevant to the sentence (*Kouadio* The Times, 21 February 1991).

(e) How 'high up in the drug operation' the defendant was is also relevant to the sentence (*Hussain* The Times, 27 June 1990).

In *Morris* [2001] 1 Cr App R 4, the Court of Appeal gave further detailed guidance. It was said that, in considering the need to test for the purity of drugs for the purposes of sentencing defendants convicted of drugs offences, courts should take account of the following matters: the amount of Class A or B drugs with which a defendant is involved is a very important, but not solely determinative, factor. Evidence as to the scale of dealing can come from many sources other than the amount of drugs with which a defendant is directly connected. Amount should generally be based on the weight of drug involved at 100% purity, not on its street value. Reference to the street value of the same weight of different drugs may, however, be pertinent by way of cross-check. Purity of drugs such as cocaine or heroin, not in tablet or dosage form and often contaminated by other substances, and amphetamine powder, can appropriately be determined only by analysis. The weight of drugs such as ecstasy, in tablet, or LSD in dosage, form can generally be assessed by reference to the number of tablets or doses and an assumed average purity of 100mg of ecstasy and 50 micrograms of LSD, unless prosecution or defence expert evidence shows to the contrary. Purity analysis is essential for sentencing purposes for cases of importation or in other circumstances where 500g or more of cocaine, heroin or amphetamine are seized, and may be desirable in respect of smaller quantities. However, bearing in mind the cost of purity analysis and that analysis may cause delay, analysis will not generally be necessary or desirable on behalf of prosecution or defence where a defendant is in possession of only a small quantity of cocaine, heroin or amphetamine consistent with personal use or only limited supply to others. In such a case the court can be expected to sentence on the basis of low level retail dealing only, but taking into account all the other circumstances of the case. However, as purity can indicate proximity to the primary source of supply, if there is a reason for the prosecution to believe that a defendant in possession of a small quantity of drugs is close to the source of supply, and is wholesaling rather than retailing, it will be necessary for purity analysis to be undertaken before a court can be invited to proceed on this more serious basis. In the absence of purity analysis or expert evidence, it is not open to a court to find or assume levels of purity, except in the case of ecstasy and LSD in the circumstances referred to above.

In due course, these guidelines will be superseded by guidance issued by the Sentencing Guidelines Council.

The Drugs Act 2005 inserts a s 4A into the Misuse of Drugs Act, making it an aggravating factor if the drug dealing happens in or near school premises *and* a courier under the age of 18 is used to deliver drugs or drug money.

6.6.3 Forfeiture

Section 27(1) of the 1971 Act allows the court to order forfeiture (and destruction, if appropriate) of 'anything shown to the satisfaction of the court to relate to the offence'. In *Cuthbertson* [1980] 2 All ER 401, Lord Diplock said (at p 406) that forfeiture orders apply to 'tangible' items such as 'the drugs involved, apparatus for making them, vehicles used for transporting them [as in *Bowers* (1994) 15 Cr App R (S) 315], or cash ready to be, or having just been handed over for them'.

The point was made in *Cuthbertson* that the aim of forfeiture orders was not to strip drug traffickers of the profits of their crime. That objective is achieved instead through the Proceeds of Crime Act 2002.

6.7   Confiscation orders under the Proceeds of Crime Act 2002

The Proceeds of Crime Act 2002 replaces the pre-existing dual scheme for the confiscation of the proceeds of crime, previously contained in the Drug Trafficking Act 1994 and the Criminal Justice Act 1988.

6.7.1 Making of confiscation order

The basic procedure for making a confiscation order under the Proceeds of Crime Act (PCA) 2002 is set out in s 6.

The power to make a confiscation order arises if the defendant is:

(a) convicted of one or more offences in the Crown Court; or

(b) committed to the Crown Court for sentence in respect of one or more offences under ss 3, 4 or 6 of the Powers of Criminal Courts (Sentencing) Act 2000; or

(c) committed to the Crown Court in respect of one or more offences under s 70 of the PCA 2002, which empowers the magistrates court to commit a defendant to the Crown Court with a view to a confiscation order being considered.

Under s 97 of the Serious Organised Crime and Police Act 2005, magistrates' courts are empowered to make confiscation orders up to £10,000.

A confiscation order can only be made if either:

- the prosecutor (or the Director of the Assets Recovery Agency) asks the court to proceed under s 6; or
- the court believes it is appropriate for it to proceed under s 6.

Where s 6 is invoked, the court has to proceed as follows:

(a) The court must first decide whether the defendant has 'a criminal lifestyle'.

(b) If it decides that the defendant has a criminal lifestyle, it must then decide whether he or she has benefited from 'general criminal conduct'.

(c) If the court decides that the defendant does not have a criminal lifestyle and has not benefited from 'general criminal conduct', it must then decide whether the defendant has benefited from 'particular criminal conduct' (ie the offence(s) of which he or she has been convicted in the present proceedings).

(d) If the court decides that the defendant has benefited from general criminal conduct or particular criminal conduct, the court must go on to:

(i) decide the recoverable amount; and

(ii) make a confiscation order requiring the defendant to pay that amount.

If the court believes that any victim of the defendant's criminal conduct has started, or intends to start, proceedings against the defendant in respect of loss, injury or damage sustained in connection with the conduct, then the court is no longer obliged to decide the recoverable amount and to make a confiscation order; nonetheless, the court retains the power to do so in such a case.

In deciding whether the defendant has a criminal lifestyle, whether he has benefited from particular or general criminal conduct, and in determining the recoverable amount, the court must decide any question which arises on a balance of probabilities (s 6(7)).

The phrase 'criminal lifestyle' is comprehensively defined in s 75. Under s 75(2), a defendant has a criminal lifestyle if (and only if) the offence, or any of the offences:

(a) is specified in Sch 2 to the Act (s 75(2)(a));

(b) constitutes conduct forming part of a course of criminal activity and the offender has obtained benefit from this conduct of at least £5,000 (s 75(2)(b)); or

(c) is an offence committed over a period of at least six months, and the defendant has obtained benefit of at least £5,000 from the conduct which constitutes the offence (s 75(2)(c)).

The offences specified in Sch 2 include:

(a) Drug trafficking: offences under the Misuse of Drugs Act 1971, s 4(2) or (3), 5(3), 8 and 20; offences under the Customs and Excise Management Act 1979, s 50(2) or (3), 68(2) or 170 (if committed in connection with a prohibition or restriction on importation or exportation which has effect by virtue of the Misuse of Drugs Act 1971); offences under the Criminal Justice (International Co-operation) Act 1990, s 12 or 19.

(b) Money laundering: offences under the PCA 2002, s 327 or 328.

(c) Directing terrorism (the Terrorism Act 2000, s 56).

(d) People trafficking (the Immigration Act 1971, s 25(1)).

(e) Arms trafficking: offences under the Customs and Excise Management Act 1979, s 68(2) or 170 (if committed in connection with a firearm or ammunition) or under the Firearms Act 1968, s 3(1).

(f) Counterfeiting (the Forgery and Counterfeiting Act 1981, s 14, 15, 16 or 17).

(g) Intellectual property: offences under the Copyright, Designs and Patents Act 1988, s 107(1) or (2), 198(1) or 297A or under the Trade Marks Act 1994, s 92(1), (2) or (3).

(h) Pimps and brothels: offences under the Sexual Offences Act 1956, s 2, 3, 9, 22, 24, 28, 29, 30, 31, 33 or 34 or under the Sexual Offences Act 1967, s 5.

(i) Blackmail (the Theft Act 1968, s 21).

(j) Inchoate offences of attempt, conspiracy or incitement of an offence specified above or aiding, abetting, counselling or procuring the commission of such an offence.

Under s 75(3), conduct forms part of a course of criminal activity for the purposes of s 75(2)(b) where the offender has benefited from the conduct, and:

(a) in the proceedings in which he was convicted, he was convicted of three or more other offences, each of three or more of them constituting conduct from which he has benefited (s 75(3)(a)); or

(b) in the period of six years ending with the day when those proceedings were started (or, if there is more than one such day, the earliest day), he was convicted on at least two separate occasions of an offence constituting conduct from which he has benefited (s 75(3)(b)).

Under s 75(5), relevant 'benefit', for the purposes of s 75(2)(b), is benefit from conduct which constitutes the offence, or benefit from any other conduct which forms part of the course of criminal activity and which constitutes an offence of which the offender has been convicted, or benefit from conduct which constitutes an offence which has been or will be taken into consideration in sentencing, and relevant 'benefit' for the purposes of s 75(2)(c) is benefit from conduct which constitutes the offence, or benefit from conduct which constitutes an offence which has been or will be taken into consideration in sentencing.

The terms 'criminal conduct', 'general criminal conduct' and 'particular criminal conduct' are defined in s 76:

(a) 'Criminal conduct' is conduct which constitutes an offence in England and Wales.

(b) 'General criminal conduct' is all the offender's criminal conduct, it being irrelevant whether the conduct occurred before or after the passing of the PCA 2002, or whether property constituting a benefit from conduct was obtained before or after the passing of the Act.

(c) 'Particular criminal conduct' is all the offender's criminal conduct which is:
   (i)   conduct which constitutes the offence or offences concerned,
   (ii) conduct which constitutes offences of which he was convicted in the same proceedings, or
   (iii) conduct which constitutes offences which the court will be taking into consideration in sentencing.

6.7.2 Recoverable amount

Section 7(1) of the PCA 2002 defines the 'recoverable amount' for the purposes of s 6 as being 'an amount equal to the defendant's benefit from the conduct concerned'. However, under s 7(2), if the defendant shows that the available amount is less than that benefit, the recoverable amount is 'the available amount' or, if the available amount is nil, a nominal amount. Section 7(5) states that the court must include in the confiscation order a statement of its findings as to the matters relevant for deciding the available amount.

Section 8 of the PCA 2002 provides that, in deciding whether the defendant has benefited from conduct, and in deciding his benefit from the conduct, the court must take account of conduct occurring up to the time it makes its decision and must take account of property obtained up to that time.

Section 9 provides that, for the purposes of deciding the recoverable amount, the 'available amount' is the aggregate of:

(a) the total of the values (at the time the confiscation order is made) of all the free property (ie property that is not subject to a forfeiture order: see s 82) then held by the defendant minus the total amount payable in pursuance of obligations which then have priority (ie a fine in respect of an earlier conviction or a preferential debt as defined by s 386 of the Insolvency Act 1986), and

(b) the total of the values (at that time) of all tainted gifts (if the court has decided that the defendant has a criminal lifestyle, a gift is to be regarded as tainted if either:

(i)   it was made by the defendant at any time during the period of six years before the start of the proceedings for the present offence; or

(ii) it was made by the defendant at any time and was of property obtained by the defendant as a result of, or in connection with, general criminal conduct;

if the court has decided that the offender does not have a criminal lifestyle, a gift is to be regarded as tainted if it was made by the defendant at any time after the date on which the present offence was committed: see s 77).

Under s 9(2), an obligation has priority if it is an obligation of the defendant:

(a) to pay an amount due in respect of a fine or other order of a court which was imposed or made on conviction of an offence and at any time before the time the confiscation order is made, or

(b) to pay a sum which would be included among the preferential debts if the defendant's bankruptcy had commenced on the date of the confiscation order or his or her winding up had been ordered on that date.

Under s 76(4) and (7), a person 'benefits' from conduct if he or she obtains property as a result of, or in connection with, the conduct. The 'benefit' is the value of the property so obtained. If a person obtains a pecuniary advantage as a result of, or in connection with the conduct, he or she is to be regarded as having obtained a sum of money equal to the value of the pecuniary advantage (s 76(5)).

Valuation of property obtained by a defendant from his or her criminal conduct is dealt with by s 80 of the PCA 2002. Under s 80(2) the value of the property at the material time (the court makes its decision) is the greater of the following:

• the value of the property (at the time the person obtained it) adjusted to take account of later changes in the value of money;

• the value (at the material time) of the property found under s 80(3).

The property found under s 80(3) is as follows:

- if the person holds the property obtained, the property found under this subsection is that property;
- if he or she holds no part of the property obtained, the property found under this subsection is any property which directly or indirectly represents it in their hands;
- if he or she holds part of the property obtained, the property found under this subsection is that part and any property which directly or indirectly represents the other part in their hands.

In *R v Ahmed; R v Qureshi* [2004] EWCA Crim 2599; [2005] 1 WLR 122, the Court of Appeal said that, when assessing realisable assets for the purpose of making a confiscation order (under the Criminal Justice Act 1988), the court is bound to include the convicted person's share in the value of the matrimonial home, irrespective of whether that might prejudice the interests of the spouse or family. If the court is later asked to make an order for the sale of the matrimonial home, Article 8 of the ECHR is engaged, and the court will have to consider whether or not it would be proportionate to make the order in the circumstances of the particular case. It is submitted that the same approach is applicable to confiscation orders made under the Proceeds of Crime Act 2002.

6.7.3 Criminal lifestyle: assumptions

Section 10 of the PCA 2002 states that if the court decides that the defendant has a criminal lifestyle it must make four assumptions for the purpose of deciding whether the defendant has benefited from general criminal conduct, and deciding the value of the benefit from that conduct. Those assumptions are as follows:

(a) that any property transferred to the defendant at any time after the relevant day was obtained as a result of the general criminal conduct, and at the earliest time the defendant appears to have held it;

(b) that any property held by the defendant at any time after the date of conviction was obtained as a result of the general criminal conduct, and at the earliest time the defendant appears to have held it;

(c) that any expenditure incurred by the defendant at any time after the relevant day was met from property obtained by the defendant as a result of his or her general criminal conduct;

(d) that, for the purpose of valuing any property obtained (or assumed to have been obtained) by the defendant, he or she obtained it free of any other interests in it.

Under s 10(8), the 'relevant day' is the first day of the period of six years ending with the day when proceedings for the present offence were started against the defendant or, if there are two or more offences and proceedings for them were started on different days, the earliest of those days.

By virtue of s 10(6), the court must not make a required assumption in relation to particular property or expenditure if either:

- the assumption is shown to be incorrect, or
- there would be a serious risk of injustice if the assumption were made.

If the court does not make one or more of the required assumptions it must state its reasons (s 10(7)).

In *Rezvi* [2002] UKHL 1; [2003] 1 AC 1099, the House of Lords held that similar assumptions to be made in confiscation proceedings under the CJA 1988 were not incompatible with the rights of a defendant under the ECHR. In *Benjafield* [2002] 1 All ER 801, the House of Lords reached the same conclusion as regards the assumptions in confiscation proceedings under the Drug Trafficking Act 1994. In *Phillips v UK* (2001) 11 BHRC 280, the European Court of Human Rights held that the statutory assumptions contained in the Drug Trafficking Act 1994 did not contravene Article 6 of the Convention.

6.7.4 Statements of information

Under s 16 of the PCA 2002, where the prosecutor or the Director of the Assets Recovery Agency has asked the court to proceed under s 6, the prosecutor or the Director (as the case may be) must give the court a statement of information within the period specified by the court.

If the court is proceeding under s 6 of its own motion, it may order the prosecutor to give it a statement of information within a specified period.

If the prosecutor or the Director (as the case may be) believes that the defendant has a criminal lifestyle, the statement of information must take the form of a statement of matters that the prosecutor or the Director believes are relevant in connection with deciding whether the defendant has a criminal lifestyle, whether he or she has benefited from his or her general criminal conduct and his or her benefit from the conduct. It must also include information the prosecutor or Director believes to be relevant in connection with the making by the court of a required assumption under s 10 and for the purpose of enabling the court to decide if the circumstances are such that it must not make such an assumption (s 16(3), (4)).

If the prosecutor or the Director (as the case may be) does not believe the defendant has a criminal lifestyle, the statement of information should take the form of a statement of matters which the prosecutor or the Director believes to be relevant in connection with deciding whether the defendant has benefited from particular criminal conduct and the benefit from that conduct (s 16(5)).

Under s 17(1), if the prosecutor or the Director gives the court a statement of information and a copy is served on the defendant, the court may order the defendant to indicate (within the period it orders) the extent to which he or she accepts each allegation in the statement and, in so far as he or she does not accept such an allegation, to give particulars of any matters he or she proposes to rely on.

If the defendant accepts to any extent an allegation in a statement of information, the court may treat this acceptance as conclusive of the matters to which it relates for the purpose of deciding the issues referred to in s 16(3) or (5): s 17(2).

If the defendant fails in any respect to comply with an order under s 17(1), he or she may be treated as accepting every allegation in the statement of information apart from any allegation in respect of which he or she has complied with the requirement and any allegation that he or she has benefited from general or particular criminal conduct.

Section 18 empowers the court, for the purpose of obtaining information to help it in carrying out its functions, to order the defendant to give it information specified in the order.

If the defendant fails without reasonable excuse to comply with an order under s 18, the court may draw such inference as it believes is appropriate (s 18(4)). It should also be borne in mind that the failure to comply with the order could also amount to contempt of court.

If the prosecutor or the Director (as the case may be) accepts to any extent an allegation made by the defendant in giving information required by an order under s 18, or in any other statement given to the court in relation to any matter relevant to deciding the available amount under s 9, the court may treat that acceptance as conclusive of the matters to which it relates.

6.7.5   Time for payment

Section 11 of the PCA 2002 provides that the amount ordered to be paid under a confiscation order must normally be paid when the order is made. However, where the offender is unable to pay immediately, the court may make an order allowing payment to be made within a specified period; this time must not exceed six months from the date on which the confiscation order is made. The offender may, in exceptional circumstances, apply to the court for an extension of that period (up to a total of 12 months from the date of the confiscation order).

6.7.6   Effect of confiscation order on the sentencing powers of the court

Under s 13 of the PCA 2002, the court must take account of the confiscation order before imposing a fine on the defendant, or (for example) a forfeiture order under s 27 of the Misuse of Drugs Act 1971. Apart from that, the court must leave the confiscation order out of account in deciding the appropriate sentence for the defendant (s 13(4)).

If the court makes both a confiscation order and a compensation order under s 130 of the Powers of Criminal Courts (Sentencing) Act 2000 against the same person in the same proceedings, and the court believes that the offender does not have sufficient means to satisfy both the orders in full, the court must direct that so much of the compensation as it specifies is to be paid out of any sums recovered under the confiscation order. The amount it specifies must be the amount it believes will not be recoverable because of the insufficiency of the offender's means.

6.7.7   Enforcement

Detailed provisions on the enforcement of confiscation orders are contained in the PCA 2002, ss 34 to 69. Sections 34 to 37 enable the appointment by the court of the Director of the Assets Recovery Agency as enforcement authority for the order. Sections 38 and 39 provide for the setting of a term of imprisonment in default of payment of the amount ordered to be paid under a confiscation order. The maximum terms to be served in default are the same as in relation to fines (see *Blackstone's Criminal Practice*, 2005, E17.3).

Where the defendant is ordered to serve a term of imprisonment in default of payment of a confiscation order, this term does not start to run until the defendant has served any prison sentence imposed for the offence(s) which led to the confiscation order being made. If the defendant does serve a sentence in default of payment, that does not prevent the order from continuing to apply for the purposes of enforcement by other means (see s 38(5)).

Sections 40 to 69 deal with restraint orders and receivership. In *J v CPS* [2005] EWCA Civ 746; The Times, 12 July 2005, the Court of Appeal gave guidance on restraint orders in connection with confiscation proceedings. Whilst, in a case where dishonesty is charged, the risk of dissipation will generally speak for itself, prosecutors should nevertheless be alive to the possibility that there might be no risk in fact. If no asset dissipation has occurred over a long period, particularly after a defendant has been charged, the prosecutor should explain why asset dissipation is feared at the date of the application for a restraint order, when it had not been feared before. If the court considers that a prosecutor has failed to consider whether there is a risk of dissipation when he should have done, or has failed to put relevant documentary material before the court, but that the public interest still requires the making of a restraint order, the judge can deprive the prosecution of its costs, but still make the order. The duty to make full and frank disclosure applies as much to applicants for restraint orders as to applicants for freezing orders. The fact that the Crown acts in the public interest generally militates against the sanction of discharging the order because of a failure to disclose if the court thinks that an order is appropriate.

The Serious Organised Crime and Police Act 2005 inserts ss 245A–245D into the 2002 Act, providing for applications (made in the High Court) for 'property freezing orders'.

In *Crowther v UK* (App No 53741/00); The Times, 11 February 2005, the ECtHR held that Article 6(1) of the ECHR applies throughout the entirety of the proceedings for 'the determination of . . . any criminal charge', including proceedings whereby a sentence is fixed. Confiscation proceedings are analogous to the determination by a court of the amount of a fine or the length of a period of imprisonment to be imposed on a properly convicted offender. It follows that the authorities have to ensure that the proceedings are completed within a reasonable time.

6.7.8 Postponement

The court should normally proceed under s 6 of the PCA 2002 before it sentences the offender for the offence(s) of which the defendant has been convicted. However, s 14 enables the court to postpone proceedings under s 6 for a specified period. Such a period of postponement may be extended, but it should not (unless there are exceptional circumstances) extend for more than two years from the date of conviction (s 14(3)).

If the offender appeals against sentence, proceedings under s 6 may be postponed for a period of up to three months after the appeal is determined or disposed of (s 14(6)). A postponement or extension may be made on application by the offender, the prosecutor or the Director of the Assets Recovery Agency, or may be made by the court of its own motion.

Section 15 provides that if proceedings under s 6 are postponed, the court may proceed to sentence the offender for the offence(s), but must not impose a fine or make a compensation order. When the postponement period comes to an end, the court may vary the sentence by imposing one or more of the financial orders, but it must do so within 28 days of the end of the postponement period (s 15(4)).

6.7.9 Reconsideration

Sections 19 to 22 of the PCA 2002 enable questions relating to confiscation orders to be reopened. Section 19 provides that where the court did not proceed against the offender under s 6, and there is now evidence available to the prosecutor which was not then available, the Director may apply to the Crown Court for consideration of the evidence at any time prior to the end of the period of six years from the date of conviction.

Section 20 provides that where the court proceeded against the offender under s 6 but found that he or she had not benefited from general criminal conduct, or particular criminal conduct, and there is now evidence available to the prosecutor which was not then available, the Director may apply to the Crown Court for consideration of the evidence at any time prior to the end of the period of six years from the date of conviction.

Section 21 provides that where the court has made a confiscation order, and there is now evidence available to the prosecutor which was not then available, the Director may apply to the Crown Court to make a new calculation of the offender's benefit from the conduct concerned.

Sections 22 to 25 allow for applications to be made to the court for reconsideration of the available amount, and for variation or discharge of the confiscation order in light of the inadequacy of the available amount.

Where there is a right to reopen the issue of confiscation (reopening the issues of the amount of benefit or the amount that might be realised), then the reasonable time requirement extends throughout the period in question. Reconsideration therefore has to take place within a reasonable time (see *Saggar* [2005] EWCA Civ 174; The Times, 14 March 2005).

6.7.10   Appeals by the prosecution

Section 31 of the PCA 2002 enables the prosecutor or the Director to appeal to the Court of Appeal against a decision of the court not to make a confiscation order, or in respect of the amount of a confiscation order which has been made.

6.7.11   Useful websites containing information on the PCA 2002

The following sites contain useful information about the operation of the PCA 2002:

Bar Council Guidance on the PCA 2002:
http://www.barcouncil.org.uk/document.asp?   languageid = 1&documentid = 2523#
ParaLink
Assets Recovery Agency: http://www.assetsrecovery.gov.uk
National Criminal Intelligence Service: http://www.ncis.co.uk
Joint Money Laundering Steering Group: htttp://www.jmlsg.org.uk

6.7.12   Case law on the Proceeds of Crime Act 2002

PCA 2002, s 328, provides that a person commits an offence if he or she enters into, or becomes concerned in, an arrangement knowing or suspecting that it facilitates the acquisition, retention, use or control of criminal property by or on behalf of another person unless he or she makes an authorised disclosure under s 338 of the Act (to the Serious Organised Crime Agency), and has the appropriate consent or else intended to make such a disclosure but has a reasonable excuse for not doing so.

In *Bowman v Fels* [2005] EWCA Civ 226, the Court of Appeal considered the effect of s 328, holding that the ordinary conduct of litigation cannot be said to involve the carrying out of a transaction related to money laundering, even if assets which happen to be the proceeds of money laundering might be the subject of claims in the proceedings, or be retained or used to satisfy any liability according to the outcome of the proceedings. The Court said that there is nothing in the language of s 328 to suggest that Parliament expressly intended to override legal professional privilege. Even if s 328 is to be interpreted as including legal proceedings within its purview, it cannot be interpreted as meaning either that legal professional privilege is to be overridden or that a lawyer is to breach his duty to the court by disclosing to a third party external to the litigation documents revealed to him through the disclosure processes. This decision effectively overrules *P v P (Ancillary Relief: Proceeds of Crime)* [2003] EWHC 2260 (Fam), [2004] Fam 1.

6.8 Further reading

Bucknell, P., *Misuse of Drugs*, 3rd edn., London: Sweet & Maxwell, 1996.

Forston, R., *Misuse of Drugs and Drug Trafficking Offences*, 4th edn., London: Sweet & Maxwell, 2002.

Gumpert, B., *Proceeds of Crime Act 2002: A Practical Guide*, Bristol: Jordans, 2003.

Mitchell, A., *Mitchell, Taylor and Talbot on Confiscation and the Proceeds of Crime*, 3rd edn., London: Sweet & Maxwell, 2002.

Public order offences

7.1 Introduction

Offences relating to public order have been created by a number of statutes. The main statutes dealt with in this chapter are the Criminal Law Act 1977, the Sporting Events (Control of Alcohol etc) Act 1985, the Public Order Act 1986, the Football Spectators Act 1989, the Football (Offences) Act 1991, the Criminal Justice and Public Order Act 1994, the Protection from Harassment Act 1997, the Crime and Disorder Act 1998, the Criminal Justice and Police Act 2001, the Football (Disorder) Act 2000 and the Serious Organised Crime and Police Act 2005.

Details of the relevant provisions are to be found in *Blackstone's Criminal Practice*, 2005, B11 and B13.

7.2 Riot

Riot is the most serious offence against public order and is triable only on indictment. It is defined by the Public Order Act 1986, s 1, as follows:

(1) *Where 12 or more persons who are present together use or threaten unlawful violence for a common purpose and the conduct of them (taken together) is such as would cause a person of reasonable firmness present at the scene to fear for his personal safety, each of the persons using unlawful violence for the common purpose is guilty of riot.*

(2) *It is immaterial whether or not the 12 or more use or threaten unlawful violence simultaneously.*

(3) *The common purpose may be inferred from conduct.*

(4) *No person of reasonable firmness need actually be, or be likely to be, present at the scene.*

(5) *Riot may be committed in private as well as in public places.*

Section 1(6) of the Act provides for a maximum penalty of a term of 10 years, or a fine or both.

Section 6(1) of the Act provides that a person is guilty of riot only if he intends to use violence or is aware that his conduct may be violent. Section 6(7) provides that s 6(1) does not affect the determination for the purposes of riot of the number of persons who use or threaten violence, thus one of 12 or more persons may be guilty of riot even though the *mens rea* of riot cannot be proved against the remaining persons.

As for aiding and abetting, see *Jefferson, Skerritt, Keogh and Readman* [1994] 1 All ER 270.

'Violence' is defined in s 8 of the Act as follows:

In this Part—

   . . .

'violence' means any violent conduct, so that—

    (a)   except in the context of affray, it includes violent conduct towards property as well as violent conduct towards persons, and

(b) it is not restricted to conduct causing or intended to cause injury or damage but includes any other violent conduct (for example, throwing at or towards a person a missile of a kind capable of causing injury which does not hit or falls short).

The Act makes special provision for the intoxicated defendant in s 6(5) and (6) as follows:

(5) For the purposes of this section a person whose awareness is impaired by intoxication shall be taken to be aware of that of which he would be aware if not intoxicated, unless he shows either that his intoxication was not self-induced or that it was caused solely by the taking or administration of a substance in the course of medical treatment.

(6) In subsection (5) 'intoxication' means any intoxication, whether caused by drink, drugs or other means, or by a combination of means.

7.3 Violent disorder

Violent disorder is an offence which is triable either way. Section 2(5) of the Public Order Act 1986 provides that it is punishable on indictment with a term of five years, or a fine or both, or on summary conviction, with six months' imprisonment, or a fine not exceeding the statutory maximum or both.

The offence is defined in s 2 of the Act as follows:

(1) Where three or more persons who are present together use or threaten unlawful violence and the conduct of them (taken together) is such as would cause a person of reasonable firmness present at the scene to fear for his personal safety, each of the persons using or threatening unlawful violence is guilty of violent disorder.

(2) It is immaterial whether or not the three or more use or threaten unlawful violence simultaneously.

(3) No person of reasonable firmness need actually be, or be likely to be, present at the scene.

(4) Violent disorder may be committed in private as well as in public places.

There is no need for a common purpose. Each of at least three persons must be using or threatening unlawful violence. See *Mahroof* (1989) 88 Cr App R 317, *Fleming* (1989) 153 JP 517, *Worton* (1990) 154 JP 201, *McGuigan* [1991] Crim LR 719, *Rothwell and Barton* [1993] Crim LR 626.

7.4 Affray

Affray is an offence which is triable either way. Section 3(7) of the Public Order Act 1986 provides that it is punishable on indictment with a term of three years, or a fine or both, or on summary conviction, with six months' imprisonment, or a fine not exceeding the statutory maximum or both.

The offence is defined in s 3 of the Act as follows:

(1) A person is guilty of affray if he uses or threatens unlawful violence towards another and his conduct is such as would cause a person of reasonable firmness present at the scene to fear for his personal safety.

(2) Where two or more persons use or threaten the unlawful violence, it is the conduct of them taken together that must be considered for the purposes of subsection (1).

(3) For the purposes of this section a threat cannot be made by the use of words alone.

(4) No person of reasonable firmness need actually be, or be likely to be, present at the scene.

(5) Affray may be committed in private as well as in public places.

(6) A constable may arrest without warrant anyone he reasonably suspects is committing affray.

In the context of this offence, 'violence' relates to persons and does not include violent conduct towards property. See s 8 and *Davison* [1992] Crim LR 31, *Charles* (1989) 11 Cr App R (S) 125, *Walsh* (1990) 12 Cr App R (S) 243, *DPP v Cotcher* [1993] COD 181, *Dixon* [1993] Crim LR 579, *Robinson* [1993] Crim LR 581 and *Stanley and Knight* [1993] Crim LR 618. Note further that it is the 'hypothetical, reasonable bystander who must be put in fear for his personal safety, not the victim himself', per Simon Brown LJ in *Sanchez* (1996) 160 JP 321 at p 323.

See further, *Thind* [1999] Crim LR 842, where the Court of Appeal held that the conviction was not unsafe even though the judge's summing up had not made it sufficiently clear that the person put in fear had to be the hypothetical bystander.

The threat of unlawful violence must, however, be directed towards a person or persons present at the scene (*I and others v DPP* [2001] 2 WLR 765, HL). It was held in this case that where a group of young people had been arrested in possession of petrol bombs, the offence of affray had not been committed, as there was no use or threat of unlawful violence 'towards another'. The notional bystander had to be in the presence of both the offender and the victim and there was no evidence that there was a victim.

7.5 Fear or provocation of violence

The offence under s 4 of the Public Order Act 1986 is triable summarily only and is punishable with six months' imprisonment, or a fine not exceeding level 5 or both. The offence is defined as follows:

(1) A person is guilty of an offence if he—

(a) uses towards another person threatening, abusive or insulting words or behaviour, or

(b) distributes or displays to another person any writing, sign or other visible representation which is threatening, abusive or insulting,

with intent to cause that person to believe that immediate unlawful violence will be used against him or another by any person, or to provoke the immediate use of unlawful violence by that person or another, or whereby that person is likely to believe that such violence will be used or it is likely that such violence will be provoked.

(2) An offence under this section may be committed in a public or a private place, except that no offence is committed where the words or behaviour are used, or the writing, sign or other visible representation is distributed or displayed, by a person inside a dwelling and the other person is also inside that or another dwelling.

(3) A constable may arrest without warrant anyone he reasonably suspects is committing an offence under this section.

The four ways in which the offence may be committed were set out in *Winn v DPP* (1992) 156 JP 881. See also *Loade v DPP* [1990] 1 QB 1052, *Horseferry Road Metropolitan Stipendiary Magistrate, ex p Siadatan* [1991] 1 QB 260, *O'Brien* [1993] Crim LR 70, *Afzal* [1993] Crim LR 791, *Rukwira and others v DPP* [1993] Crim LR 882 and *Swanston v DPP* (1997) 161 JP 203.

It was held by the Divisional Court in *DPP v Ramos* [2000] Crim LR 768 that a letter threatening that a bomb would be detonated, but which did not state when the detonation would take place, was capable of being a threat, as the state of mind of the victim was an important factor.

7.5.1   Intentional harassment, alarm or distress

The offence under s 4A of the Public Order Act 1986 is triable summarily only and is punishable with six months' imprisonment, or a fine not exceeding level 5, or both. The offence is defined as follows:

4A.—(1) A person is guilty of an offence if, with intent to cause a person harassment, alarm or distress, he—

  (a)   uses threatening, abusive or insulting words or behaviour, or disorderly behaviour, or

  (b)   displays any writing, sign or other visible representation which is threatening, abusive or insulting,

  thereby causing that or another person harassment, alarm or distress.

  (2) An offence under this section may be committed in a public or a private place, except that no offence is committed where the words or behaviour are used, or the writing, sign or other visible representation is displayed, by a person inside a dwelling and the person who is harassed, alarmed or distressed is also inside that or another dwelling.

  [(3) provides a specific defence.]

  (4) A constable may arrest without warrant anyone he reasonably suspects is committing an offence under this section.

  (5) A person guilty of an offence under this section is liable on summary conviction to imprisonment for a term not exceeding 6 months or a fine not exceeding level 5 on the standard scale or both.

The following statutory defence is provided in s 4A(3) as follows:

  (3) It is a defence for the accused to prove—

  (a)   that he was inside a dwelling and had no reason to believe that the words or behaviour used, or the writing, sign or other visible representation displayed, would be heard or seen by a person outside that or any other dwelling, or

  (b)   that his conduct was reasonable.

7.6   Harassment, alarm or distress

The offence under s 5 of the Public Order Act 1986 is triable summarily only and is punishable with a fine not exceeding level 3. The offence is defined as follows:

  (1) A person is guilty of an offence if he—

  (a)   uses threatening, abusive or insulting words or behaviour, or disorderly behaviour, or

  (b)   displays any writing, sign or other visible representation which is threatening, abusive or insulting,

  within the hearing or sight of a person likely to be caused harassment, alarm or distress thereby.

  [(2) and

  (3) concern the place of commission of the offence and a specific defence.]

  (4) A constable may arrest a person without warrant if—

  (a)   he engages in offensive conduct which a constable warns him to stop, and

  (b)   he engages in further offensive conduct immediately or shortly after the warning.

  (5) In subsection (4) 'offensive conduct' means conduct the constable reasonably suspects to constitute an offence under this section, and the conduct mentioned in paragraph (a) and the further conduct need not be of the same nature.

See *Lodge v DPP* The Times, 26 October 1988, *DPP v Orum* [1989] 1 WLR 88, *Ball* (1990) 90 Cr App R 378, *Chappell v DPP* (1989) 89 Cr App R 82, *Groom v DPP* [1991] Crim LR 713, *DPP v Clarke* (1992) 94 Cr App R 359, *Chambers and Edwards v DPP* [1995] Crim LR 896 and *Vigon v DPP* (1998) 162 JP 115.

A specific defence is set out in s 5(3) as follows:

(3) *It is a defence for the accused to prove—*

   (a) *that he had no reason to believe that there was any person within hearing or sight who was likely to be caused harassment, alarm or distress, or*

   (b) *that he was inside a dwelling and had no reason to believe that the words or behaviour used, or the writing, sign or other visible representation displayed, would be heard or seen by a person outside that or any other dwelling, or*

   (c) *that his conduct was reasonable.*

See *Kwasi Poku v DPP* [1993] Crim LR 705 and *Morrow and others v DPP and others* [1994] Crim LR 58.

In *Percy v DPP* [2002] Crim LR 835, the defendant had defaced an American flag at an American air base and had put it on the ground and stood on it. The Divisional Court held that her conviction of an offence under s 5 should be quashed as it was incompatible with the right to freedom of expression contained in Article 10 of the ECHR. See also *Norwood v DPP* [2003] Crim LR 888 and *DPP v Hammond* The Times, 28 January 2004.

7.7 Racially or religiously aggravated public order offences

Sections 29 to 32 of the Crime and Disorder Act 1998 create racially or religiously aggravated offences. The public order offences which may be racially or religiously aggravated are offences contrary to ss 4, 4A and 5 of the Public Order Act 1986 and harassment contrary to ss 2 and 4 of the Protection from Harassment Act 1997. The definition of 'racially or religiously aggravated' is provided in s 28 of the Crime and Disorder Act 1998:

(1) *An offence is racially or religiously aggravated for the purposes of sections 29 to 32 below if—*

   (a) *at the time of committing the offence, or immediately before or after doing so, the offender demonstrates towards the victim of the offence hostility based on the victim's membership (or presumed membership) of a racial or religious group; or*

   (b) *the offence is motivated (wholly or partly) by hostility towards members of a racial or religious group based on their membership of that group.*

(2) *In subsection (1)(a) above—*

   'membership', in relation to a racial or religious group, includes association with members of that group;

   'presumed' means presumed by the offender.

(3) *It is immaterial for the purposes of paragraph (a) or (b) of subsection (1) above whether or not the offender's hostility is also based, to any extent, on any other factor not mentioned in that paragraph.*

(4) *In this section 'racial group' means a group of persons defined by reference to race, colour, nationality (including citizenship) or ethnic or national origins.*

(5) *In this section 'religious group' means a group of persons defined by reference to religious belief or lack of religious belief.*

In *Norwood v DPP* [2003] Crim LR 888, the appellant, a regional director of the British National Party, had displayed a poster which contained information said to be offensive to Muslims. He appealed by way of case stated against his conviction for an offence of causing alarm, or distress under s 5(1)(b) of the Public Order Act 1986 which was religiously aggravated in the manner provided by ss 28 and 31 of the Crime and Disorder Act 1998, as amended by s 39 of the Anti-Terrorism, Crime and Security Act 2001. The Administrative Court held that the judge was justified in finding on the evidence before the court, that the aggravated offence had been made out and that the appellant's right to freedom of expression under Article 10(1) of the ECHR had been restricted.

The Court of Appeal indicated in *Saunders* [2000] 1 Cr App R 458 and in *Kelly* [2001] 2 Cr App R (S) 341, that when sentencing for racially aggravated public order offences, the sentencer should consider the appropriate sentence for the offence in the absence of racial aggravation and then add a further term to reflect the racial element.

7.8 Offences of stirring up racial hatred

Sections 18 to 23 of the Public Order Act 1986 create six distinct offences. They are triable either way and are punishable on indictment with a term of two years' imprisonment or a fine or both, or on summary conviction, with six months' imprisonment, or a fine not exceeding the statutory maximum or both. Proceedings require the consent of the Attorney-General (s 27(3)).

7.8.1 Use of words or behaviour or display of written material stirring up racial hatred

The s 18 offence is defined as follows:

> (1) *A person who uses threatening, abusive or insulting words or behaviour, or displays any written material which is threatening, abusive or insulting, is guilty of an offence if—*
>
>   (a)   *he intends thereby to stir up racial hatred, or*
>
>   (b)   *having regard to all the circumstances racial hatred is likely to be stirred up thereby.*

'Racial hatred' is defined by s 17 as follows:

In this part 'racial hatred' means hatred against a group of persons in Great Britain defined by reference to colour, race, nationality (including citizenship) or ethnic or national origins.

The *mens rea* of the offence is referred to in s 18(5):

A person who is not shown to have intended to stir up racial hatred is not guilty of an offence under this section if he did not intend his words or behaviour, or the written material, to be, and was not aware that it might be, threatening, abusive or insulting.

Section 18(2) stipulates where the offence may be committed and s 18(4) sets out a statutory defence:

> (2) *An offence under this section may be committed in a public or a private place, except that no offence is committed where the words or behaviour are used, or the written material is displayed, by a person inside a dwelling and are not heard or seen except by other persons in that or another dwelling.*
>
> (4) *In proceedings for an offence under this section it is a defence for the accused to prove that he was inside a dwelling and had no reason to believe that the words or behaviour used, or the written material displayed, would be heard or seen by a person outside that or any other dwelling.*

7.8.2 Publishing or distributing written material stirring up racial hatred

The Public Order Act 1986, s 19 offence is defined as follows:

> (1) *A person who publishes or distributes written material which is threatening, abusive or insulting is guilty of an offence if—*
>
>   (a)   *he intends thereby to stir up racial hatred, or*
>
>   (b)   *having regard to all the circumstances racial hatred is likely to be stirred up thereby.*

This offence is an arrestable offence in accordance with s 24(2) of the Police and Criminal Evidence Act 1984 (s 155 of the CJPOA 1994).

7.8.3 Public performance of play stirring up racial hatred

The Public Order Act 1986, s 20 offence is defined as follows:

(1) *If a public performance of a play is given which involves the use of threatening, abusive or insulting words or behaviour, any person who presents or directs the performance is guilty of an offence if—*

   (a) *he intends thereby to stir up racial hatred, or*

   (b) *having regard to all the circumstances (and, in particular, taking the performance as a whole) racial hatred is likely to be stirred up thereby.*

The following statutory defences are provided in s 20:

(2) *If a person presenting or directing the performance is not shown to have intended to stir up racial hatred, it is a defence for him to prove—*

   (a) *that he did not know and had no reason to suspect that the performance would involve the use of the offending words or behaviour, or*

   (b) *that he did not know and had no reason to suspect that the offending words or behaviour were threatening, abusive or insulting, or*

   (c) *that he did not know and had no reason to suspect that the circumstances in which the performance would be given would be such that racial hatred would be likely to be stirred up.*

(3) *This section does not apply to a performance given solely or primarily for one or more of the following purposes—*

   (a) *rehearsal,*

   (b) *making a recording of the performance, or*

   (c) *enabling the performance to be included in a programme service,*

   but if it is proved that the performance was attended by persons other than those directly concerned with the giving of the performance or the doing in relation to it of the things mentioned in paragraph (b) or (c), the performance shall, unless the contrary is shown, be taken not to have been given solely for the purposes mentioned above.

(4) *For the purposes of this section—*

   (a) *a person shall not be treated as presenting a performance of a play by reason only of his taking part in it as a performer,*

   (b) *a person taking part as a performer in a performance directed by another shall be treated as a person who directed the performance if without reasonable excuse he performs otherwise than in accordance with that person's direction, and*

   (c) *a person shall be taken to have directed a performance of a play given under his direction notwithstanding that he was not present during the performance;*

   and a person shall not be treated as aiding or abetting the commission of an offence under this section by reason only of his taking part in a performance as a performer.

7.8.4 Distributing, showing or playing a recording stirring up racial hatred

The Public Order Act 1986, s 21 offence is defined as follows:

(1) *A person who distributes, or shows or plays, a recording of visual images or sounds which are threatening, abusive or insulting is guilty of an offence if—*

   (a) *he intends thereby to stir up racial hatred, or*

   (b) *having regard to all the circumstances racial hatred is likely to be stirred up thereby.*

The following statutory defence is provided in s 21:

(3) *In proceedings for an offence under this section it is a defence for an accused who is not shown to have intended to stir up racial hatred to prove that he was not aware of the content of the*

recording and did not suspect, and had no reason to suspect, that it was threatening, abusive or insulting.

(4) *This section does not apply to the showing or playing of a recording solely for the purpose of enabling the recording to be included in a programme service.*

7.8.5 Broadcasting or including programme in cable programme service stirring up racial hatred

The Public Order Act 1986, s 22 offence is defined as follows:

(1) *If a programme involving threatening, abusive or insulting visual images or sound is included in a programme service, each of the persons mentioned in subsection (2) is guilty of an offence if—*

   (a) *he intends to stir up racial hatred, or*

   (b) *having regard to all the circumstances racial hatred is likely to be stirred up thereby.*

(2) *The persons are—*

   (a) *the person providing the programme service,*

   (b) *any person by whom the programme is produced or directed, and*

   (c) *any person by whom offending words or behaviour are used.*

The following statutory defences are provided in s 22:

(3) *If the person providing the service, or a person by whom the programme was produced or directed, is not shown to have intended to stir up racial hatred, it is a defence for him to prove that—*

   (a) *he did not know and had no reason to suspect that the programme would involve the offending material, and*

   (b) *having regard to the circumstances in which the programme was included in a programme service, it was not reasonably practicable for him to secure the removal of the material.*

(4) *It is a defence for a person by whom the programme was produced or directed who is not shown to have intended to stir up racial hatred to prove that he did not know and had no reason to suspect—*

   (a) *that the programme would be included in a programme service, or*

   (b) *that the circumstances in which the programme would be so included would be such that racial hatred would be likely to be stirred up.*

(5) *It is a defence for a person by whom offending words or behaviour were used and who is not shown to have intended to stir up racial hatred to prove that he did not know and had no reason to suspect—*

   (a) *that a programme involving the use of the offending material would be included in a programme service, or*

   (b) *that the circumstances in which a programme involving the use of the offending material would be so included, or in which a programme so included would involve the use of the offending material, would be such that racial hatred would be likely to be stirred up.*

(6) *A person who is not shown to have intended to stir up racial hatred is not guilty of an offence under this section if he did not know, and had no reason to suspect, that the offending material was threatening, abusive or insulting.*

7.8.6 Possession of racially inflammatory material stirring up racial hatred

The Public Order Act 1986, s 23 offence is defined as follows:

(1) *A person who has in his possession written material which is threatening, abusive or insulting, or a recording of visual images or sound which are threatening, abusive or insulting, with a view to—*

   (a) *in the case of written material, its being displayed, published, distributed, or included in a programme service, whether by himself or another, or*

   (b) *in the case of a recording, its being distributed, shown, played, or included in a programme service, whether by himself or another,*

> is guilty of an offence if he intends racial hatred to be stirred up thereby or, having regard to all the circumstances, racial hatred is likely to be stirred up thereby.
>
> (2) For this purpose regard is to be had to such display, publication, distribution, showing, playing, or inclusion in a programme service as he has, or it may reasonably be inferred that he has, in view.

A statutory defence is provided in s 23(3):

> (3) In proceedings for an offence under this section it is a defence for an accused who is not shown to have intended to stir up racial hatred to prove that he was not aware of the content of the written material or recording and did not suspect, and had no reason to suspect, that it was threatening, abusive or insulting.

7.9   Football and sporting offences

7.9.1   Throwing of objects, chanting of indecent or racialist nature, going onto playing area

Sections 2, 3 and 4 of the Football (Offences) Act 1991 create offences which are triable summarily only. The maximum penalty is a fine not exceeding level 3 on the standard scale (s 5(2)). They provide as follows:

> 2. It is an offence for a person at a designated football match to throw anything at or towards—
>
> (a) the playing area, or any area adjacent to the playing area to which spectators are not generally admitted, or
>
> (b) any area in which spectators or other persons are or may be present, without lawful authority or lawful excuse (which shall be for him to prove).
>
> 3.—(1) It is an offence to take part at a designated football match in chanting of an indecent or racialist nature.
>
> (2) For this purpose—
>
> (a) 'chanting' means the repeated uttering of any words or sounds in concert with one or more others; and
>
> (b) 'of racialist nature' means consisting of or including matter which is threatening, abusive or insulting to a person by reason of his colour, race, nationality (including citizenship) or ethnic or national origins.
>
> 4. It is an offence for a person at a designated football match to go onto the playing area, or any area adjacent to the playing area to which spectators are not generally admitted, without lawful authority or lawful excuse (which shall be for him to prove).

The Divisional Court held in *DPP v Stoke-on-Trent Magistrates' Court* [2003] 3 All ER 1096 that the use of the phrase 'You're just a town full of Pakis' chanted at a football match was insulting and racially abusive within the meaning of s 3(2)(b).

7.9.2   Alcohol offences at sporting events

Section 1 of the Sporting Events (Control of Alcohol etc) Act 1985 creates offences which are triable summarily only and are punishable by a fine not exceeding level 4 on the standard scale in the case of an offence under s 1(2), level 3 in the case of an offence under s 1(3), and level 2 in the case of an offence under s 1(4). The offences are defined as follows:

> (2) A person who knowingly causes or permits intoxicating liquor to be carried on a vehicle to which this section applies is guilty of an offence—
>
> (a) if the vehicle is a public service vehicle and he is the operator of the vehicle or the servant or agent of the operator, or

> *(b)   if the vehicle is a hired vehicle and he is the person to whom it is hired or the servant or agent of that person.*
>
> *(3)   A person who has intoxicating liquor in his possession while on a vehicle to which this section applies is guilty of an offence.*
>
> *(4)   A person who is drunk on a vehicle to which this section applies is guilty of an offence.*

Section 2 offences are also triable summarily only and are punishable by a fine not exceeding level 3 on the standard scale, or by imprisonment for a term not exceeding three months or both in the case of an offence under s 2(1), and a fine not exceeding level 2 in the case of an offence under s 2(2). The offences are defined as follows:

> *(1)   A person who has intoxicating liquor or an article to which this section applies in his possession—*
>
> *(a)   at any time during the period of a designated sporting event when he is in any area of a designated sports ground from which the event may be directly viewed, or*
>
> *(b)   while entering or trying to enter a designated sports ground at any time during the period of a designated sporting event at that ground, is guilty of an offence.*
>
> *(2)   A person who is drunk in a designated sports ground at any time during the period of a designated sporting event at that ground or is drunk while entering or trying to enter such a ground at any time during the period of a designated sporting event at that ground is guilty of an offence.*

7.9.3   Banning orders

The Football Spectators Act 1989 provides that a court by or before which a person has been convicted of certain offences may make a banning order against him. The relevant offences are set out in Sch 1, as substituted by the Football (Disorder) Act 2000 which came into force on 28 August 2000. It was held by the Court of Appeal in *Gough and Smith v Chief Constable of Derbyshire* [2002] 2 All ER 985, that international banning orders under the Act contravened neither European law on freedom of movement of persons nor the ECHR.

7.10   Offences relating to public processions and assemblies

7.10.1   Failure to give notice to the police

A person organising a public procession is required by s 11 of the Public Order Act 1986 to satisfy requirements concerning the giving of notice of the procession to the police.

The offence under s 11(7) of the Public Order Act 1986 is triable summarily only and is punishable with a fine not exceeding level 3. The offence is defined as follows:

> *(7)   Where a public procession is held each of the persons organising it is guilty of an offence if—*
>
> *(a)   the requirements of this section as to notice have not been satisfied, or*
>
> *(b)   the date when it is held, the time when it starts, or its route, differs from the date, time or route specified in the notice.*

The following statutory defences are provided in s 11(8) and (9):

> *(8)   It is a defence for the accused to prove that he did not know of, and neither suspected nor had reason to suspect, the failure to satisfy the requirements or (as the case may be) the difference of date, time or route.*

(9) To the extent that an alleged offence turns on a difference of date, time or route, it is a defence for the accused to prove that the difference arose from circumstances beyond his control or from something done with the agreement of a police officer or by his direction.

7.10.2   Failure to comply with conditions imposed on public procession

The three offences under the Public Order Act 1986, s 12 are triable summarily and are defined in s 12(4) to (6) as follows:

(4) A person who organises a public procession and knowingly fails to comply with a condition imposed under this section is guilty of an offence, but it is a defence for him to prove that the failure arose from circumstances beyond his control.

(5) A person who takes part in a public procession and knowingly fails to comply with a condition imposed under this section is guilty of an offence, but it is a defence for him to prove that the failure arose from circumstances beyond his control.

(6) A person who incites another to commit an offence under subsection (5) is guilty of an offence.

The penalty for each of the s 12(4) offence is imprisonment for a term not exceeding three months, or a fine not exceeding level 4 or both.

The penalty for the s 12(5) offence is a fine not exceeding level 3 and for the s 12(6) offence, imprisionment for a term not exceeding three months, or a fine not exceeding level 4 or both.

7.10.3   Contravening prohibition of public procession

The three offences under s 13 of the 1986 Act are triable summarily and are defined in s 13(7) to (9) as follows:

(7) A person who organises a public procession the holding of which he knows is prohibited by virtue of an order under this section is guilty of an offence.

(8) A person who takes part in a public procession the holding of which he knows is prohibited by virtue of an order under this section is guilty of an offence.

(9) A person who incites another to commit an offence under subsection (8) is guilty of an offence.

The penalty for each of the s13(7) and (9) offences is imprisonment for a term not exceeding three months or a fine not exceeding level 4 or both, and for the s 13(8) offence is a fine not exceeding level 3.

7.10.4   Failure to comply with conditions imposed on public assembly

The three offences under the Public Order Act 1986, s 14 are triable summarily only and are defined in s 14(4) to (6) as follows:

(4) A person who organises a public assembly and knowingly fails to comply with a condition imposed under this section is guilty of an offence, but it is a defence for him to prove that the failure arose from circumstances beyond his control.

(5) A person who takes part in a public assembly and knowingly fails to comply with a condition imposed under this section is guilty of an offence, but it is a defence for him to prove that the failure arose from circumstances beyond his control.

(6) A person who incites another to commit an offence under subsection (5) is guilty of an offence.

The penalty for the s 14(4) and (6) offences is imprisonment for a term not exceeding three months, or a fine not exceeding level 4 or both, and for the s 14(5) offence, a fine not exceeding level 3. See *DPP v Baillie* [1995] Crim LR 426.

7.11   Bomb hoaxes

An offence under s 51(1) of the Criminal Law Act 1977 is triable either way and is punishable on indictment with a term of seven years' imprisonment, and on summary conviction with a term not exceeding six months' imprisonment, or a fine not exceeding the statutory maximum or both (s 51(4)).

The offence is defined as follows:

(1) *A person who—*
   (a) *places any article in any place whatever, or*
   (b) *dispatches any article by post, rail or any other means whatever of sending things from one place to another,*
   with the intention (in either case) of inducing in some other person a belief that it is likely to explode or ignite and thereby cause personal injury or damage to property is guilty of an offence.

   In this subsection 'article' includes substance.

(2) *A person who communicates any information which he knows or believes to be false to another person with the intention of inducing in him or any other person a false belief that a bomb or other thing liable to explode or ignite is present in any place or location whatever is guilty of an offence.*

See *Browne* (1984) 6 Cr App R (S) 5, *Dunbar* (1987) 9 Cr App R (S) 393 and *Wilburn* (1992) 13 Cr App R (S) 309.

7.12   Offences in relation to collective trespass or nuisance on land

7.12.1   Powers regarding trespass

Section 61(1)–(3) of the Criminal Justice and Public Order Act 1994 (CJPOA 1994) enables a senior police officer to make a direction for two or more trespassers to leave land.

61.—(1) *If the senior police officer present at the scene reasonably believes that two or more persons are trespassing on land and are present there with the common purpose of residing there for any period, that reasonable steps have been taken by or on behalf of the occupier to ask them to leave and—*
   (a) *that any of those persons has caused damage to the land or to property on the land or used threatening, abusive or insulting words or behaviour towards the occupier, a member of his family or an employee or agent of his, or*
   (b) *that those persons have between them six or more vehicles on the land,*
   he may direct those persons, or any of them, to leave the land and to remove any vehicles or other property they have with them on the land.

(2) *Where the persons in question are reasonably believed by the senior police officer to be persons who were not originally trespassers but have become trespassers on the land, the officer must reasonably believe that the other conditions specified in subsection (1) are satisfied after those persons became trespassers before he can exercise the power conferred by that subsection.*

(3) *A direction under subsection (1) above, if not communicated to the persons referred to in subsection (1) by the police officer giving the direction, may be communicated to them by any constable at the scene.*

The offence under s 61(4) is defined as follows:

(4) *If a person knowing that a direction under subsection (1) above has been given which applies to him—*
   (a) *fails to leave the land as soon as reasonably practicable, or*
   (b) *having left again enters the land as a trespasser within the period of three months beginning with the day on which the direction was given,*

> *he commits an offence and is liable on summary conviction to imprisonment for a term not exceeding three months or a fine not exceeding level 4 on the standard scale, or both.*

Section 61(5) confers a power of arrest without a warrant on a police officer in uniform. The following statutory defence is provided in s 61(6):

> *(6) In proceedings for an offence under this section it is a defence for the accused to show—*
>
> > *(a)   that he was not trespassing on the land, or*
> >
> > *(b)   that he had a reasonable excuse for failing to leave the land as soon as reasonably practicable or, as the case may be, for again entering the land as a trespasser.*

Section 61(9) defines various terms including 'common land', 'occupier', 'trespass' and 'vehicle'.

7.12.2   Powers regarding raves

Section 63(1)–(5) of the CJPOA 1994 enables a police officer of at least the rank of superintendent to give a direction for persons to leave land if two or more of them are preparing for a rave, or ten or more of them are waiting for, or attending a rave.

> 63.—*(1)   This section applies to a gathering on land in the open air of 100 or more persons (whether or not trespassers) at which amplified music is played during the night (with or without intermissions) and is such as, by reason of its loudness and duration and the time at which it is played, is likely to cause serious distress to the inhabitants of the locality; and for this purpose—*
>
> > *(a)   such a gathering continues during intermissions in the music and, where the gathering extends over several days, throughout the period during which amplified music is played at night (with or without intermissions); and*
> >
> > *(b)   'music' includes sounds wholly or predominantly characterised by the emission of a succession of repetitive beats.*
>
> *(2)   If, as respects any land in the open air, a police officer of at least the rank of superintendent reasonably believes that—*
>
> > *(a)   two or more persons are making preparations for the holding there of a gathering to which this section applies,*
> >
> > *(b)   ten or more persons are waiting for such a gathering to begin there, or*
> >
> > *(c)   ten or more persons are attending such a gathering which is in progress,*
>
> *he may give a direction that those persons and any other persons who come to prepare or wait for or to attend the gathering are to leave the land and remove any vehicles or other property which they have with them on the land.*
>
> *(3)   A direction under subsection (2) above, if not communicated to the persons referred to in subsection (2) by the police officer giving the direction, may be communicated to them by any constable at the scene.*
>
> *(4)   Persons shall be treated as having had a direction under subsection (2) above communicated to them if reasonable steps have been taken to bring it to their attention.*
>
> *(5)   A direction under subsection (2) above does not apply to an exempt person.*

The offence under s 63(6) is defined as follows:

> *(6)   If a person knowing that a direction has been given which applies to him—*
>
> > *(a)   fails to leave the land as soon as reasonably practicable, or*
> >
> > *(b)   having left again enters the land within the period of 7 days beginning with the day on which the direction was given,*
>
> *he commits an offence and is liable on summary conviction to imprisonment for a term not exceeding three months or a fine not exceeding level 4 on the standard scale, or both.*

Section 63(8) confers a power of arrest without a warrant on a police officer in uniform.

The following statutory defence is provided in s 63(7):

(7) In proceedings for an offence under this section it is a defence for the accused to show that he had a reasonable excuse for failing to leave the land as soon as reasonably practicable or, as the case may be, for again entering the land.

Section 63(9) provides that licensed gatherings are not included in the section and an 'exempt person' is defined in s 63(10) as an occupier, any member of his family, his employee or agent and any person whose home is on the land.

Section 65(1)–(3) enables a police officer in uniform to stop a person on his way to a rave within a radius of five miles of the site of the rave and to direct him not to proceed to the rave.

65.—(1) If a constable in uniform reasonably believes that a person is on his way to a gathering to which section 63 applies in relation to which a direction under section 63(2) is in force, he may, subject to subsections (2) and (3) below—

(a)   stop that person, and

(b)   direct him not to proceed in the direction of the gathering.

(2) The power conferred by subsection (1) above may only be exercised at a place within 5 miles of the boundary of the site of the gathering.

(3) No direction may be given under subsection (1) above to an exempt person.

The offence under s 65(4) is defined as follows:

(4) If a person knowing that a direction under subsection (1) above has been given to him fails to comply with that direction, he commits an offence and is liable on summary conviction to a fine not exceeding level 3 on the standard scale.

Section 65(5) confers a power of arrest without a warrant on a police officer in uniform.

Powers of entry, seizure, retention and charges in respect of seized property are provided by ss 64, 66 and 67.

7.12.3 Aggravated trespass

The offence of aggravated trespass is triable summarily only and carries a maximum penalty of three months' imprisonment, or a fine not exceeding level 4, or both (s 68(3)).

It is defined in s 68 of the CJPOA 1994 as follows:

68.—(1) A person commits the offence of aggravated trespass if he trespasses on land in the open air and, in relation to any lawful activity which persons are engaging in or are about to engage in on that or adjoining land in the open air, does there anything which is intended by him to have the effect—

(a)   of intimidating those persons or any of them so as to deter them or any of them from engaging in that activity,

(b)   of obstructing that activity, or

(c)   of disrupting that activity.

(2) Activity on any occasion on the part of a person or persons on land is 'lawful' for the purposes of this section if he or they may engage in the activity on the land on that occasion without committing an offence or trespassing on the land.

Section 68(4) confers a power of arrest without a warrant on a police officer in uniform.

Section 69 enables a senior police officer present to direct disruptive or intending disruptive trespassers to leave land.

69.—(1) If the senior police officer present at the scene reasonably believes—

(a)   that a person is committing, has committed or intends to commit the offence of aggravated trespass on land in the open air; or

(b)   *that two or more persons are trespassing on land in the open air and are present there with the common purpose of intimidating persons so as to deter them from engaging in a lawful activity or of obstructing or disrupting a lawful activity,*

he may direct that person or (as the case may be) those persons (or any of them) to leave the land.

(2)   *A direction under subsection (1) above, if not communicated to the persons referred to in subsection (1) by the police officer giving the direction, may be communicated to them by any constable at the scene.*

The offence under s 69(3) is defined as follows:

(3)   *If a person knowing that a direction under subsection (1) above has been given which applies to him—*

(a)   *fails to leave the land as soon as practicable, or*

(b)   *having left again enters the land as a trespasser within the period of three months beginning with the day on which the direction was given,*

he commits an offence and is liable on summary conviction to imprisonment for a term not exceeding three months or a fine not exceeding level 4 on the standard scale, or both.

Section 69(5) confers a power of arrest without a warrant on a police officer in uniform. The following statutory defence is provided in s 69(4):

(4)   *In proceedings for an offence under subsection (3) it is a defence for the accused to show—*

(a)   *that he was not trespassing on the land, or*

(b)   *that he had a reasonable excuse for failing to leave the land as soon as practicable or, as the case may be, for again entering the land as a trespasser.*

7.12.4   Trespassory assemblies

Section 14A of the Public Order Act 1986 enables a chief officer of police to apply to a district council for an order prohibiting trespassory assemblies.

The offences in s 14B are defined as follows:

14B.—(1)   A person who organises an assembly the holding of which he knows is prohibited by an order under section 14A is guilty of an offence.

(2)   *A person who takes part in an assembly which he knows is prohibited by an order under section 14A is guilty of an offence.*

(3)   *In England and Wales, a person who incites another to commit an offence under subsection (2) is guilty of an offence.*

Offences under s 14B(1) and (3) are triable summarily only and are punishable with imprisonment for a term not exceeding three months or a fine not exceeding level 4, or both, and in the case of an offence under s 14B(2) with a fine not exceeding level 3 (s 14B(5)–(7)).

In *DPP v Jones* [1999] 2 WLR 625, the defendants had taken part in a peaceful, non-obstructive assembly on the highway adjacent to the monument at Stonehenge in respect of which there was in force an order under s 14A. The House of Lords held that the public had a right to use the highway for such reasonable and usual activities, including peaceful assembly, as were consistent with the primary right to use it for passage and repassage, and that a peaceful assembly for a reasonable period that did not unreasonably obstruct the highway was not necessarily unlawful, nor did it necessarily constitute a trespassory assembly. Each case had to be decided in the light of its particular facts, and the right of public assembly could, in certain circumstances, be exercised on the highway provided that it caused no obstruction to persons passing along the highway and that the tribunal of fact made a finding that it had been a reasonable user.

Section 14C of the Public Order Act 1986 enables a police officer in uniform to stop persons on their way to trespassory assemblies and to direct them not to proceed in that direction.

> 14C.—(1) *If a constable in uniform reasonably believes that a person is on his way to an assembly within the area to which an order under section 14A applies which the constable reasonably believes is likely to be an assembly which is prohibited by that order, he may, subject to subsection (2) below—*
>
> (a) *stop that person, and*
>
> (b) *direct him not to proceed in the direction of the assembly.*
>
> (2) *The power conferred by subsection (1) may only be exercised within the area to which the order applies.*

The offence under s 14C is triable summarily only and is punishable with a fine not exceeding level 3 (s 14C(5)).

The offence is defined as follows:

> (3) *A person who fails to comply with a direction under subsection (1) which he knows has been given to him is guilty of an offence.*

Section 14C(4) confers a power of arrest without a warrant on a police officer in uniform.

7.12.5   Removal of unauthorised campers

Section 77 of the CJPOA 1994 enables a local authority to give a direction for removal of unauthorised campers from land.

> 77.—(1) *If it appears to a local authority that persons are for the time being residing in a vehicle or vehicles within that authority's area—*
>
> (a) *on any land forming part of a highway;*
>
> (b) *on any other unoccupied land; or*
>
> (c) *on any occupied land without the consent of the occupier,*
>
> *the authority may give a direction that those persons and any others with them are to leave the land and remove the vehicle or vehicles and any other property they have with them on the land.*
>
> (2) *Notice of a direction under subsection (1) must be served on the persons to whom the direction applies, but it shall be sufficient for this purpose for the direction to specify the land and (except where the direction applies to only one person) to be addressed to all occupants of the vehicles on the land, without naming them.*

The offence under s 77(3) is defined as follows:

> (3) *If a person knowing that a direction under subsection (1) above has been given which applies to him—*
>
> (a) *fails, as soon as practicable, to leave the land or remove from the land any vehicle or other property which is the subject of the direction, or*
>
> (b) *having removed any such vehicle or property again enters the land with a vehicle within the period of three months beginning with the day on which the direction was given,*
>
> *he commits an offence and is liable on summary conviction to a fine not exceeding level 3 on the standard scale.*

Guidance relating to the making of removal directions and to service of notices of directions was provided by the Divisional Court in *Wealden DC, ex p Wales* The Times, 22 September 1995.

Section 78(1)–(3) enables a local authority to apply to a magistrates' court for an order requiring the removal of vehicles or property from the land where a direction has been breached.

> 78.—(1) *A magistrates' court may, on a complaint made by a local authority, if satisfied that persons and vehicles in which they are residing are present on land within that authority's area in*

contravention of a direction given under section 77, make an order requiring the removal of any vehicle or other property which is so present on the land and any person residing in it.

(2) *An order under this section may authorise the local authority to take such steps as are reasonably necessary to ensure that the order is complied with and, in particular, may authorise the authority, by its officers and servants—*

   (a) *to enter upon the land specified in the order; and*

   (b) *to take, in relation to any vehicle or property to be removed in pursuance of the order, such steps for securing entry and rendering it suitable for removal as may be so specified.*

(3) *The local authority shall not enter upon any occupied land unless they have given to the owner and occupier at least 24 hours' notice of their intention to do so, or unless after reasonable inquiries they are unable to ascertain their names and addresses.*

The offence under s 78(4) is defined as follows:

(4) *A person who wilfully obstructs any person in the exercise of any power conferred on him by an order under this section commits an offence and is liable on summary conviction to a fine not exceeding level 3 on the standard scale.*

Section 78(5) provides that it is not necessary for the names of the occupants of vehicles on the land in question to be named in any summonses sent to them.

7.13 Harassment

Offences of harassment are defined in ss 1, 2 and 4 of the Protection from Harassment Act 1997.

Section 1 provides:

(1) *A person must not pursue a course of conduct—*

   (a) *which amounts to harassment of another, and*

   (b) *which he knows or ought to know amounts to harassment of the other.*

(1A) *A person must not pursue a course of conduct—*

   (a) *which involves harassment of two or more persons, and*

   (b) *which he knows or ought to know involves harassment of those persons, and*

   (c) *by which he intends to persuade any person (whether or not one of those mentioned above)—*

      (i) *not to do something that he is entitled or required to do, or*

      (ii) *to do something that he is not under any obligation to do.*

(2) *For the purposes of this section, the person whose course of conduct is in question ought to know that it amounts to or involves harassment of another if a reasonable person in possession of the same information would think the course of conduct amounted to or involved harassment of the other.*

(3) *Subsection (1) or (1A) does not apply to a course of conduct if the person who pursued it shows—*

   (a) *that it was pursued for the purpose of preventing or detecting crime,*

   (b) *that it was pursued under any enactment or rule of law or to comply with any condition or requirement imposed by any person under any enactment, or*

   (c) *that in the particular circumstances the pursuit of the course of conduct was reasonable.*

Section 2 provides:

(1) *A person who pursues a course of conduct in breach of section 1(1) or (1A) is guilty of an offence.*

(2) *A person guilty of an offence under this section is liable on summary conviction to imprisonment for a term not exceeding six months, or a fine not exceeding level 5 on the standard scale, or both.*

Section 4 provides:

(1) A person whose course of conduct causes another to fear, on at least two occasions, that violence will be used against him is guilty of an offence if he knows or ought to know that his course of conduct will cause the other so to fear on each of those occasions.

(2) For the purposes of this section, the person whose course of conduct is in question ought to know that it will cause another to fear that violence will be used against him on any occasion if a reasonable person in possession of the same information would think the course of conduct would cause the other so to fear on that occasion.

(3) It is a defence for a person charged with an offence under this section to show that—

    (a)   his course of conduct was pursued for the purpose of preventing or detecting crime,

    (b)   his course of conduct was pursued under any enactment or rule of law or to comply with any condition or requirement imposed by any person under any enactment, or

    (c)   the pursuit of his course of conduct was reasonable for the protection of himself or another or for the protection of his or another's property.

(4) A person guilty of an offence under this section is liable—

    (a)   on conviction on indictment, to imprisonment for a term not exceeding five years, or a fine, or both, or

    (b)   on summary conviction, to imprisonment for a term not exceeding six months, or a fine not exceeding the statutory maximum, or both.

(5) If on the trial on indictment of a person charged with an offence under this section the jury find him not guilty of the offence charged, they may find him guilty of an offence under section 2.

(6) The Crown Court has the same powers and duties in relation to a person who is by virtue of subsection (5) convicted before it of an offence under section 2 as a magistrates' court would have on convicting him of the offence.

7.14 Harassment alarm or distress of a person in a dwelling

This offence is defined in s. 42A of the Criminal Justice and Police Act 2001 as follows:

(1) A person commits an offence if—

    (a)   that person is present outside or in the vicinity of any premises that are used by any individual ('the resident') as his dwelling;

    (b)   that person is present there for the purpose (by his presence or otherwise) of representing to the resident or another individual (whether or not one who uses the premises as his dwelling), or of persuading the resident or such another individual—

        (i)   that he should not do something that he is entitled or required to do; or

        (ii)   that he should do something that he is not under any obligation to do;

    (c)   that person—

        (i)   intends his presence to amount to the harassment of, or to cause alarm or distress to, the resident; or

        (ii)   knows or ought to know that his presence is likely to result in the harassment of, or to cause alarm or distress to, the resident; and

    (d)   the presence of that person—

        (i)   amounts to the harassment of, or causes alarm or distress to, any person falling within subsection (2); or

        (ii)   is likely to result in the harassment of, or to cause alarm or distress to, any such person.

(2) A person falls within this subsection if he is—

    (a)   the resident,

    (b)   a person in the resident's dwelling, or

    (c)   a person in another dwelling in the vicinity of the resident's dwelling.

(3) The references in subsection (1)(c) and (d) to a person's presence are references to his presence either alone or together with that of any other persons who are also present.

(4) For the purposes of this section a person (A) ought to know that his presence is likely to result in the harassment of, or to cause alarm or distress to, a resident if a reasonable person in possession of the same information would think that A's presence was likely to have that effect.

(5) A person guilty of an offence under this section shall be liable, on summary conviction, to imprisonment for a term not exceeding 51 weeks or to a fine not exceeding level 4 on the standard scale, or to both.

(6) In relation to an offence committed before the commencement of section 281(5) of the Criminal Justice Act 2003 (alteration of penalties for summary offences), the reference in subsection (5) to 51 weeks is to be read as a reference to 6 months.

(7) In this section 'dwelling' has the same meaning as in Part 1 of the Public Order Act 1986.

7.15 Trespassing on a designated site

The offence of trespassing on a designated site has been created by s 128 of the Serious Organised Crime and Police Act 2005 and is defined by the section as follows:

(1) A person commits an offence if he enters, or is on, any designated site in England and Wales or Northern Ireland as a trespasser.

(2) A 'designated site' means a site—

(a) specified or described (in any way) in an order made by the Secretary of State, and

(b) designated for the purposes of this section by the order.

(3) The Secretary of State may only designate a site for the purposes of this section if—

(a) it is comprised in Crown land; or

(b) it is comprised in land belonging to Her Majesty in Her private capacity or to the immediate heir to the Throne in his private capacity; or

(c) it appears to the Secretary of State that it is appropriate to designate the site in the interests of national security.

(4) It is a defence for a person charged with an offence under this section to prove that he did not know, and had no reasonable cause to suspect, that the site in relation to which the offence is alleged to have been committed was a designated site.

(5) A person guilty of an offence under this section is liable on summary conviction—

(a) to imprisonment for a term not exceeding 51 weeks, or

(b) to a fine not exceeding level 5 on the standard scale, or to both.

(6) No proceedings for an offence under this section may be instituted against any person—

(a) in England and Wales, except by or with the consent of the Attorney General, or

(b) in Northern Ireland, except by or with the consent of the Attorney General for Northern Ireland.

(7) For the purposes of this section a person who is on any designated site as a trespasser does not cease to be a trespasser by virtue of being allowed time to leave the site.

(8) In this section—

(a) 'site' means the whole or part of any building or buildings, or any land, or both;

(b) 'Crown land' means land in which there is a Crown interest or a Duchy interest.

(9) For this purpose—

'Crown interest' means an interest belonging to Her Majesty in right of the Crown, and

'Duchy interest' means an interest belonging to Her Majesty in right of the Duchy of Lancaster or belonging to the Duchy of Cornwall.

(10) In the application of this section to Northern Ireland, the reference to 51 weeks in subsection (5)(a) is to be read as a reference to 6 months.

7.16   Demonstrating without authorisation in a designated area

Section 132 of the Serious Organised Crime and Police Act 2005 creates an offence of demonstrating in a designated area without authorisation. The section provides:

(1) Any person who—

   (a)   organises a demonstration in a public place in the designated area, or

   (b)   takes part in a demonstration in a public place in the designated area, or

   (c)   carries on a demonstration by himself in a public place in the designated area, is guilty of an offence if, when the demonstration starts, authorisation for the demonstration has not been given under section 134(2).

(2) It is a defence for a person accused of an offence under subsection (1) to show that he reasonably believed that authorisation had been given.

(3) Subsection (1) does not apply if the demonstration is—

   (a)   a public procession of which notice is required to be given under subsection (1) of section 11 of the Public Order Act 1986 (c. 64), or of which (by virtue of subsection (2) of that section) notice is not required to be given, or

   (b)   a public procession for the purposes of section 12 or 13 of that Act.

(4) Subsection (1) also does not apply in relation to any conduct which is lawful under section 220 of the Trade Union and Labour Relations (Consolidation) Act 1992 (c. 52).

(5) If subsection (1) does not apply by virtue of subsection (3) or (4), nothing in sections 133 to 136 applies either.

(6) Section 14 of the Public Order Act 1986 (imposition of conditions on public assemblies) does not apply in relation to a public assembly which is also a demonstration in a public place in the designated area.

(7) In this section and in sections 133 to 136—

   (a)   'the designated area' means the area specified in an order under section 138,

   (b)   'public place' means any highway or any place to which at the material time the public or any section of the public has access, on payment or otherwise, as of right or by virtue of express or implied permission,

   (c)   references to any person organising a demonstration include a person participating in its organisation,

   (d)   references to any person organising a demonstration do not include a person carrying on a demonstration by himself,

   (e)   references to any person or persons taking part in a demonstration (except in subsection (1) of this section) include a person carrying on a demonstration by himself.

7.17   Further reading

Card, R., *Public Order Law*, Bristol: Jordans, 2000.

8

Offensive weapons

8.1 Introduction

This chapter deals with some of the more common offences relating to weapons that a junior practitioner is likely to come across in early practice. It does not deal with firearms legislation, which is extensive, and for which reference should be made to textbooks or practitioner works.

8.2 Prevention of Crime Act 1953

Section 1 provides:

> (1) Any person who without lawful authority or reasonable excuse, the proof whereof shall lie on him, has with him in any public place any offensive weapon shall be guilty of an offence.

This is an offence that is triable either way, and is punishable on indictment with a term of four years' imprisonment or a fine or both, or on summary conviction with six months' imprisonment or a fine not exceeding the prescribed sum or both. Section 1(2) permits the court on conviction of an offence under s 1 to make an order for the forfeiture or disposal of any weapon in respect of which the offence was committed.

It should be noted that generally offences relating to weapons are used to deal with those people who *carry* weapons with them: those who actually *use* a weapon to inflict, say, an assault, are usually charged with the relevant substantive assault charge. A person who, on the spur of the moment, uses a lawfully carried article to attack another is unlikely to have committed an offence under s 1 (although that person is likely to be liable for some form of assault). On this point see, eg, *Jura* [1954] 1 QB 503, *Ohlson v Hylton* [1975] 1 WLR 724, *Bates v Bulman* [1979] 1 WLR 1190, and *Veasey* [1999] Crim LR 158.

8.2.1 'Has with him'

It must be proved that the defendant had the article with him knowingly, although forgetting that the article is in one's possession is not an excuse (*McCalla* (1988) 87 Cr App R 372). However, on the question of whether forgetfulness can amount to reasonable excuse (see **8.2.4**), see *Glidewell* (1999) 163 JP 557.

8.2.2 'Public place'

Public place is defined as including any highway and any other premises or place to which at the material time the public have or are permitted to have access, whether on payment or otherwise (s 1(4)).

8.2.3 'Offensive weapon'

Section 1(4) defines an offensive weapon as:

. . . any article made or adapted for use for causing injury to the person, or intended by the person having it with him for such use by him or by some other person.

The Court of Appeal in *Simpson* (1983) 78 Cr App R 115 explained this as meaning that there were three categories of offensive weapon: articles made for causing injury to the person (often known as weapons offensive *per se*); articles adapted for that purpose; and articles not so made or adapted, but which were carried with an intention to use to cause injury to the person.

The distinction between the first two categories and the third one is important, for in the third category the prosecution is required to prove the accused had the requisite intent to cause injury. In the first two categories such additional intent is not needed.

Where intent must be proved, it must be shown that the accused had the requisite intent at the time and place specified in the charge. Evidence which shows only that he had the intent at an earlier stage will not be sufficient (see *Allamby* [1974] 1 WLR 1494).

The question of whether an article is offensive *per se* is usually a question of fact for the jury to decide; however, in some cases the judge can take judicial notice that an article is offensive *per se* and direct the jury accordingly. For examples of both types of situation see *Gibson v Wales* [1983] 1 WLR 393 and *Simpson* (1983) 78 Cr App R 115 (flick knives), *DPP v Hynde* [1998] 1 WLR 1222 (butterfly knives, on similar legislation), *Houghton v Chief Constable of Greater Manchester* (1986) 84 Cr App R 319 (a police truncheon), *Copus v DPP* [1989] Crim LR 577 (a rice flail) and *Butler* [1988] Crim LR 696 (a sword stick).

Articles adapted for causing injury would include articles such as a deliberately broken bottle. Articles that are not made or adapted for use for causing injury to the person (eg, a baseball bat or sandbag) can still class as offensive weapons if the prosecution can show that the article was carried with the intention of using it to cause injury.

8.2.4 'Lawful authority or reasonable excuse'

If a person has with him an offensive weapon in a public place with lawful authority or reasonable excuse, no offence is committed. The burden of proving lawful authority or reasonable excuse lies with the defendant: it is not for the prosecution to disprove it as part of its case (see **8.3.1**). As with other legal burdens of proof cast on the defence, the standard of proof is on a balance of probabilities.

What constitutes lawful authority or reasonable excuse will depend on the circumstances of each case. Some people are permitted by the nature of their employment to carry offensive weapons at times, a common example being a police officer carrying a truncheon. A more common claim made by a defendant is that of reasonable excuse: carrying a police truncheon as part of a police uniform worn at a fancy dress party may amount to reasonable excuse (*Houghton v Chief Constable of Greater Manchester* (1986) 84 Cr App R 319). A defendant who carried a machete and a catapult in order to kill squirrels to feed wild birds which he kept under licence was held to have reasonable excuse (*Southwell v Chadwick* (1986) 85 Cr App R 235). On whether lack of knowledge that an object is an offensive weapon amounts to a reasonable excuse, see *Densu* [1998] 1 Cr App R 400.

Often the defendant says that he carried the article in self-defence, and claims this to amount to reasonable excuse. A number of cases have considered this point, and the answer is ultimately one of degree. A person who habitually carries a weapon with him on his person or in his vehicle on the off chance that he may be attacked is unlikely to satisfy the test. However, carrying an offensive weapon following an assault which might be repeated may amount to reasonable excuse. See *Evans v Hughes* (1972) 56 Cr App R 813, *Peacock* [1973] Crim LR 639 and *Malnik v DPP* [1989] Crim LR 451.

8.3   Criminal Justice Act 1988

8.3.1   Section 139

Section 139 of the 1988 Act states:

(1) *Subject to subsections (4) and (5) below, any person who has an article to which this section applies with him in a public place shall be guilty of an offence.*

(2) *Subject to subsection (3) below, this section applies to any article which has a blade or is sharply pointed except a folding pocketknife.*

(3) *This section applies to a folding pocketknife if the cutting edge of its blade exceeds 3 inches.*

This section creates an offence which is triable either way, and is punishable on indictment with a term of imprisonment of up to two years and/or a fine, and on summary conviction by a term of six months' imprisonment and/or a fine not exceeding the prescribed amount.

Certain articles that are carried may not fall within the ambit of the Prevention of Crime Act 1953, s 1, but may come within the scope of the Criminal Justice Act 1988, s 139, eg a sheath knife for which there is no evidence of the specific intent necessary to make it an offensive weapon.

A folding pocket knife which locks in position when opened does not come within the term 'folding pocketknife' used by the section (*Harris v DPP* (1992) 96 Cr App R 235, followed in *Deegan* [1998] 2 Cr App R 121).

A screwdriver has been held not to be a bladed article within the meaning of s 139 (*Davis* [1998] Crim LR 564).

'Public place' includes any place to which at the material time the public have or are permitted access, whether on payment or otherwise (s 139(7)).

Section 139(4) makes it a defence for the defendant to prove that he had good reason or lawful authority for having the article with him in a public place. This is a legal burden that lies on the defendant. The statutory imposition on the defendant of a legal burden of proof has been the subject of challenge in a number of cases, on the basis that the burden concerned is incompatible with Article 6 of the ECHR. Such challenges have sometimes been successful (see eg *Lambert* [2002] 2 AC 545 (Misuse of Drugs Act 1971) and *Sheldrake v DPP* [2003] 2 All ER 497 (Road Traffic Act 1988)). However, claims that the legal burden imposed under the Criminal Justice Act, s 139 is incompatible have failed (see *L v DPP* [2003] QB 137 and *Mark Anthony Mathews* [2003] EWCA Crim 813). A failure to leave to the jury the issue of whether self-defence amounted to good reason has resulted in the conviction being quashed (see *Emmanuel* [1998] Crim LR 347).

Section 139(5) additionally provides that, without prejudice to the generality of subsection (4), it shall be a defence for the accused to prove that he had the article for use at work; for religious reasons; or as part of any national costume. For an example of an attempt to rely on the 'use at work' defence, see *Manning* [1998] Crim LR 198.

8.3.2   Section 139A

Section 139A provides an additional triable either way offence of having an article within the meaning of s 139 or an offensive weapon within the meaning of the Prevention of

Crime Act 1953, s 1 on school premises. This is subject to the defence of good reason or lawful authority, and to the use at work/religious reasons/national dress defence, as well as an additional one of having the article on the premises for educational purposes. Punishment depends on whether the article comes within s 139, in which case punishment is the same as s 139 itself, or whether it comes within the Prevention of Crime Act 1953, s 1, in which case punishment is the same as s 1.

Section 139B provides search and seizure powers for the police to enter school premises and search people thereon.

8.4   Other offences

In addition to the commonly used offences under the Prevention of Crime Act 1953 and the Criminal Justice Act 1988 there are a number of other pieces of legislation that seek to restrict the carrying, manufacture, sale, hire, purchase and use of weapons. These include the Restriction of Offensive Weapons Act 1959, ss 141 and 141A of the Criminal Justice Act 1988 (introduced by the Offensive Weapons Act 1996), the Crossbows Act 1987 and the Knives Act 1997. Reference to practitioner works such as *Archbold* or *Blackstone's Criminal Practice* should be made for details of these offences.

9

Road traffic offences: general

9.1 Introduction

This chapter deals with the offences of dangerous driving, careless (or inconsiderate) driving, failing to stop after an accident and failing to report an accident. The various offences related to drinking and driving are dealt with in **Chapter 10**. Between them, these offences constitute a representative sample of the road traffic offences likely to confront counsel in early practice.

The standard reference work for practitioners is Wilkinson, *Road Traffic Offences* (London: Sweet & Maxwell). Section C of *Blackstone's Criminal Practice* is devoted to driving offences.

There is one point which is of general application to road traffic offences, but has particular relevance to dangerous and careless driving. The Highway Code is often used by the courts as a guide to what constitutes safe or careful driving. The position in law is that a failure to observe a provision of the Code does not of itself constitute an offence. Any such failure may, however, be relied upon by any party to civil or criminal proceedings as tending to prove or disprove liability in those proceedings (Road Traffic Act 1988, s 38(7)). In practice it is common for advocates, and the court, to place reliance upon the Code's provisions in evaluating the evidence in the case.

9.2 Dangerous driving

The offence of dangerous driving is defined in s 2A of the Road Traffic Act 1988 (RTA), which was inserted by the RTA 1991. It reads as follows:

2A.—(1) *For the purposes of sections 1 and 2 above a person is to be regarded as driving dangerously if (and, subject to subsection (2) below, only if)—*

    (a) *the way he drives falls far below what would be expected of a competent and careful driver, and*

    (b) *it would be obvious to a competent and careful driver that driving in that way would be dangerous.*

  (2) *A person is also to be regarded as driving dangerously for the purposes of sections 1 and 2 above if it would be obvious to a competent and careful driver that driving the vehicle in its current state would be dangerous.*

  (3) *In subsections (1) and (2) above 'dangerous' refers to danger either of injury to any person or of serious damage to property; and in determining for the purposes of those subsections what would be expected of, or obvious to, a competent and careful driver in a particular case, regard shall be had not only to the circumstances of which he could be expected to be aware but also to any circumstances shown to have been within the knowledge of the accused.*

*(4) In determining for the purposes of subsection (2) above the state of a vehicle, regard may be had to any-
     thing attached to or carried on or in it and to the manner in which it is attached or carried.*

The offence of dangerous driving was not in fact an entirely new one. It was on the statute
books until 1977, when it was replaced by 'reckless driving'. The offence of reckless
driving, which was not statutorily defined, gave rise to voluminous case law as the courts
attempted to grapple with the concept of recklessness. In its revived form, the offence of
dangerous driving is arguably somewhat more widely drawn than the concept of reckless
driving, and is subject to a statutory definition.

The core of that definition is contained in s 2A(1), and it poses two questions in relation
to the allegedly dangerous driving:

(a) Did the driving fall far below the standard which would be expected of a competent
     and careful driver? Clearly the word upon which the defence will frequently
     focus in argument is 'far', and its presence in the definition appears to be one of
     the features which distinguishes this offence from that of careless driving (see **9.3**).

(b) Would it be obvious to that hypothetical competent and careful driver that driving
     in such a way would be dangerous? The key words in this formulation would seem
     to be 'obvious' and 'dangerous'. As far as 'dangerous' is concerned, some assistance
     is provided by the opening words to s 2A(3), which tie the concept to danger of
     injury to the person or serious damage to property. In view of the fact that the word
     'danger' is unqualified, it would seem that danger to any person, even though
     slight, would suffice, provided that it is not *de minimis*.

The prosecution must prove both elements (a) and (b) above before s 2A(1) is satisfied
(*Aitken* v *Lees* 1994 SLT 182).

As can be seen from the wording of s 2A(3), in interpreting s 2A(1) and (2), regard must
be had:

- to circumstances of which a competent and careful driver could be expected to be
  aware; and

- to circumstances which are shown to be within the (actual) knowledge of the
  accused.

9.2.1 Evidence of dangerous driving

What, then, constitutes evidence of dangerousness to measure against the statutory
definition? Obviously, it depends upon the particular facts of the case, and precedents are
of little, if any, assistance. Some guidance can be gleaned from the *Driving Offences
Charging Standard* which was agreed by the police and the Crown Prosecution Service in
January 1996, a summary of which can be found online at www.cps.gov.uk/legal/section 9/
chapter 6.html. It must be stressed, however, that the *Charging Standard* provides
guidance for police and prosecutors, and is not authoritative as far as the courts are
concerned. The *Charging Standard* gives the following as examples of driving which may
support an allegation of dangerous driving (see para 7.7):

(a) racing or competitive driving;

(b) prolonged, persistent or deliberate bad driving;

(c) speed which is highly inappropriate for the prevailing road or traffic conditions;

(d) aggressive or intimidatory driving, such as sudden lane changes, cutting into a line
     of vehicles or driving much too close to the vehicle in front, especially when the

purpose is to cause the other vehicle to pull to one side to allow the accused to overtake;

(e) disregard of traffic lights and other road signs, which, on an objective analysis, would appear to be deliberate;

(f) failure to pay proper attention, amounting to something significantly more than a momentary lapse;

(g) overtaking which could not have been carried out with safety;

(h) driving a vehicle with a load which presents a danger to other road users.

9.2.2   Notice of intended prosecution

Dangerous driving, like careless driving, is one of the offences to which s 1 of the Road Traffic Offenders Act 1988 (RTOA) applies. This states:

1.—(1) Subject to section 2 of this Act, a person shall not be convicted of an offence to which this section applies unless—

(a) *he was warned at the time the offence was committed that the question of prosecuting him for some one or other of the offences to which this section applies would be taken into consideration, or*

(b) *within 14 days of the commission of the offence a summons . . . for the offence was served on him, or*

(c) *within 14 days of the commission of the offence a notice of the intended prosecution specifying the nature of the alleged offence and the time and place where it is alleged to have been committed, was—*

(i) *in the case of an offence under section 28 or 29 of the Road Traffic Act 1988 (cycling offences), served on him,*

(ii) *in the case of any other offence, served on him or on the person, if any, registered as the keeper of the vehicle at the time of the commission of the offence.*

(1A) A notice required by this section to be served on that person may be served on that person

(a) *by delivering it to him;*

(b) *by addressing it to him and leaving it at his last known address;*

(c) *by sending it by registered post, recorded delivery service or first class post addressed to him at his last known address.*

(2) A notice shall be deemed for the purposes of subsection (1)(c) above to have been served on a person if it was sent by registered post or recorded delivery service addressed to him at his last known address, notwithstanding that the notice was returned undelivered or was for any other reason not received by him.

(3) The requirement of subsection (1) above shall in every case be deemed to have been complied with unless and until the contrary is proved.

(4) Schedule 1 to this Act shows the offences to which this section applies.

The offences in respect of which there is an obligation under s 1 include a number of the most common road traffic offences, eg dangerous driving (contrary to RTA 1988, s 2), careless driving (s 3), leaving a vehicle in a dangerous position (s 22), dangerous cycling (s 28), careless cycling (s 29), failing to comply with traffic directions (s 35) or signs (s 36).

The warning must have been understood by the defendant. In *Gibson v Dalton* [1980] RTR 410, Donaldson LJ (as he then was) put it like this (pp 413–4):

The obligation on the prosecutor is to warn the accused, not merely to address a warning to him or to give a warning. The mischief to which this section is directed is clear. It is that motorists are entitled to have it brought to their attention at a relatively early stage there is likely to be a prosecution in order that they may recall and, it may be, record the facts as they occurred at the time . . . But a warning which does not get through to the accused person is of no value at all.

If, viewing the matter objectively, one would expect that the words addressed to the accused person would have been heard and understood by him, then prima facie he was warned within the meaning of the statute. But it is only a prima facie case. It is open to the defendant to prove, if he can, that he did not understand or hear or appreciate the warning and therefore that he was not warned.

Section 2 of the RTOA 1988, however, lays down certain circumstances in which no notice of intended prosecution is required:

2.—(1) The requirement of section 1(1) of this Act does not apply in relation to an offence if, at the time of the offence or immediately after it, an accident occurs owing to the presence on a road of the vehicle in respect of which the offence was committed.

(2) . . .

(3) Failure to comply with the requirement of section 1(1) of this Act is not a bar to the conviction of the accused in a case where the court is satisfied—

(a) that neither the name and address of the accused nor the name and address of the registered keeper, if any, could with reasonable diligence have been ascertained in time for a summons, or, as the case may be, a complaint to be served or for a notice to be served or sent in compliance with the requirement, or

(b) that the accused by his own conduct contributed to the failure.

(4) Failure to comply with the requirement of section 1(1) of this Act in relation to an offence is not a bar to the conviction of a person of that offence by virtue of the provision of—

(a) section 24 of this Act, or

(b) any of the enactments mentioned in section 24(6);

but a person is not to be convicted of an offence by virtue of any of those provisions if section 1 applies to the offence with which he was charged and the requirement of section 1(1) was not satisfied in relation to the offence charged.

As can be seen, there is no requirement to warn of an intended prosecution in the case of an accident. If the accident was so trivial that the defendant was unaware of it, however, a notice will still be necessary (*Bentley v Dickinson* [1983] RTR 356).

The rationale was set out by Bingham LJ in *DPP v Pidhajeckvj* [1991] RTR 136:

The point of a notice is to alert the driver to the risk of prosecution so that he can promptly investigate the facts and prepare his defence. Ordinarily there is no need for such a notice where there has been an accident, because the driver is alerted to the situation and the possibility of proceedings. But there is a need where the driver is unaware of any accident, because then he has nothing to alert him to the possibility of proceedings.

The point which arose in *Pidhajeckvj* was whether a notice was required where the accident was so serious that its effects resulted in amnesia (contrast *Bentley* where it was so trivial that the defendant could not remember it). The Divisional Court in *Pidhajeckvj* held that this situation was distinguishable from that in *Bentley*. Where the defendant could not remember the details after an accident, but it was apparent that one had occurred, the exemption still applied and no notice of intended prosecution was required. As Bingham LJ put it:

Parliament cannot have intended oral warnings to be given to the unconscious survivors of serious motor accidents, not the giving of written notices to survivors so badly injured as to be unable to read them or understand their effect.

Note that there is a presumption in favour of compliance (see RTOA 1988, s 1(3)). In other words, the prosecution do not have to prove a warning as part of their case. Hence, if the defence challenge the prosecution on this basis, they bear the burden of proof on a balance of probabilities. This can be a difficult onus to discharge, since it requires evidence from both the driver and the keeper of the vehicle in order to establish that neither of them was served in accordance with RTOA, s 1(1)(c)(i). The prosecution may of course make an admission that one or other was not served. Once the defence establishes that there was no service, the prosecution can prove that a notice was sent to the last known address by recorded or registered delivery.

9.2.3 Alternative verdict

Section 24 of the RTOA 1988 lays down a series of alternative verdicts which can be brought in in road traffic cases. The relevant part reads as follows:

24.—(1) Where—

    (a)   a person charged with an offence under a provision of the Road Traffic Act 1988 specified in the first column of the Table below (where the general nature of the offences is also indicated) is found not guilty of that offence, but

    (b)   the allegations in the indictment or information (or in Scotland complaint) amount to or include an allegation of an offence under one or more of the provisions specified in the corresponding entry in the second column,

he may be convicted of that offence or of one or more of those offences.

Offence charged	Alternative
Section 1 (causing death by dangerous driving)	Section 2 (dangerous driving)
	Section 3 (careless, and inconsiderate, driving)
Section 2 (dangerous driving)	Section 3 (careless, and inconsiderate, driving)
Section 3A (causing death by careless driving when under influence of drink or drugs)	Section 3 (careless, and inconsiderate, driving)
	Section 4(1) (driving when unfit to drive through drink or drugs)
	Section 5(1)(a) (driving with excess alcohol in breath, blood or urine)
	Section 7(6) (failing to provide specimen)
Section 4(1) (driving or attempting to drive when unfit to drive through drink or drugs)	Section 4(2) (being in charge of a vehicle when unfit to drive through drink or drugs)
Section 5(1)(a) (driving or attempting to drive with excess alcohol in breath, blood or urine)	Section 5(1)(b) (being in charge of a vehicle with excess alcohol in breath, blood or urine)
Section 28 (dangerous cycling)	Section 29 (careless, and inconsiderate, cycling)

    (2)   Where the offence with which a person is charged is an offence under section 3A of the Road Traffic Act 1988, subsection (1) above shall not authorise his conviction of any offence of attempting to drive.

    (3)   Where a person is charged with having committed an offence under section 4(1) or 5(1)(a) of the Road Traffic Act 1988 by driving a vehicle, he may be convicted of having committed an offence under the provision in question by attempting to drive.

    (4)   Where by virtue of this section a person is convicted before the Crown Court of an offence triable only summarily, the court shall have the same powers and duties as a magistrates' court would have had on convicting him of that offence.

    . . .

    (6)   This section has effect without prejudice to section 6(3) of the Criminal Law Act 1967 (alternative verdicts on trial on indictment) . . . and section 23 of this Act.

As will be apparent, the offence of careless, and inconsiderate, driving is an alternative which the magistrates can find where they decide not to convict the accused of dangerous driving.

9.2.4 Punishment

Dangerous driving is punishable:

- on indictment, with two years' imprisonment, or an unlimited fine or both;
- after summary trial, six months' imprisonment or a fine of £5,000 or both.

There is a minimum disqualification period of 12 months, unless special reasons (see **11.4**) can be established by the defence. Where the driver is disqualified, retesting by way of an extended driving test is mandatory. Endorsement is obligatory in the absence of special reasons (3 to 11 points unless the defendant is disqualified, in which case there is endorsement but without penalty points).

9.2.5 Sentencing guidelines

In *Cooksley* [2004] 1 Cr App R (S) 1, the Court of Appeal, following the advice of the Sentencing Advisory Panel, issued fresh guidelines in relation to the offence of causing death by dangerous driving. Causing death by dangerous driving is a much more serious offence, carrying a maximum penalty of 14 years. However, the judgment nevertheless provides useful guidance as to the aggravating and mitigating factors to which the court will have regard in sentencing an offender for dangerous driving.

The Court prefaced the issuing of the new guidelines by making the general remark that although the offence of causing death by dangerous driving is one which does not require an intention to drive dangerously or an intention to injure, because before an offender can be convicted of dangerous driving, his driving has to fall 'far below' the standard of driving that would be expected of a competent and careful driver and the driving must be such that it would be obvious to the same competent and careful driver that driving in that way would be dangerous, it will usually be obvious to the offender that the driving was dangerous and he therefore deserves to be punished accordingly. It is submitted that the same is true of dangerous driving.

The Court then went on to adopt the series of aggravating and mitigating factors which had been set out by the Sentencing Advisory Panel, but stressed that they should not be regarded as an exhaustive statement of the factors. The judgment went on to stress that it is also important to appreciate that the significance of the factors could differ. There could be a case with three or more aggravating factors, which were not as serious as a case providing a bad example of one factor. The factors, insofar as they are relevant to dangerous driving, are as follows:

Aggravating Factors
Highly culpable standard of driving at time of offence

- (a) the consumption of drugs (including legal medication known to cause drowsiness) or of alcohol, ranging from a couple of drinks to a 'motorised pub crawl';
- (b) greatly excessive speed; racing; competitive driving against another vehicle; 'showing off';
- (c) disregard of warnings from fellow passengers;
- (d) a prolonged, persistent and deliberate course of very bad driving;
- (e) aggressive driving (such as driving much too close to the vehicle in front, persistent inappropriate attempts to overtake, or cutting in after overtaking);
- (f) driving while the driver's attention is avoidably distracted, eg, by reading or by use of a mobile phone (especially if hand-held);
- (g) driving when knowingly suffering from a medical condition which significantly impairs the offender's driving skills;

(h) driving when knowingly deprived of adequate sleep or rest;

(i) driving a poorly maintained or dangerously loaded vehicle, especially where this has been motivated by commercial concerns.

Driving habitually below acceptable standard

(j) other offences committed at the same time, such as driving without ever having held a licence; driving while disqualified; driving without insurance; driving while a learner without supervision; taking a vehicle without consent; driving a stolen vehicle;

(k) previous convictions for motoring offences, particularly offences which involve bad driving or the consumption of excessive alcohol before driving;

. . .

Irresponsible behaviour at time of offence

(n) behaviour at the time of the offence, such as failing to stop, falsely claiming that one of the victims was responsible for the crash, or trying to throw the victim off the bonnet of the car by swerving in order to escape;

. . .

(p) offence committed while the offender was on bail.

Mitigating Factors

(a) a good driving record;

(b) the absence of previous convictions;

(c) a timely plea of guilty;

(d) genuine . . . remorse;

(e) the offender's age (but only in cases where lack of driving experience has contributed to the commission of the offence); and

(f) the fact that the offender has also been seriously injured as a result of the accident caused by the dangerous driving.

In *Howells* [2003] 1 Cr App R (S) 61, the Court of Appeal held that for 'road rage' cases of dangerous driving, where no accident nor injury results, and where there is no consumption of alcohol, but where there is ample evidence to suggest furious driving in temper with an intent of causing fear and possible injury, the appropriate sentencing bracket lies between six and 12 months.

9.3 Careless driving

Section 3 of the RTA 1988 states:

3. If a person drives a mechanically propelled vehicle on a road or other public place without due care and attention, or without reasonable consideration for other persons using the road or place, he is guilty of an offence.

As will be seen from the statute, the offence is not defined, but it may take one of two forms:

(a) Driving without due care and attention. The test is whether the defendant has failed to exercise 'the degree of care and attention which a reasonable prudent driver would exercise' (*Simpson v Peat* [1952] 2 QB 447).

(b) Driving without reasonable consideration. The test is whether other road users were inconvenienced by the defendant's inconsiderate driving.

The *Driving Offences Charging Standard* (see **9.2.1** for comment on its status) gives the following as examples of driving which may support an allegation of careless driving:

- Acts of driving caused by more than momentary inattention and where the safety of road users is affected, such as:
  - overtaking on the inside;
  - driving inappropriately close to another vehicle;
  - driving through a red light;
  - emerging from a side road into the path of another vehicle;
  - turning into a minor road and colliding with a pedestrian.
- Conduct which clearly caused the driver not to be in a position to respond in the event of an emergency on the road, for example:
  - using a hand held mobile telephone while the vehicle is moving, especially when at speed;
  - tuning a car radio;
  - reading a newspaper/map;
  - selecting and lighting a cigarette/cigar/pipe;
  - talking to and looking at a passenger which causes the driver more than momentary inattention;
  - leg and/or arm in plaster;
  - fatigue/nodding off.

The *Charging Standard* makes the point, however, that it is the manner of the driving rather than the explanation for it which is crucial in deciding whether to charge careless driving. The list detailed above really consists of a series of examples which explain the driver's conduct, and usually where they occur, a charge of careless driving will be appropriate, but the manner of driving must be considered in the context of the other facts in the case to decide the most appropriate way forward (see para 5.6 of the *Charging Standard*). In addition, the *Charging Standard* suggests that the public interest will tend to be against a prosecution for careless driving where:

- the incident is of a type such as frequently occurs at parking places, roundabouts, junctions or in traffic queues, involving minimal carelessness such as momentary inattention or a minor error of judgment;
- only the person at fault suffered injury and damage, if any, which was mainly restricted to the vehicle or property owned by that person.

As far as the second limb of the offence, inconsiderate driving, is concerned, the accused must be shown to have fallen below the standard of a reasonable, prudent and competent driver *and* to have done so without reasonable consideration for others. It follows that a person who drives without reasonable consideration for other road users can be convicted of driving without due care and attention, but the reverse does not necessarily apply. The *Charging Standard* (para 6.4) suggests that an allegation of inconsiderate driving is appropriate 'when the driving amounts to a clear act of selfishness, impatience or aggressiveness' resulting in 'some inconvenience to other road users, for example, forcing other drivers to move over and/or brake as a consequence'.

It gives the following examples of conduct appropriate to a charge of driving without reasonable consideration:

- flashing of lights to *force* other drivers in front to give way;
- misuse of any lane to avoid queuing or gain some other advantage over other drivers;
- unnecessarily remaining in an overtaking lane;
- unnecessarily slow driving or braking without good cause;
- driving with undipped headlights which dazzle oncoming drivers;
- driving through a puddle causing pedestrians to be splashed.

The usual basis on which the prosecution puts its case under s 3, however, is an allegation of careless driving. In determining whether the defendant fell short of the necessary standard, the court must not judge him or her with hindsight. An illustration is provided by *Bristol Crown Court, ex p Jones* [1986] RTR 259. The defendant's lights suddenly failed when he was driving at night. He pulled on to the motorway's hard shoulder and collided with an unlit parked vehicle of which he was unaware. It was held that his behaviour was reasonable, and the offence was not proved.

Where the defendant is unable to explain an accident, the facts of the case may lead to an irresistible inference that it resulted from careless driving. Thus, in *Rabjohns v Burgar* [1971] RTR 234, the defendant's car collided with the wall of a bridge, leaving skid marks on the road. The weather was fine and the road dry. There was no evidence of the involvement of any other vehicle, and no witnesses. The defendant did not give evidence or put forward any explanation. The Divisional Court held that the only conclusion possible on this evidence was that the defendant had driven carelessly.

Where the defendant does put forward an exculpatory explanation, however, it is incumbent on the prosecution to disprove it, provided that it is not fanciful. For example, in *Butty v Davey* [1972] RTR 75, rain had made the road unexpectedly slippery. The defendant's car slid to the wrong side of the road and hit another vehicle. The magistrates found that this did not constitute driving without due care and attention, and their decision was upheld. Similarly, in *Lodwick v Jones* [1983] RTR 273, the defendant put forward the existence of an unexpected icy patch as an explanation for skidding. Again, this was accepted by the justices and it was held that they were entitled to do so.

9.3.1 Procedural matters

By s 24 of the RTOA 1988, a verdict of careless driving is an alternative where dangerous driving is charged (see **9.2.3**). Careless driving is one of those specified offences for which a notice of intended prosecution is usually necessary (see **9.2.2**). But note that by s 2(4) of the RTOA 1988, a failure to warn a suspect of an intended prosecution does not act as a bar to conviction of one of the alternative offences specified in s 24, ie provided that notice has been given in relation to the original offence, the defendant can be convicted of one of the alternatives.

9.3.2 Punishment

Careless driving is a summary offence, punishable by a fine of up to £2,500, with discretionary disqualification. Endorsement is obligatory (3 to 9 points), except where there are special reasons.

9.4　Failing to stop/failing to report

This offence is created by s 170 of the RTA 1988:

170.—(1)　This section applies in a case where, owing to the presence of a mechanically propelled vehicle on a road or other public place, an accident occurs by which—

　　(a)　personal injury is caused to a person other than the driver of that mechanically propelled vehicle, or

　　(b)　damage is caused—

　　　　(i)　to a vehicle other than that mechanically propelled vehicle or a trailer drawn by that mechanically propelled vehicle, or

　　　　(ii)　to an animal other than an animal in or on that mechanically propelled vehicle or a trailer drawn by that mechanically propelled vehicle, or

　　　　(iii)　to any other property constructed on, fixed to, growing in or otherwise forming part of the land on which the road in question is situated or land adjacent to such land.

(2)　The driver of the mechanically propelled vehicle must stop and, if required to do so by any person having reasonable grounds for so requiring, give his name and address and also the name and address of the owner and the identification marks of the vehicle.

(3)　If for any reason the driver of the mechanically propelled vehicle does not give his name and address under subsection (2) above, he must report the accident.

(4)　A person who fails to comply with subsection (2) or (3) above is guilty of an offence.

(5)　If, in a case where this section applies by virtue of subsection (1)(a) above, the driver of a motor vehicle does not at the time of the accident produce such a certificate of insurance or security, or other evidence, as is mentioned in section 165(2)(a) of this Act—

　　(a)　to a constable, or

　　(b)　to some person who, having reasonable grounds for so doing has required him to produce it, the driver must report the accident and produce such a certificate or other evidence.

This subsection does not apply to the driver of an invalid carriage.

(6)　To comply with a duty under this section to report an accident or to produce such a certificate of insurance or security, or other evidence, as is mentioned in section 165(2)(a) of this Act, the driver—

　　(a)　must do so at a police station or to a constable, and

　　(b)　must do so as soon as is reasonably practicable and, in any case, within twenty-four hours of the occurrence of the accident.

(7)　A person who fails to comply with a duty under subsection (5) above is guilty of an offence, but he shall not be convicted by reason only of a failure to produce a certificate or other evidence if, within [seven] days after the occurrence of the accident, the certificate or other evidence is produced at a police station that was specified by him at the time when the accident was reported.

(8)　In this section 'animal' means horse, cattle, ass, mule, sheep, pig, goat or dog.

By s 170(2), then, the driver of a vehicle involved in an accident which falls within the definition laid down in s 170(1), must stop and, if reasonably required to do so, give appropriate details. If the driver does not give his or her name and address, then he or she must report the accident to the police as soon as possible and, in any event, within 24 hours of the accident (s 170(3)).

A contravention of s170 is a summary offence, punishable by up to six months' imprisonment or a fine of up to £5,000 or both. It carries discretionary disqualification, and obligatory endorsement (5 to 10 points), subject to special reasons (see **11.4**).

Drink driving offences

10.1 Introduction

Alcohol is a major cause of road accidents. One in five drivers killed in road accidents have levels of alcohol which are over the legal limit. The seriousness with which the problem of drink driving is viewed is reflected not only by the range of offences created in the Road Traffic Acts (driving with excess alcohol, failure to provide a specimen for analysis etc) but also by the very severe penalties imposed for those offences (see **Chapter 11**).

10.2 Prescribed limits and specimen tests

Under the drink driving provisions, drink means an alcoholic drink and drugs can refer to medicines as well as prohibited drugs and substances which affect the control of the body (eg, *Bradford v Wilson* [1993] Crim LR 482, toluene inhaled when glue sniffing). The prescribed limits are 35 microgrammes (µg) of alcohol in 100 ml of breath, or 80 mg of alcohol in 100 ml of blood or 107 mg of alcohol in 100 ml of urine. This level can be achieved by a man drinking about $3\frac{1}{2}$ to 5 units within an hour and a woman drinking about $2\frac{1}{2}$ to 4 units within an hour. (A unit of alcohol is approximately equal to a half pint of ordinary beer, lager or cider, or a single measure of spirits (whisky, vodka, gin, bacardi, etc) or a glass of wine or small glass of sherry.) There is no sure way of telling how much an individual can drink before reaching this limit. It varies with each person depending on weight, age, sex, whether the person has just eaten and the sort of drinks which have been consumed. These factors may also affect the rate of absorption of alcohol into the blood. Most of the alcohol drunk is rapidly absorbed into the bloodstream. Nearly all the alcohol has to be burnt up by the liver, the rest is disposed of either in sweat or urine. Only time can remove the alcohol from the bloodstream. In an average sized man it may be broken down at the rate of about one unit per hour.

There are three ways of providing a specimen for analysis: breath, blood or urine. The roadside breath test is really a preliminary test on an approved device where the driver inflates a small bag by blowing into it. The bag has to be inflated by a single breath and there should be no smoking immediately before or during the test as this may affect the result. In addition, 20 minutes ought to have elapsed between the last drink of alcohol and the use of the device. This also relates to other aromatic drinks and mouth sprays. In *DPP v Kay* [1999] RTR 109, the Divisional Court held that the failure of officers to ask questions such as when the defendant had last drank or smoked did not invalidate the roadside breath test or the subsequent arrest. The Home Office has warned that the operation of breath test devices may be affected by police radio equipment operating within inches of the devices. Where the police require the breath sample to be analysed the driver has to attend the police station and provide a sample of breath on an approved device, either the Lion Intoximeter or Camic Breath Analyser. These two machines analyse the alcohol level in breath and produce a print-out of two samples of breath taken within a short time. The lower of the two readings is the one that the prosecution will rely on in determining whether a prosecution can be founded. The machines also operate a self-check system to indicate that they are operating accurately. The driver is given a copy of the print-out. The print-out forms part of the admissible evidence against the defendant. In *DPP v Spurrier* [2000] RTR 60, the Divisional Court held that it was not always necessary for magistrates to hear expert evidence to rebut the presumption of reliability of a Lion Intoximeter when the defendant's evidence of consumption was contradicted by the device. The defendant had not driven erratically, was not unsteady on her feet and her eyes were not glazed but she produced a reading of 143 mg (four times over the limit). She claimed to have consumed two cans of lager and a significant proportion of a bottle of whisky, 12 hours previously. Accepting her evidence the justices concluded that the Lion Intoximeter could not have been reliable and that there was no need to call evidence on that point.

Where the machine is broken or unavailable or the suspected offence may be due to a drug rather than alcohol, or there are medical reasons for not requiring a sample of breath the police constable will offer the driver the chance to provide a blood specimen (for which a doctor will be called) or a urine sample (which does not need to be taken by a doctor). The choice of whether to provide a blood or urine sample is that of the police officer and not the driver (s 7(4)).

In *Stewart v DPP* [2003] All ER (D) 164, it was held that even where the machine gave an unreliable reading and the police officer offered the defendant the choice of either providing two more specimens of breath or specimens of blood or urine, the officer had not acted unlawfully in requiring or giving the defendant the option to provide two further specimens of breath.

10.3 Driving, attempting to drive or being in charge of a vehicle when unfit

Under RTA 1988, s 4 it is an offence to drive, to attempt to drive, or to be in charge of a mechanically propelled vehicle on a road or other public place when under the influence of drink or drugs. The relevant parts read as follows:

4.—(1) A person who, when driving or attempting to drive a mechanically propelled vehicle on a road or other public place, is unfit to drive through drink or drugs is guilty of an offence.

   (2) Without prejudice to subsection (1) above, a person who, when in charge of a [mechanically propelled vehicle] which is on a road or other public place, is unfit to drive through drink or drugs is guilty of an offence.

   (3) For the purposes of subsection (2) above, a person shall be deemed not to have been in charge of a mechanically propelled vehicle if he proves that at the material time the circumstances were such that there was no likelihood of his driving it so long as he remained unfit to drive through drink or drugs.

   (4) The court may, in determining whether there was such a likelihood as is mentioned in subsection (3) above, disregard any injury to him and any damage to the vehicle.

   (5) For the purposes of this section, a person shall be taken to be unfit to drive if his ability to drive properly is for the time being impaired.

(6) A constable may arrest a person without warrant if he has reasonable cause to suspect that person is or has been committing an offence under this section.

(7) For the purpose of arresting a person under the power conferred by subsection (6) above, a constable may enter (if need be by force) any place where that person is or where the constable, with reasonable cause, suspects him to be.

The essence of driving is the use of the driver's controls to direct the movement of the vehicle (*McDonagh* [1974] QB 48). Being in charge is a wide concept, see *DPP v Watkins* [1989] QB 821. The owner or a person who has recently driven the vehicle would be in charge unless he or she has put the vehicle in someone else's charge or unless there was no realistic possibility of resuming control of the vehicle. It is a question of fact and degree if someone is in charge, see *DPP v Watkins* [1989] QB 821.

'Road' is defined in s 192 as 'any highway and any other road to which the public has access'. The other public place need not be a road but must be a place to which the public has access eg a car park.

Evidence of unfitness may be provided by specimen sample of blood/breath/urine. Opinion evidence may also be received of the defendant's state (eg eyes glazed, speech slurred, unsteady on feet, etc) but not of whether or not the defendant was fit to drive (*Davies* [1962] 3 All ER 97). In *Leethams v DPP* (1999) RTR 29 officers gave evidence that the defendant's eyes were red, his speech slurred and slow. He admitted smoking a cannabis cigarette some hours earlier. The blood sample showed no alcohol but cannabis consumption some time before the sample. (The effect of cannabis begins immediately after use, rises to a maximum after 20 minutes and disperses after two to four hours.) The Divisional Court held that despite lack of evidence from a doctor the officers had proved the case by the evidence of the appellant's driving, his appearance, behaviour and admission.

The offence under s 4(1) is punishable with six months' imprisonment or a £5,000 fine, or both, and obligatory disqualification. Where penalty points are endorsed the range is 3 to 11 points. The offence under s 4(2) is punishable with three months' imprisonment or a £2,500 fine, or both, and discretionary disqualification. Endorsement carries 10 penalty points.

10.4   Driving or being in charge above the prescribed limit

The offence of driving, attempting to drive or being in charge when over the prescribed limit is dealt with in s 5:

5.—(1) If a person—

(a)   drives or attempts to drive a motor vehicle on a road or other public place, or

(b)   is in charge of a motor vehicle on a road or other public place,

after consuming so much alcohol that the proportion of it in his breath, blood or urine exceeds the prescribed limit he is guilty of an offence.

(2) It is a defence for a person charged with an offence under subsection (1)(b) above to prove that at the time he is alleged to have committed the offence the circumstances were such that there was no likelihood of his driving the vehicle whilst the proportion of alcohol in his breath, blood or urine remained likely to exceed the prescribed limit.

(3) The court may, in determining whether there was such a likelihood as is mentioned in subsection (2) above, disregard any injury to him and any damage to the vehicle.

In *DPP v H* [1998] RTR 200 it was affirmed that driving with excess alcohol was an offence of strict liability, so that *mens rea* was not an issue and the defence of insanity was not available.

The prosecution are entitled to do a back-calculation to show that at the time of driving, attempting to drive or being in charge, the alcohol in the driver's breath was in excess of the prescribed amount. In *Gumbley v Cunningham* [1988] QB 170, the appellant was involved in a fatal accident before midnight. He gave a specimen of blood with a reading of 59 Bg at 3.35 am the following morning. The prosecution adduced evidence of a calculation showing that a person with the appellant's age and physical characteristics would eliminate blood alcohol at the rate of 10 to 25 µg per hour and therefore his blood alcohol level at the time of the accident would have been between 120 and 130 µg of alcohol per 100 ml of blood. This means that where a specimen contains less than the legal limit, but it can be shown by back calculation that the driver had excess alcohol at the time of the offence then a conviction will follow. Mann J said, 'those who drive whilst above the prescribed limits cannot necessarily escape punishment because of the lapse of time'. He further stressed that:

. . . the prosecution should not seek to rely on evidence of back-calculation save where that evidence is easily understood and clearly persuasive of the presence of excess alcohol at the time when a defendant was driving. Moreover, justices must be very careful especially where there is conflicting evidence not to convict unless, upon the scientific and other evidence which they find it safe to rely on, they are sure an excess of alcohol was in the defendant's body when he was actually driving as charged.

10.4.1   The hip-flask defence

Where the defendant wishes to claim that a post-driving drink took him over the limit (the hip-flask defence) the burden of proof lies on him to show that on a balance of probabilities. The court is entitled to assume that the alcohol level at the time of driving was not less than that at the time of the test (RTOA 1988, s 15(2)). This statutory assumption will not be made if the defendant proves that he consumed alcohol after he stopped driving, attempting to drive or being in charge and before he provided a specimen, and that had he not done so the proportion of alcohol in his breath/blood/urine would not have exceeded the prescribed limit. See *DPP v Williams* [1989] Crim LR 382.

10.4.2   No likelihood of driving

Under s 5(2) it is a defence for a person to prove that there was no likelihood of him driving whilst the proportion of alcohol in his blood/breath or urine remained likely to exceed the prescribed limit. A similar defence is afforded under s 4(3), where the allegation relates to being unfit through drink or drugs.

The s 5(2) defence potentially conflicted with the presumption of innocence guaranteed by Article 6 of the ECHR insofar as it placed the legal burden on the defendant. However, in *Sheldrake v DPP* [2005] 1 AC 264, the House of Lords held that the imposition of the legal burden on a defendant under s 5(2) did not infringe Article 6 as the imposition of a legal burden upon the defendant did not go beyond what was necessary and reasonable, and was not in any way arbitrary. Thus, under s 5(2) it is for the defendant to show, on the balance of probabilities, that there was no likelihood of him driving the vehicle of which he was in charge.

10.4.3   Laced drinks

It is not a defence to the charge but the fact that drinks may have been laced may be put forward as a reason for not disqualifying. The defendant would have to show that he or she had been misled by a third party and would be expected to have made some enquiry about what he or she was drinking. The person lacing the drinks may be convicted of procuring a person to commit an offence under RTA 1988, s 5. See *Attorney-General's Reference (No 1 of 1975)* [1975] QB 773.

The offence under s 5(1)(a) is punishable with six months' imprisonment or a £5,000 fine, or both, and obligatory disqualification. Where penalty points are endorsed the range is 3 to 11 points. The offence under s 5(1)(b) is punishable with three months' imprisonment or a £2,500 fine, or both, and discretionary disqualification. Endorsement carries 10 penalty points.

10.5   Failure to provide a specimen

10.5.1   Breath tests

Under RTA 1988, s 6(4) (the roadside breath test), failure without reasonable excuse to provide a specimen of breath for a breath test when required to do so by a police constable in uniform is an offence. The section reads as follows:

6.—(1) Where a constable in uniform has reasonable cause to suspect—

(a)   that a person driving or attempting to drive or in charge of a motor vehicle on a road or other public place has alcohol in his body or has committed a traffic offence whilst the vehicle was in motion, or

(b)   that a person has been driving or attempting to drive or been in charge of a motor vehicle on a road or other public place with alcohol in his body and that that person still has alcohol in his body, or

(c)   that a person has been driving or attempting to drive or been in charge of a motor vehicle on a road or other public place and has committed a traffic offence whilst the vehicle was in motion,

he may, subject to section 9 of this Act, require him to provide a specimen of breath for a breath test.

(2)   If an accident occurs owing to the presence of a motor vehicle on a road or other public place, a constable may, subject to section 9 of this Act, require any person who he has reasonable cause to believe was driving or attempting to drive or in charge of the vehicle at the time of the accident to provide a specimen of breath for a breath test.

(3)   A person may be required under subsection (1) or subsection (2) above to provide a specimen either at or near the place where the requirement is made or, if the requirement is made under subsection (2) above and the constable making the requirement thinks fit, at a police station specified by the constable.

(4)   A person who, without reasonable excuse, fails to provide a specimen of breath when required to do so in pursuance of this section is guilty of an offence.

(5)   A constable may arrest a person without warrant if—

(a)   as a result of a breath test he has reasonable cause to suspect that the proportion of alcohol in that person's breath or blood exceeds the prescribed limit, or

(b)   that person has failed to provide a specimen of breath for a breath test when required to do so in pursuance of this section and the constable has reasonable cause to suspect that he has alcohol in his body,

but a person shall not be arrested by virtue of this subsection when he is at a hospital as a patient.

(6)   A constable may, for the purpose of requiring a person to provide a specimen of breath under subsection (2) above in a case where he has reasonable cause to suspect that the accident involved injury to another person or of arresting him in such a case under subsection (5) above, enter (if need

be by force) any place where that person is or where the constable, with reasonable cause, suspects him to be.

Evidence has to be adduced to establish a reasonable cause to suspect the presence of alcohol. A court cannot infer reasonable cause from the mere fact of asking for a breath test (*Siddiqui v Swain* [1979] RTR 454). There is no restriction on random stopping of motorists but a subsequent request for a breath test can be made only if the constable has reasonable cause to suspect alcohol has been taken (*Chief Constable of Gwent v Dash* [1986] RTR 41). The constable's suspicions may arise after the defendant has been stopped. Although the absence of a reasonable cause may invalidate an arrest it will not invalidate the subsequent procedure (*DPP v Godwin* [1991] RTR 303). The court may always, of course, exercise its discretion to exclude the evidence under PACE 1984, s 78.

The offence is punishable with a fine of £1,000, discretionary disqualification and endorsement of 4 penalty points.

10.5.2   Specimens for analysis

Section 7 of the 1988 Act deals with provision of a specimen for analysis:

7.—(1) *In the course of an investigation into whether a person has committed an offence under section 3A, 4 or 5 of this Act a constable may, subject to the following provisions of this section and section 9 of this Act, require him—*

    (a)   *to provide two specimens of breath for analysis by means of a device of a type approved by the Secretary of State, or*

    (b)   *to provide a specimen of blood or urine for a laboratory test.*

  (2)   *A requirement under this section to provide specimens of breath can only be made at a police station.*

  (3)   *A requirement under this section to provide a specimen of blood or urine can only be made at a police station or at a hospital; and it cannot be made at a police station unless—*

    (a)   *the constable making the requirement has reasonable cause to believe that for medical reasons a specimen of breath cannot be provided or should not be required, or*

    (b)   *at the time the requirement is made a device or a reliable device of the type mentioned in subsection (1)(a) above is not available at the police station or it is then for any other reason not practicable to use such a device there, or*

    (bb) *a device of the type mentioned in subsection (1)(a) above has been used at the police station but the constable who required the specimens of breath has reasonable cause to believe that the device has not produced a reliable indication of the proportion of alcohol in the breath of the person concerned, or*

    (c)   *the suspected offence is one under section 3A or 4 of this Act and the constable making the requirement has been advised by a medical practitioner that the condition of the person required to provide the specimen might be due to some drug;*

    but may then be made notwithstanding that the person required to provide the specimen has already provided or been required to provide two specimens of breath.

  (4)   *If the provision of a specimen other than a specimen of breath may be required in pursuance of this section the question whether it is to be a specimen of blood or a specimen of urine and, in the case of a specimen of blood, the question who is to be asked to take it shall be decided (subject to subsection (4A)) by the constable making the requirement.*

  (4A) *Where a constable decides for the purposes of subsection (4) to require the provision of a specimen of blood, there shall be no requirement to provide such a specimen if—*

    (a)   *the medical practitioner who is asked to take the specimen is of the opinion that, for medical reasons, it cannot or should not be taken; or*

    (b)   *the registered health care professional who is asked to take it is of that opinion and there is no contrary opinion from a medical practitioner;*

    and, where by virtue of this subsection there can be no requirement to provide a specimen of blood, the constable may require a specimen of urine instead.

(5) *A specimen of urine shall be provided within one hour of the requirement for its provision being made and after the provision of a previous specimen of urine.*

(6) *A person who, without reasonable excuse, fails to provide a specimen when required to do so in pursuance of this section is guilty of an offence.*

(7) *A constable must, on requiring any person to provide a specimen in pursuance of this section, warn him that a failure to provide it may render him liable to prosecution.*

The section requires two specimens of breath for analysis and the prosecution rely on the lower reading for their case. Where the lower reading is not more than 50 μg of alcohol in 100 ml of breath, the person providing the sample may request that it should be replaced by a blood or urine sample (s 8(2)). Although the accused can express a preference for a particular sample, the choice will be made by the officer (see *DPP v Warren* [1993] RTR 58). The only right of the defendant to object to giving blood and to give urine instead will be for medical reasons to be determined by the medical practitioner. In *Epping Justices, ex p Quy* [1998] RTR 158 the Divisional Court held that a fear of needles was capable of being a medical reason. In that case the officer should have asked further questions and/or called a medical practitioner. A specimen of blood must be taken with the accused's consent and by a medical practitioner. The officer must warn the accused that failure to provide the specimen of breath, blood or urine is an offence that may render the accused liable to prosecution and also carries the penalty of disqualification (s 7(7)). Failure to give the warning renders the results of the test inadmissible (*Murray v DPP* [1993] Crim LR 968).

Guidance and clarification as to the procedures to be followed by the police under s 7(3) or s 8(2) following *DPP v Warren*, was set out by the House of Lords in *DPP v Jackson; Stanley v DPP* [1998] 3 All ER 769. It was held *inter alia*, that (i) it was for the police officer to decide whether the specimen was to be of blood or urine (s 7(4)); (ii) the specimen of blood was to be taken by a doctor (s 11(4)). In addition, the right of the police officer to choose whether the specimen was to be of blood or urine was subject to the qualification that if a medical reason was raised why a specimen of blood could not or should not be taken, the issue was to be decided by a doctor and not by the police officer; (iii) an offence under s 7(6) for failure to provide a specimen of blood or urine or an offence under s 5(1), proved by a specimen of breath where the driver had not claimed under s 8(2) to replace it with a specimen of blood or urine was an unusual offence in that the driver had the choice to make, in the police station prior to the charge being made; (iv) it was not a mandatory requirement but a driver should be aware, whether in a s 7(3) case or a s 8(2) case of the role of a doctor in the taking of a specimen of blood and in determining any medical objections which he might raise to the giving of such a specimen. The mandatory requirements were: (a) in a s 7(3) case the warning as to the risk of prosecution required by s 7(7); (b) in a s 7(3) case the statement of the reason under the subsection why breath specimens could not be taken or used; and (c) in a s 8(2) case the statement that the specimen of breath which the driver had given containing the lower proportion of alcohol did not exceed 50 μg of alcohol in 100 ml of breath.

In *Richardson v DPP* [2003] All ER (D) 282, the defendant, who produced a sample of breath with a reading of 93 μg, requested a blood sample. That request was refused and he argued before the court that the refusal to allow him to provide a blood sample violated Article 6(3) of the ECHR. In dismissing his appeal, the Administrative Court noted that s 8(2) provided a person with a safeguard where the proportion of alcohol in his breath was low enough to permit a possible error, 50 μg but no greater. Article 6(3) only provided that a defendant had to be provided with adequate facilities to challenge the evidence against him and the present case did not indicate any risk that the defendant had been denied his right to a fair trial.

10.5.3 Failure

What constitutes failure is a question of fact. Failure includes a refusal and also includes a conditional agreement (eg only allowing blood to be taken from an inappropriate part of the body, *Solesbury v Pugh* [1969] 2 All ER 1171). A refusal may be implied from conduct. In *Smyth v DPP* [1996] RTR 59, the defendant said 'no' when asked to provide a specimen, but within five seconds said that he wanted to change his mind. He was convicted by the magistrates. The Queen's Bench Division, allowing his appeal and concluding he had not refused to provide a specimen, said that the tribunal should have had regard to all the defendant's words and conduct.

10.5.4 Reasonable excuse

The issue of reasonable excuse has to be raised by the defendant; the burden is on the prosecution to disprove it beyond reasonable doubt. A physical inability to provide a specimen may amount to a reasonable excuse.

No fear short of a phobia recognised by medical science to be as strong and inhibiting as, for instance, claustrophobia can be allowed to excuse failure to provide a specimen for a laboratory test, and in most if not all cases where the fear of providing it is claimed to be invincible the claim will have to be supported by medical evidence (per Lord Widgery CJ in *Harding* [1974] RTR 325).

An inability to understand what is being said due to a limited grasp of English may also be a reasonable excuse (*Chief Constable of Avon and Somerset v Singh* [1988] RTR 107). In *Harling* [1970] RTR 441, a reasonable excuse was said to exist where the defendant lost confidence in the doctor's ability after the doctor had made three unsuccessful attempts to take blood.

Cases in which the defence of reasonable excuse have failed are *Sykes v White* [1983] RTR 419 (dislike of blood not amounting to a phobia); *DPP v Fountain* [1988] Crim LR 123 (fear of contracting AIDS through the use of needles, but compare *DeFreitas v DPP* [1993] RTR 98, a genuine but unreasonable phobia of contracting AIDS was found to be a reasonable excuse); *Woolman v Lenton* [1985] Crim LR 516 (difficulty in blowing through the nose); *Daniels v DPP* [1992] RTR 140 (a belief that no offence had been committed); *DPP v Coyle* The Times, 20 July 1995 (motorist not told of necessity to provide required specimen within a total of three minutes, see also *Cosgrove v DPP* The Times, 29 March 1996); *Thomas v DPP* [1991] RTR 292 (a previous unlawful arrest was not relevant to the subsequent procedures and could not amount to a reasonable excuse, see also *Matto v Wolverhampton Crown Court* [1987] RTR 337).

In *DPP v Varley* [1999] Crim LR 753, the defendant asked for legal advice before he would agree to the breath test procedure. The sergeant said that he was not prepared to wait for the duty solicitor. The magistrates concluded that the defendant had a reasonable excuse and acquitted him. The Divisional Court held that those facts were not capable of amounting to a reasonable excuse; generally a reasonable excuse existed when a defendant was mentally or physically unable to provide a specimen.

In *Kennedy v DPP* [2002] All ER (D) 77, the defendant appealed against his conviction for refusal to provide a specimen after he had relied on PACE 1984, s 58 that he had not been given the opportunity to consult a solicitor as soon as was practicable. Where the offence suspected was under s 5, public interest required that the obtaining of breath specimens could not be delayed to any significant extent to allow a defendant to take legal advice. In this case the defendant had only indicated a general desire to have legal advice and there was no reason why the custody officer should not continue to take details and contact the solicitor's call centre at the first convenient opportunity.

Where the specimen is required to ascertain ability to drive, or the proportion of alcohol at the time the accused was driving, or attempting to drive, the offence is punishable with six months' imprisonment or a £5,000 fine, or both, and obligatory disqualification. Endorsement carries 3 to 11 penalty points. In all other cases it is three months' imprisonment, discretionary disqualification or 10 penalty points.

10.5.5   Protection for hospital patients

If the accused is in hospital as a patient there can be no requirement to provide a specimen unless the medical practitioner in charge of the case has been notified and the specimen is provided at the hospital. If the medical practitioner decides that the provision of a specimen or the warning required under s 7(7) would be prejudicial to the proper care and treatment of the patient, then the requirement must not be made (s 9).

10.5.6   Failure to give permission to for laboratory test

Section 7A of the 1988 Act authorises a constable to request a medical practitioner to take a specimen of blood from a person who has been involved in an accident and is incapable of giving valid consent (ie the person is unconscious). However, while a person is at a hospital as a patient, no specimen of blood shall be taken from him under s 7A if the medical practitioner in immediate charge of his case objects under s 9 (see **10.5.5** above). Any specimen taken shall not be subjected to a laboratory test unless the person from whom it was taken has given his permission (s 7A(4)). While a person is at a hospital as a patient, he shall not be required to give his permission for a laboratory test of a specimen if the medical practitioner in immediate charge of his case objects under s 9. It is an offence for a person, without reasonable excuse, to fail to give permission (s 7A(6)). The section reads as follows:

7A.—(1) *A constable may make a request to a medical practitioner for him to take a specimen of blood from a person ('the person concerned') irrespective of whether that person consents if—*

(a)   *that person is a person from whom the constable would (in the absence of any incapacity of that person and of any objection under section 9) be entitled under section 7 to require the provision of a specimen of blood for a laboratory test;*

(b)   *it appears to that constable that that person has been involved in an accident that constitutes or is comprised in the matter that is under investigation or the circumstances of that matter;*

(c)   *it appears to that constable that that person is or may be incapable (whether or not he has purported to do so) of giving a valid consent to the taking of a specimen of blood; and*

(d)   *it appears to that constable that that person's incapacity is attributable to medical reasons.*

(2) *A request under this section—*

(a)   *shall not be made to a medical practitioner who for the time being has any responsibility (apart from the request) for the clinical care of the person concerned; and*

(b)   *shall not be made to a medical practitioner other than a police medical practitioner unless—*

(i)   *it is not reasonably practicable for the request to made to a police medical practitioner; or*

(ii)   *it is not reasonably practicable for such a medical practitioner (assuming him to be willing to do so) to take the specimen.*

(3) *It shall be lawful for a medical practitioner to whom a request is made under this section, if he thinks fit—*

(a)   *to take a specimen of blood from the person concerned irrespective of whether that person consents; and*

(b)   *to provide the sample to a constable.*

(4) If a specimen is taken in pursuance of a request under this section, the specimen shall not be subjected to a laboratory test unless the person from whom it was taken—

    (a)   has been informed that it was taken; and

    (b)   has been required by a constable to give his permission for a laboratory test of the specimen; and

    (c)   has given his permission.

(5) A constable must, on requiring a person to give his permission for the purposes of this section for a laboratory test of a specimen, warn that person that a failure to give the permission may render him liable to prosecution.

(6) A person who, without reasonable excuse, fails to give his permission for a laboratory test of a specimen of blood taken from him under this section is guilty of an offence.

(7) In this section 'police medical practitioner' means a medical practitioner who is engaged under any agreement to provide medical services for purposes connected with the activities of a police force.

Where the test would be for ascertaining ability to drive, or the proportion of alcohol at the time the offender was driving, or attempting to drive, the offence is punishable with six months' imprisonment or a £5,000 fine, or both, and obligatory disqualification. Endorsement carries 3 to 11 points. In all other cases, it is three months' imprisonment or a £2,500 fine, or both, discretionary disqualification or 10 penalty points.

10.6 Causing death by careless driving when under the influence of drink or drugs

The offence under RTA 1988, s 3A is indictable only and reads as follows:

(1) If a person causes the death of another person by driving a mechanically propelled vehicle on a road or other public place without due care and attention, or without reasonable consideration for other persons using the road or place, and—

    (a)   he is, at the time when he is driving, unfit to drive through drink or drugs, or

    (b)   he has consumed so much alcohol that the proportion of it in his breath, blood or urine at that time exceeds the prescribed limit, or

    (c)   he is, within 18 hours after that time, required to provide a specimen in pursuance of section 7 of this Act, but without reasonable excuse fails to provide it,

    he is guilty of an offence.

(2) For the purposes of this section a person shall be taken to be unfit to drive at any time when his ability to drive properly is impaired.

(3) Subsection (1)(b) and (c) above shall not apply in relation to a person driving a mechanically propelled vehicle other than a motor vehicle.

A jury acquitting a defendant of an offence under s 3A may convict on an alternative offence under s 3 (careless and inconsiderate driving), s 4(1) (driving when unfit through drink or drugs), s 5(1)(a) (driving with excess alcohol in breath, blood or urine), or s 7(6) (failing to provide a specimen). Alternative verdicts are set out in RTOA 1988, s 24; see **9.2.3**.

The s3A offence is punishable with 10 years' imprisonment or a fine, or both. Disqualification is obligatory.

10.7   Cycling when under the influence of drink or drugs

Section 30 of the RTA 1988 states:

A person who, when riding a cycle on a road or other public place, is unfit through drink or drugs (that is to say, is under the influence of drink or a drug to such an extent as to be incapable of having proper control of the cycle) is guilty of an offence.

The offence covers riding a bicycle, tricycle or other cycle having four or more wheels, but not being a motor vehicle, on a road. The offence is committed on public highways as well as footways. The police cannot require the cyclist to provide a specimen of breath, blood or urine but if one is provided it may be used in a prosecution.

The offence is summary only and punishable by a maximum fine of £1,000.

10.8   Procedure and sentence

Most motoring offences are summary only offences and are brought to court by way of summons, but in most drink driving cases the motorist will have been charged at the police station. The defendant is generally bailed to appear at the magistrates' court. Advance disclosure is not available in summary only offences. As the drink driving offences carry punishment of disqualification, which cannot be ordered in the defendant's absence, the offences cannot be dealt with by way of postal written pleas of guilty.

Public funding is rarely given in road traffic cases, but the criteria set out in Access to Justice Act 1999, Sch 3, para 5(2), for considering the grant of a representation order may be satisfied in some drink driving cases.

For sentencing see **Chapter 11** generally. Driving with excess alcohol carries a maximum six months' imprisonment. The Magistrates' Association Guidelines state that those driving with more than 115 µg in 100 ml of breath (ie over three times the limit) should be considered for a custodial sentence; see also *Shoult* [1996] RTR 298. Aggravating features identified by the Magistrates' Association include; police chase, causing injury/fear/damage, carrying passengers for reward, large goods vehicle, nature of driving, high reading.

Road traffic offences: penalties

11.1 Introduction

The distinctive penalties for road traffic offences are endorsement and disqualification from driving. It is common for the court to impose a fine for a driving offence, although in appropriate cases a custodial or community sentence might be imposed. This chapter concentrates on endorsement and disqualification.

11.2 Endorsement

An endorsement involves entering details of the conviction on the offender's driving licence. If the endorsement is obligatory, then the court must cause it to be carried out. It is 'part of the penalty'. The matters to be endorsed include the convicting court, the dates of offence, conviction and sentence, the particulars of offence and the sentence imposed.

11.2.1 Expiry of the endorsement

The endorsement will remain on the defendant's licence until he or she can apply for a clean one, surrendering the one which has been endorsed and paying an administrative fee. Application for a clean licence can be made:

- after 11 years from the date of conviction for an excess alcohol offence;
- after four years from the date of conviction where the defendant was disqualified, or the offence is one of dangerous driving;
- after four years from the date of the offence in other cases.

11.2.2 Production of licence

The defendant is under an obligation to produce a driving licence when convicted of an offence involving endorsement. It is an offence to fail to do so. If the defendant is unable to produce a licence, then the court will lack vital information in determining sentence. It may therefore decide to adjourn for the licence to be produced, or a printout of the defendant's driving record to be produced from DVLA, so as to establish any previous endorsements. When it does come to sentence the offender, the court may take into account any endorsements, including old ones which are no longer effective for 'totting up' purposes (see 11.3.1.2).

11.2.3   Penalty points

The framework for the imposition of penalty points is set out in the Road Traffic Offenders Act (RTOA) 1988, s 28:

28.—(1) Where a person is convicted of an offence involving obligatory endorsement, then, subject to the following provisions of this section, the number of penalty points to be attributed to the offence is—

    (a) the number shown in relation to the offence in the last column of part I or part II of schedule 2 to this Act, or

    (b) where a range of numbers is shown, a number within that range.

(2) Where a person is convicted of an offence committed by aiding, abetting, counselling or procuring, or inciting to the commission of, an offence involving obligatory disqualification, then, subject to the following provisions of this section, the number of penalty points to be attributed to the offence is 10.

(3) Where both a range of numbers and a number followed by the words '(fixed penalty)' is shown in the last column of part I of schedule 2 to this Act in relation to an offence, that number is the number of penalty points to be attributed to the offence for the purposes of sections 57(5) and 77(5) of this Act; and, where only a range of numbers is shown there, the lowest number in the range is the number of penalty points to be attributed to the offence for those purposes.

(4) Where a person is convicted (whether on the same occasion or not) of two or more offences committed on the same occasion and involving obligatory endorsement, the total number of penalty points to be attributed to them is the number or highest number that would be attributed on a conviction of one of them (so that if the convictions are on different occasions the number of penalty points to be attributed to the offences on the later occasion or occasions shall be restricted accordingly).

(5) In a case where (apart from this subsection) subsection (4) above would apply to two or more offences, the court may if it thinks fit determine that that subsection shall not apply to the offences (or, where three or more offences are concerned, to any one or more of them).

(6) Where a court makes such a determination it shall state its reasons in open court and, if it is a magistrates' court . . . shall cause them to be entered in the register . . . of its proceedings.

The penalty points applicable to those offences which carry them are set out in RTOA 1988, Sch 2, extracts from which are reprinted below.

For most offences carrying penalty points, the number of points is fixed, eg 3 points for failing to comply with a traffic sign (by jumping a red light, for instance). Other offences have a range, from which the sentencer can select the most appropriate, eg 3 to 6 points for speeding.

What if the defendant is convicted of two or more offences on the same occasion, and both carry penalty points? Say, for example, that the defendant is convicted of careless driving (for which a range of 3 to 9 points is laid down) and driving without insurance (6 to 8 points). Assume further that the episode of careless driving took place while the defendant was uninsured. The situation used to be that the court had to decide which of the offences committed on the same occasion was the more serious, and fix the appropriate number of points for that offence. It could not then impose any extra points for the other offence(s) (*Johnson v Finbow* [1983] 1 WLR 879).

The position is now governed by RTOA 1988, s 28(5). The court can now, if it thinks fit, impose penalty points for more than one offence committed on the same occasion. In the example given above, that would mean that the court could, for example, impose 9 points for the careless driving, and an additional 6 points for the driving without insurance, thus triggering off a penalty points disqualification (see **11.3.1.2**). The normal practice, however, is still to impose penalty points only for the most serious offence. If the court wishes to exercise its powers under s 28(5), it must state its reasons in open court and they must be put on the register.

ROAD TRAFFIC OFFENDERS ACT 1988 SCHEDULE 2 (EXTRACTS)
PROSECUTION AND PUNISHMENT OF OFFENCES
PART I
OFFENCES UNDER THE TRAFFIC ACTS

(1) Provision creating offence	(2) General nature of offence	(3) Mode of prosecution	(4) Punishment	(5) Disqualification	(6) Endorsement	(7) Penalty points
Offences under the Road Traffic Regulation Act 1984						
RTRA section 16(1)	Contravention of temporary prohibition or restriction.	Summarily.	Level 3 on the standard scale.	Discretionary if committed in respect of a speed restriction.	Obligatory if committed in respect of a speed restriction.	3–6 or 3 (fixed penalty).
RTRA section 17(4)	Use of special road contrary to scheme or regulations.	Summarily.	Level 4 on the standard scale.	Discretionary if committed in respect of a motor vehicle otherwise than by unlawfully stopping or allowing the vehicle to remain at rest on a part of a special road on which vehicles are in certain circumstances permitted to remain at rest.	Obligatory if committed as mentioned in the entry in column 5.	3–6 or 3 (fixed penalty if committed in respect of a speed restriction, 3 in any other case.
RTRA section 25(5)	Contravention of pedestrian crossing regulations.	Summarily.	Level 3 on the standard scale.	Discretionary if committed in respect of a motor vehicle.	Obligatory if committed in respect of a motor vehicle.	3
RTRA section 28(3)	Not stopping at school crossing	Summarily.	Level 3 on the standard scale.	Discretionary if committed in respect of a motor vehicle.	Obligatory if commited in respect of a motor vehicle.	3
RTRA section 29(3)	Contravention of order relating to street playground.	Summarily.	Level 3 on the standard scale.	Discretionary if committed in respect of a motor vehicle.	Obligatory if committed in respect of a motor vehicle.	2
RTRA section 89(1)	Exceeding speed limit.	Summarily.	Level 3 on the standard scale.	Discretionary.	Obligatory.	3–6 or 3 (fixed penalty).
Offences under the Road Traffic Act 1988						
RTA section 1	Causing death by dangerous driving.	On indictment.	14 years.	Obligatory.	Obligatory.	3–11
RTA section 2	Dangerous Driving.	(a) Summarily.	(a) 6 months or the statutory maximum or both.	Obligatory.	Obligatory.	3–11
		(b) On indictment.	(b) 2 years or a fine or both.			
RTA section 3	Careless, and inconsiderate, driving.	Summarily.	Level 4 on the standard scale.	Discretionary.	Obligatory.	3–9
RTA section 3A	Causing death by careless driving when under influence of drink or drugs.	On indictment.	14 years or a fine or both.	Obligatory.	Obligatory.	3–11
RTA section 4(1)	Driving or attempting to drive when unfit to drive through drink or drugs.	Summarily.	6 months or level 5 on the standard scale or both.	Obligatory.	Obligatory.	3–11
RTA section 4(2)	Being in charge of a mechanically propelled vehicle when unfit to drive through drink or drugs.	Summarily.	51 weeks or level 4 on the scale or both.	Discretionary.	Obligatory.	10

(1) Provision creating offence	(2) General nature of offence	(3) Mode of prosecution	(4) Punishment	(5) Disqualification	(6) Endorsement	(7) Penalty points
RTA section 5(1)(a)	Driving or attempting to drive with excess alcohol in breath, blood or urine.	Summarily.	6 months or level 5 on the standard scale or both.	Obligatory.	Obligatory.	3–11
RTA section 5(1)(b)	Being in charge of a mechanically propelled vehicle with excess alcohol in breath blood or urine.	Summarily.	51 weeks or level 4 on the standard scale or both.	Discretionary	Obligatory.	10
RTA section 6	Failing to provide a specimen of breath for a breath test.	Summarily.	Level 3 on the standard scale.	Discretionary.	Obligatory.	4
RTA section 7	Failing to provide specimen for analysis or laboratory test.	Summarily.	(a) Where the specimen was required to ascertain ability to drive or proportion of alcohol at the time offender was driving or attempting to drive, 6 months or level 5 on the standard scale or both. (b) In any other case, 51 weeks or level 4 on the standard scale or both.	(a) Obligatory in case mentioned in column 4(a). (b) Discretionary in any other case.	Obligatory.	(a) 3-11 in case mentioned in column 4(a). (b) 10 in any case.
RTA Section 7 A	Failing to allow specimen to be subjected to laboratory test.	Summarily.	(a) Where the test would be for ascertaining ability to drive or proportion of alcohol at the time offender was driving or attempting to drive, 6 months or level 5 on the standard scale or both. (b) In any other case, 51 weeks or level 4 on the standard scale or both.	(a) Obligatory in the case mentioned in column 4(a). (b) Discretionary in any other case.	Obligatory.	3–11, in case mentioned in column 4(a). 10 in any other case.
RTA section 12	Motor racing and speed trials on public ways.	Summarily.	Level 4 on the standard scale.	Obligatory.	Obligatory.	3–11
RTA section 22	Leaving vehicles in dangerous positions.	Summarily.	Level 3 on the standard scale.	Discretionary if committed in respect of a motor vehicle.	Obligatory if commited in respect of a motor vehicle.	3
RTA section 22A	Causing danger to road users.	(a) Summarily. (b) On indictment.	(a) 6 months or the statutory maximum or both. (b) 7 years or a fine or both.			
RTA section 23	Carrying passenger on motor-cycle contrary to section 23.	Summarily.	Level 3 on the standard scale.	Discretionary.	Obligatory.	3

(1) Provision creating offence	(2) General nature of offence	(3) Mode of prosecution	(4) Punishment	(5) Disqualification	(6) Endorsement	(7) Penalty points
RTA section 35	Failing to comply with traffic directions.	Summarily.	Level 3 on the standard scale.	Discretionary, if committed in respect of a motor vehicle by failure to comply with a direction of a constable or traffic warden.	Obligatory if committed as described in column 5.	3
RTA section 36	Failing to comply with traffic signs.	Summarily.	Level 3 on the standard scale.	Discretionary, if committed in respect of a motor vehicle by failure to comply with an indication given by a sign specified for the purpose of this paragraph in regulations under RTA section 36.	Obligatory if committed as described in column 5.	3
RTA section 40A	Using vehicle in dangerous condition etc.	Summarily.	(a) Level 5 on the standard scale if committed in respect of a goods vehicle or a vehicle adapted to carry more than eight passengers. (b) Level 4 on the standard scale in any other case.	Discretionary.	Obligatory.	3
RTA section 41A	Breach of requirement as to brakes, steering-gear or tyres.	Summarily.	(a) Level 5 on the standard scale if committed in respect of a goods vehicle or a vehicle adapted to carry more than eight passengers. (b) Level 4 on the standard scale in any other case.	Discretionary.	Obligatory.	3
RTA section 87(1)	Driving otherwise than in accordance with a licence.	Summarily.	Level 3 on the standard scale.	Discretionary in a case where the offender's driving would not have been in accordance with any licence that could have been granted to him.	Obligatory in the case mentioned in column 5.	3–6
RTA section 92(10)	Driving after making false declaration as to physical fitness.	Summarily.	Level 4 on the standard scale.	Discretionary.	Obligatory.	3–6
RTA section 93(3)	Failure to deliver revoked licence and counterpart to Secretary of State.	Summarily.	Level 3 on the standard scale.			
RTA section 94(3)	Failure of notify Secretary of State of onset of, or deterioration in, relevant or prospective disability.	Summarily.	Level 3 on the standard scale.			
RTA section 94(3A)	Driving after such a failure.	Summarily.	Level 3 on the standard scale.	Discretionary.	Obligatory.	3–6
RTA section 94A	Driving after refusal of licence under section 92(3) or revocation under section 93 or service of a notice under section 99C or 109B.	Summarily.	6 months or level 5 on the standard scale or both.	Discretionary.	Obligatory.	3–6

(1) Provision creating offence	(2) General nature of offence	(3) Mode of prosecution	(4) Punishment	(5) Disqualification	(6) Endorsement	(7) Penalty points
RTA section 96	Driving with uncorrected defective eyesight, or refusing to submit to test of eyesight.	Summarily	Level 3 on the standard scale.	Discretionary	Obligatory.	3
RTA section 99(5)	Driving licence holder failing to surrender licence and counterpart.	Summarily.	Level 3 on the standard scale.			
RTA section 103(1)(a)	Obtaining driving licence while disqualified.	Summarily.	Level 3 on the standard scale.			
RTA section 103(1)(b)	Driving while disqualified.	Summarily.	6 months or level 5 on the standard scale or both.	Discretionary.	Obligatory.	6
RTA section 143	Using motor vehicle while uninsured or unsecured against third party risks.	Summarily.	Level 5 on the standard scale.	Discretionary.	Obligatory.	6–8
RTA section 170(4)	Failing to stop after accident and give particulars or report accident.	Summarily.	6 months or level 5 on the standard scale or both.	Discretionary.	Obligatory.	5–10
RTA section 170(7)	Failure by driver, in case of accident involving injury to another, to produce evidence of insurance or security or to report accident.	Summarily.	Level 3 on the standard scale.			
RTA section 171	Failure by owner of motor vehicle to give police information for verifying compliance with requirement of compulsory insurance or security.	Summarily.	Level 4 on the standard scale.			
RTA section 172	Failure of person keeping vehicle and others to give police information as to identity of driver, etc, in the case of certain offences.	Summarily.	Level 3 on the standard scale.	Discretionary if committed otherwise than by virtue of subsection (5) or (11).	Obligatory if committed otherwise than by virtue of subsection (5) or (11).	3

11.3 Disqualification

All orders of disqualification from driving run from the moment they are pronounced (*Meese* [1973] 1 WLR 675 (CA)). In that case, the trial judge ordered that the two periods of disqualification which he was imposing should run consecutively. The Court of Appeal held that such a sentence was unlawful, since the start of the second period would be postponed. They must run concurrently.

Disqualification can be for any period — even life. But a life disqualification is extremely rare. The danger which the appellate courts have seen with very long periods of disqualification (eg, 10 years) is that they may shut the defendant out of a substantial number of jobs, and create an incentive to disregard the law.

11.3.1 Categories of disqualification

There are three categories of disqualification: obligatory; penalty points; and discretionary. The succeeding paragraphs deal with each in turn.

11.3.1.1 Obligatory

Where an offence carries obligatory disqualification, there must be an order of disqualification unless there are special reasons (see **11.4**).

As far as the minimum period for which the court must disqualify is concerned:

(a) The minimum is usually 12 months.

(b) For certain of the most serious offences (manslaughter, causing death by dangerous driving, and causing death by careless driving while under the influence of drink or drugs) there is a longer minimum of two years.

(c) A minimum of two years must be imposed when the defendant has been disqualified for 56 days or more at least twice in the three years preceding the commission of the offence in question.

(d) There is a special minimum sentence of three years disqualification under RTOA 1988, s 34(3) where the defendant is convicted of an alcohol-related offence which was committed within 10 years of the date of conviction of an earlier alcohol-related offence.

11.3.1.2 Penalty points

This applies where the defendant 'tots up' 12 or more points within three years (RTOA 1988, s 29). Such a 'totter' is then disqualified for a minimum of six months, in the absence of clearly defined 'mitigating grounds'.

The penalty points to be taken into account are:

(a) any for the offence(s) of which the defendant is now convicted (disregarding any for which the court disqualifies);

(b) any ordered to be endorsed on a previous occasion for an offence *committed* in the preceding three years (by RTOA 1988, s 35, 'if any of the offences was committed more than three years before another, the points in respect of that offence are not to be added to those in respect of the other').

The law used to be that, if the defendant was disqualified, the slate was wiped clean and he or she started again to tot up towards 12. Now, there is no general rule that the slate will be wiped clean once there is disqualification. The rule is that all penalty points remain until there is a penalty points disqualification, whereupon they are wiped off.

The court may decide not to impose a penalty points disqualification (or impose a shorter one than six months) if there are mitigating grounds. When the term is applied to a 'totter', then it has a restricted meaning. Certain factors may not be mitigating grounds by virtue of RTOA 1988, s 35(4), ie:

- any circumstances that are alleged to make the offence(s) not a serious one;
- hardship, other than exceptional hardship;
- any circumstances taken into account as mitigating grounds in the preceding three years.

Frequently, 'exceptional hardship' is argued in relation to the offender's employment. The court might take into account the following factors, together with any others which appear from the facts:

- whether the offender requires a licence to drive as a necessary part of the job;
- whether he or she needs to drive in order to get to work;
- the distances to be travelled to work;
- the availability of public transport;
- the hours required by the job (eg, are they at a time when public transport is available);
- the offender's age and health;
- any other means of transport available;
- any particular hardship caused to the offender's family by the loss of the job or reduced wages;
- any employees dependent on the offender's ability to drive.

11.3.1.3 Discretionary

Where an offence carries discretionary disqualification the court can disqualify for the offence where it imposes less than 12 points.

11.3.1.4 Probationary period

Every driver who qualified on or after 1 June 1997 is subject to a probationary period of two years, beginning with the day on which he or she qualified (Road Traffic (New Drivers) Act 1995). A driver who acquires six or more penalty points during that probationary period, will have his or her licence revoked and must undergo retesting before a full driving licence can once again be issued.

11.3.2 Ending disqualification

In the normal course of events, the disqualification will end once the period laid down by the court expires. Prior to that, the offender can apply for his or her licence back before the period of disqualification ends, provided that a certain period of time has elapsed. That period is:

- at least two years in any event;
- half the period of disqualification if the period ordered is between four and ten years;
- five years if the disqualification is for ten years or more.

11.3.3 Order for retest

There is, however, provision for the sentencing court to lay down that the offender must pass a driving test before the disqualification comes to an end. Whilst such an order is within the court's discretion, it should not be imposed on a punitive basis, but in order to protect the safety of other road users, eg, because of the age, infirmity or lack of experience of the offender, or the nature of the offence (*Guilfoyle* [1973] 2 All ER 844). Retests are now compulsory when the court disqualifies for manslaughter or for dangerous driving (whether it causes death or not): RTOA 1988, s 36.

11.4 Special reasons

As mentioned above, where disqualification is obligatory, the court must disqualify unless there are 'special reasons'. A similar rule applies where endorsement is obligatory.

Where special reasons are necessary, these must relate to the offence, and not the circumstances of the offender. As it was put in *Whittal v Kirby* [1947] KB 194:

A 'special reason' within the exception is one which is special to the facts of the particular case, that is, special to the facts which constitute the offence. It is, in other words, a mitigating or extenuating circumstance, not amounting in law to a defence to the charge, yet directly connected with the commission of the offence, and one which the court ought properly to take into consideration when imposing punishment. A circumstance peculiar to the offender as distinguished from the offence is not a 'special reason' within the exception.

Frequently, special reasons are put forward where the defendant alleges that his or her drink was laced. Guidance has now been laid down in *DPP v O'Connor* [1992] RTR 66 as to what constitutes special reasons in these circumstances. The defence must show on the balance of probabilities:

- that the defendant's drink had been laced;
- that the defendant did not know or suspect that it had been laced;
- that, if the defendant had not taken the laced drink, his or her alcohol level would not have exceeded the prescribed limit.

Another series of cases relates to drink driving in an emergency. In *Chatters v Burke* [1986] 1 WLR 1321, the court laid down seven matters which the justices ought to take into account in such cases:

First of all they should consider how far the vehicle was in fact driven; secondly, in what manner it was driven; thirdly, what was the state of the vehicle; fourthly, whether it was the intention of the driver to drive any further; fifthly, the prevailing conditions with regard to the road and the traffic upon it; sixthly, whether there was any possibility of danger by contact with other road users; and finally, what was the reason for the vehicle being driven at all.

The argument that there are special reasons is not, however, confined to drink driving cases. For example, it also has application to a speeding case (*Police Prosecutor v Humphreys* [1970] Crim LR 234).

Further, the defendant can argue that there are special reasons not to impose penalty points.

Part III

A case to prepare

12

Introduction to the sample brief

This chapter introduces the papers for a criminal case (reproduced in **Chapter 14**) which are intended to provide you with the opportunity to make use of some of the skills which are required of a barrister in criminal practice. The issues which are involved are ones which ought to be familiar by the time you have reached this part of the manual. From time to time, however, you will find it helpful to make reference to some of the other manuals in this series, eg, the *Opinion Writing Manual*, the *Advocacy Manual* and the *Conference Skills Manual*.

The case is one where there are a number of co-defendants, who are charged with offences of violence and offences against public order. There may be a conflict of interest between the two defendants whom you are initially instructed to advise, so you must consider whether there should be separate representation for those two defendants — a point on which the barrister in criminal practice is frequently asked to advise. There are also issues relating to identification, alibi, severance of the indictment, admissibility and the overall strengths and weaknesses of the prosecution case. You need to address the question of advising on plea and on sentence. The set of papers includes a questionnaire which has to be filled in before the Plea and Case Management Hearing, so that you have to consider whether it can be filled in on the information which you have to hand, or whether more details are needed (eg from the client in conference) before you are able to do so. The consideration of the questionnaire will give you the opportunity to become familiar with a document which the barrister in criminal practice frequently has to consider. In addition, the papers include a copy of a custody record, which is a fertile source of information for both sides in a criminal trial, and needs careful consideration as you advise and prepare for trial. There are copies of other documents in common use, such as crime report.

In making use of this set of papers, it is suggested that you should proceed as follows:

- use the papers as an exercise in writing an Advice on Evidence;
- then use them to prepare for a conference with the client;
- finally, use them to prepare for the advocacy tasks involved in a trial.

Each of these suggestions is considered in more detail in the succeeding sections.

12.1 Advice on evidence

The papers take the form of a brief received by counsel, with instructions to provide an Advice on Evidence for the defendants Nicholas Spring and John Hanson (or Hanson only if there is a conflict of interest between them). Your initial use of the papers ought therefore to be as an exercise in writing an Advice on Evidence in a criminal case. Prior to doing so, you should read through **Chapter 12** of the *Opinion Writing Manual*, which deals with this task. You may also find it helpful to take a look at **Chapter 17** in the *Case Preparation Manual*. (*You should avoid looking at the sample Advice which is printed at the end of this Manual. If you do so, it will obviously destroy much of the value in doing the Advice as an exercise.*)

Once you have refreshed your memory as to the steps involved in writing an Advice on Evidence in a criminal case, you should be ready to start. In order to make sure that you manage your time effectively, and to ensure that you do not become too remote from the situation in practice, it is suggested that you work against the clock, and that you do not allow yourself more than six hours to produce the Advice, including any legal research which you need to do.

Having started the clock, you might read through the papers once, quickly, in order to get the general sense. Second and third readings are then likely to be necessary in order to be able to analyse the evidence and form an initial judgment on the points which need to be dealt with in the Advice. As you read the papers for the second or third time, you might compile a chronology, a list of issues, a schedule of the various descriptions of the defendants in whom you are particularly interested. You should also begin to make a list of the points on which your instructing solicitors need to take action, the documents which you need to see and the missing pieces of information.

Having gone through the papers several times in this way, you are in a position to make a plan of your Advice. Consider how the various points which you need to cover should be dealt with and the logical order in which you should present them. You can then write your Advice, keeping an eye on the clock so that you do not produce something which is unrealistic in terms of length and degree of detail.

Once your Advice is completed, and you have taken a pause in order to recover, look at the sample Advice, which is printed in **Chapter 14**. (*This should be the first time that you have glanced at it!*)

Consider your Advice against the sample. Bear in mind that it is a sample and not a model. Your version may be superior, at least in certain respects, to what is printed. But wherever you reach a different conclusion from the sample, you should consider which is preferable, and why. Think also about the form in which the sample is written and compare it with yours in order to gain some constructive feedback.

12.2   Preparing for conference

The next task which you might undertake with the *Hanson* papers is preparation for conference. It is not giving away any deep secret to suggest that part of the advice which you are likely to provide is that there should be a conference with the client. In preparing for this task, you may work in parallel with a friend or colleague, with each of you working separately, and then comparing your conclusions.

In any event, you will find it helpful before using the papers in this way to read the relevant sections of the *Conference Manual* — in particular **Chapter 5**. You will need to consider, among other matters, the information which you need to obtain from your client(s), and how best to obtain it; and the advice which needs to be given, for example on plea and likely sentence if convicted. Having prepared and produced a working plan for the conference, compare notes with the friend or colleague who has been performing the same task.

12.3 Preparing for trial

The papers can be used again to prepare for trial. Again you might wish to work in parallel with someone on this task. It would be sensible if the two of you worked out the answers which you have been given in the imaginary conference referred to in **12.2**. This will then give you a basis for preparation for trial, ie you prepare on the assumption that the client has given you certain answers to the questions which you asked in conference.

As to the areas which need preparation, it is suggested that you deal with each of the areas described in the following paragraphs.

12.3.1 Closing speech

It actually makes a lot of sense to prepare your closing speech before preparing the matters which you have to deal with during the course of the trial.

Your closing speech ought to be your interpretation of the points which arise in trial. If you are able to make certain realistic assumptions about what is likely to emerge during the trial, preparing your closing speech first gives the rest of your preparation a clear focus. Obviously, if the trial actually took place, the speech would need to be rewritten at intervals during its course, in order to ensure that it was based, not on assumptions, but on the evidence which in fact emerged.

12.3.2 Submissions

From the time that you prepared to write your Advice on Evidence, it will have been apparent that there would be disputes about the admissibility of certain pieces of evidence. You need to consider how you will present the argument in relation to these points of admissibility. In doing so, you are likely to find **Chapter 38** of the *Advocacy Manual* of assistance. Similarly, you should consider whether you are at all likely to be making a submission of no case to answer on behalf of your client(s). If so, prepare a framework, using **Chapter 39** of the *Advocacy Manual* to remind yourself of the process involved.

12.3.3 Cross-examination

There are two areas of cross-examination which you must prepare. First, there are the prosecution witnesses, both police and civilian. The themes and arguments which you intend to develop in your closing speech will determine the course of cross-examination here to some extent. Your cross-examination will also be affected by the instructions which you have received in the brief and those which are obtained in conference.

Consider whether there any co-defendants who stand trial with your client. If they appear on the indictment before your client, you will have to cross-examine them before your client gives evidence. In addition, consider the points to keep in mind in preparing any cross-examination (see **Chapter 22** of the *Advocacy Manual*).

12.3.4   Examination in chief

One of the most important tasks in preparing for trial as defence counsel is to consider the impression your client would make as a witness. Will it be necessary for your client to give evidence? If it is, then prepare to examine him in chief, using **Chapter 21** of the *Advocacy Manual* as a reminder of the steps you need to take.

12.3.5   Comparing notes

Once you have dealt with each of the advocacy tasks which you are likely to face, discuss your approach with your friend or colleague and compare notes.

12.4   The papers in *R v Nicholas Spring, John Hanson and others*

You can now read the brief contained in **Chapter 13**, and start preparing the Advice on Evidence. (*Remember not to look at the sample Advice in* **Chapter 14** *until you have finished.*)

13

R v Spring, Hanson and others

Contents

Instructions to counsel	120
Judge's questionnaire	122
Indictment	126
Witness statements	127
Record of tape recorded interview (Spring)	145
Record of tape recorded interview (Hanson)	147
Antecedents (Hanson)	149
Previous convictions (Hanson)	150
Antecedents (Spring)	151
Previous convictions (Spring)	152
Statement of John Hanson	153
Custody records	154
Charge sheets	160
Crime complaint/report	162
Defence statement	163

IN THE OXTON CROWN COURT
T0155/03

BETWEEN:

R

–and–

NICHOLAS SPRING
JOHN HANSON & Others

INSTRUCTIONS TO COUNSEL

Messrs. Archer & Balcombe
Centenary House,
Bray Street,
Oxton. OT5 16MM

Solicitors for the Defendants

IN THE OXTON CROWN COURT   T0155/06

BETWEEN:

R

–v–

NICHOLAS SPRING
and JOHN HANSON and Others

INSTRUCTIONS TO COUNSEL

Counsel has herewith:

1. Copy Indictment.
2. Statements of prosecution witnesses.
3. Interviews of Mr Spring & Mr Hanson.
4. Custody records.
5. Unused material.
6. Previous convictions of the Defendants.
7. Proof of Evidence of Mr Hanson.
8. Defence Statement of Mr Hanson.

Counsel is instructed on behalf of the Defendants, Nicholas Spring and John Hanson, who are charged with Violent Disorder, Causing Grievous Bodily Harm with intent to resist arrest of Nicholas Spring and on behalf of John Hanson who is charged, alone, with Attempted Robbery.

The facts of this case are set out in the various documents and Instructing Solicitors do not intend to repeat them herein. All defendants were sent for trial on 17th July.

The other Defendants are represented by Messrs Glidewell and Speed. They have informed us that Sean Baker and Martin Thompson will plead guilty to Violent Disorder whilst Louis Bucknell, Simon Bratt and Anthony Mead will plead guilty to Affray. The CPS have indicated that these pleas are acceptable.

Instructing Solicitors feel that there may be a conflict of interest so that two counsel may be required and counsel is asked to advise on separate representation, generally on evidence, and any other matters arising plea and possible sentence if convicted. If counsel is of the view that there is a conflict of interest, then such advice is requested in respect of John Hanson.

Counsel is also requested to complete the questionnaire for the Plea and Case Management Hearing, which is to be held on 21st August 2006 and to draft a defence case statement (draft enclosed).

21 July 2006

PLEA AND CASE MANAGEMENT HEARING IN THE CROWN COURT

Date of hearing: Judge:

P			represented by:		☐
D1		in custody/on bail	represented by:		☐
D2		in custody/on bail	represented by:		☐
D3		in custody/on bail	represented by:		☐
D4		in custody/on bail	represented by:		☐
D5		in custody/on bail	represented by:		☐

Tick right hand column if the advocate is instructed for trial

No. of case in Crown Court: URN:

Has the defendant been advised about credit for pleading guilty?   D1 D2 D3 D4 D5 ☐ ☐ ☐ ☐ ☐

Has the defendant been warned that if he is on bail and fails to attend, the proceedings may continue in his absence?   ☐ ☐ ☐ ☐ ☐

Is the Crown Court Case Details form up-to-date?   P ☐ ☐ ☐ ☐ ☐ ☐

Matters likely to be applicable to all trials

1) TRIAL JUDGE
Should the future management of the case be under the supervision of the trial or a nominated judge?   **YES/NO**

2) RESOLVING THE CASE WITHOUT A TRIAL   Not applicable ☐
a.   **Might the case against a defendant be resolved by a plea of guilty to some counts on the indictment or to a lesser offence?**   D1 D2 D3 D4 D5 ☐ ☐ ☐ ☐ ☐
b.   **If so, how?**
c.   **Is the prosecution prepared to resolve the case in this way?**   ☐ ☐ ☐ ☐ ☐
d.   **If no, does the court take the provisional view that the case should be resolved in this way?**   ☐ ☐ ☐ ☐ ☐
e.   *If yes, the court orders:*

3) GUILTY PLEA   Not applicable ☐
a.   **Is there a written basis of plea?**   D1 D2 D3 D4 D5 ☐ ☐ ☐ ☐ ☐

b.   **Is the basis of plea acceptable to the prosecution?**   ☐ ☐ ☐ ☐ ☐
a.   Is the basis of plea acceptable to the court?   ☐ ☐ ☐ ☐ ☐
b.   If not acceptable, section 25 (Newton Hearing) will also apply.
c.   *The defendant(s) will be sentenced on:*
d.   *The prosecution to serve any further material relevant to sentence by:*
e.   *The pre-sentence report, if required, to be received by the Crown Court and made available to the defence and the prosecution by:*
f.   *The defence to serve any material which it wishes the court to consider when sentencing the defendant by:*
g.   **Will "derogatory assertions" be made in mitigation?**   ☐ ☐ ☐ ☐ ☐
h.   *If yes, the court orders:*
i.   **Are there any other matters which should be dealt with at the same time as these proceedings (other offences/TICs)?**   ☐ ☐ ☐ ☐ ☐
j.   **If yes, give brief details:**
k.   *If there are other matters, the court orders:*
l.   *Further orders (e.g. orders re medical or psychiatric reports or confiscation proceedings):*

4) NOT GUILTY - TRIAL DATE   Not applicable ☐
a.   **If the defendant is in custody and if the provisions regarding custody time limits apply, when does the custody time limit (or any extension thereof) expire?**
     D1:   ; D2:   ; D3:   ; D4:   ; D5:   .
b.   **Set out other reasons why the trial should take place earlier or later than it might otherwise?**

c.   *If the defendant is in custody and the date of the trial is outside the custody time limit period, the court makes the following orders:*

d.   **What is the estimated length of the prosecution, defence cases?**
     Prosecution   Defence

e.   *The trial will take place on: and the length of it will be:*

5) READINESS FOR TRIAL
     The parties' case progression officers to inform the Crown Court case progression officer in writing that the case is ready for trial, that it will proceed as a trial on the date in 4e and will take no more/less time than the period in 4e, by:

6) EVIDENCE - WITNESSES
a   **Have the parties completed Annex A?**   **YES/NO**
b.   If yes, does the court approve Annex A?   YES/NO
c.   *If the list of witnesses to be called orally is not agreed or approved, agreement (which is subject to the court's approval) must be reached and notified to the court by:*
d   *Absent agreement, the prosecution shall seek further directions by:*

7) EVIDENCE - DEFENDANTS' INTERVIEWS   **Not applicable** ☐
a   **Should the interviews be edited before the trial?**

	P	D1	D2	D3	D4	D5
	☐	☐	☐	☐	☐	☐

b.   *Proposals for the editing of interviews shall be drafted by:*   *and served by:*
c.   *The other parties shall respond by:*
d   *The agreed interviews shall be filed with the Court by:*
e.   *Absent agreement, the party(ies) named in b) shall seek further directions by:*

8) DEFENCE STATEMENT
a   **Has a defence statement been served?**

	D1	D2	D3	D4	D5
a	☐	☐	☐	☐	☐
b	☐	☐	☐	☐	☐
c	☐	☐	☐	☐	☐

b.   **Is there an issue as to its adequacy?**
c.   *The court gives a warning to:*
d   *The court orders:*

9) PROSECUTION ADDITIONAL EVIDENCE   **Not applicable** ☐
a   *Any additional evidence to be served by:*
b.   **Which topic/issue will the additional evidence relate to?**

10) FURTHER PROSECUTION DISCLOSURE   **Not applicable** ☐
a   *The prosecution to complete any further disclosure by:*
b.   **Is the defence alleging that the prosecution has not complied with its obligation to disclose material?**

	D1	D2	D3	D4	D5
	☐	☐	☐	☐	☐

c.   *If yes, the court orders:*

11) EVIDENCE - ADMISSIONS/SCHEDULES
a.   **Have the parties considered which admissions/schedules can be agreed:**   **YES/NO**
b.   *If yes and if the court agrees that the proposed admissions/schedules are sufficient, they shall be drafted by:*
c.   *and sent to the other parties by:*
d.   *The other parties shall respond by:*
e.   *The agreed admissions/schedules shall be filed with the court by:*
f.   *Absent agreement, the named party in b) shall seek further directions by:*
g.   *If the answer to question a. is no or if the court does not approve the proposed admissions/schedules, the court orders:*

Matters which may apply to any trial

12) EVIDENCE - EXHIBITS
a.   **Have the parties completed and agreed Annex B?**   **YES/NO**
b.   *If Annex B is not agreed, agreement must be reached and notified to the court by:*
c.   *In the absence of agreement, the prosecution shall seek further directions by:*
d.   *If, in the view of the court, any exhibits should be presented in a particular way in order to be more easily understood by the jury, the court orders:*
e.   *Further orders:*

13) EVIDENCE - VIDEO EVIDENCE   **Not applicable** ☐
a.   **Has the prosecution delivered to the defence the transcript of video witness evidence upon which it proposes to rely?**

	D1	D2	D3	D4	D5
	☐	☐	☐	☐	☐

b.   *If no, the prosecution to do so by:*
c.   *The defence shall submit any editing proposals by:*
d.   *The prosecution shall respond by:*
e.   *The agreed transcripts and edited video shall be filed with the court by:*
f.   *Absent agreement, the prosecution shall seek further directions by:*

14) EVIDENCE - CCTV EVIDENCE   **Not applicable** ☐
a.   **Has any unedited CCTV evidence been made available in full to the other parties?**

	P	D1	D2	D3	D4	D5
	☐	☐	☐	☐	☐	☐

b.   *If yes, copy of proposed composite/edited film/stills to be served by:*
c.   *The other parties to respond by:*
d.   *Absent agreement, the party seeking to rely on the evidence shall seek directions by:*

15) EVIDENCE - EXPERT EVIDENCE   **Not applicable** ☐
a   **Expert evidence is likely to be called by:**

	P	D1	D2	D3	D4	D5
a	☐	☐	☐	☐	☐	☐

b.   **To prove/disprove:** P :
    D1/2/3/4/5:
c.   Does the court approve of the need for the identified expert evidence?   ☐   ☐   ☐   ☐   ☐   ☐
d   If no, why?
e.   *In any event the evidence to be served by:*

f. **Should the expert evidence be presented in a particular way in order to be more easily understood by the jury?** ☐ ☐ ☐ ☐ ☐ ☐
g. *If yes, the court orders:*

h. **Would it be helpful if the experts consulted together and if possible agreed a written note of points of agreement or disagreement with a summary of reasons?** ☐ ☐ ☐ ☐ ☐ ☐
i. *If yes, and if the parties agree, the court orders:*

16) ELECTRONIC EQUIPMENT – COMPATIBILITY Not applicable☐
a. **Does the trial courtroom have the appropriate equipment to allow the presentation of electronic evidence (CCTV, live link, audio recordings, DVD etc)?** P☐ D1☐ D2☐ D3☐ D4☐ D5☐
b. *If no, the court orders:*

17) EVIDENCE - SPECIAL MEASURES AND LIVE LINK Not applicable☐
a. **Any outstanding issues about special measures or live links?** D1☐ D2☐ D3☐ D4☐ D5☐
b. If yes, the court orders:

18) MISCELLANEOUS ORDERS RE. WITNESSES AND DEFENDANT Not applicable ☐
a. **Does any witness or defendant need an interpreter or have special needs for which arrangements should be made?** P☐ D1☐ D2☐ D3☐ D4☐ D5☐
b. *If yes, the court orders:*

c. **Are any special arrangements needed for a child defendant?** ☐ ☐ ☐ ☐ ☐ ☐
d. *If yes, the court orders:*

e. **Will a defendant be unrepresented at trial?** ☐ ☐ ☐ ☐ ☐ ☐
f. *If yes, the court orders:*

19) HEARSAY / BAD CHARACTER EVIDENCE Not applicable☐
a. **Further applications regarding hearsay evidence or bad character evidence are to be made by:** P☐ D1☐ D2☐ D3☐ D4☐ D5☐
b. *The court orders:*

20) PRODUCTION OF MATERIAL FROM THIRD PARTIES Not applicable☐
a. **Applications for production of material (e.g. social services, hospital, banking records) from third parties to be made by:** P☐ D1☐ D2☐ D3☐ D4☐ D5☐
b. *The court orders:*

21) PRE-TRIAL RESOLUTION OF ISSUES Not applicable ☐
a. **What are the legal or factual issues which should be resolved before the trial:**
b. *If the issues are not capable of being resolved at the plea and case management hearing, the necessary hearing will take place on   and will last:*
c. **Do the parties wish to call witnesses to give evidence orally to enable the court to resolve the issues?** P☐ D1☐ D2☐ D3☐ D4☐ D5☐
d. *If yes, and if the court approves, the court makes the following orders:*

e. *Skeleton arguments to be submitted by: P by: D1/2/3/4/5 by:*

22) PUBLIC INTEREST IMMUNITY: ON NOTICE APPLICATIONS Not applicable ☐
a. **What is the nature of the prosecution's application on notice for public interest immunity?**
b. *The court orders:*

23) FURTHER ORDERS CONCERNING THE CONDUCT OF THE TRIAL
a. *Prosecution case summary/opening, if necessary, to be served by:*
b. *To ensure that the trial does not take more time than the period in 4e., the court orders:*

24) ANY FURTHER MISCELLANEOUS ORDERS - INCLUDING ORDERS RE. LITIGATION SUPPORT

25) NEWTON HEARING Not applicable ☐
a. *The Newton hearing will take place on: and the length of it will be:*
b. *The issues to be resolved are:*
c. *The prosecution to serve any further material by: and the defence by:*
d. *The following witnesses will be called to give evidence orally:*
e. *Further orders (including any orders re. hearsay/bad character):*

Judge's signature:

ANNEX A
Witnesses upon whom the prosecution intends to rely and who will give evidence orally

Name of witness	Page No	Type of witness	Required by:						Order of calling
			P ☐	D1 ☐	D2 ☐	D3 ☐	D4 ☐	D5 ☐	
			P ☐	D1 ☐	D2 ☐	D3 ☐	D4 ☐	D5 ☐	
			P ☐	D1 ☐	D2 ☐	D3 ☐	D4 ☐	D5 ☐	
			P ☐	D1 ☐	D2 ☐	D3 ☐	D4 ☐	D5 ☐	
			P ☐	D1 ☐	D2 ☐	D3 ☐	D4 ☐	D5 ☐	
			P ☐	D1 ☐	D2 ☐	D3 ☐	D4 ☐	D5 ☐	
			P ☐	D1 ☐	D2 ☐	D3 ☐	D4 ☐	D5 ☐	
			P ☐	D1 ☐	D2 ☐	D3 ☐	D4 ☐	D5 ☐	
			P ☐	D1 ☐	D2 ☐	D3 ☐	D4 ☐	D5 ☐	
			P ☐	D1 ☐	D2 ☐	D3 ☐	D4 ☐	D5 ☐	
			P ☐	D1 ☐	D2 ☐	D3 ☐	D4 ☐	D5 ☐	
			P ☐	D1 ☐	D2 ☐	D3 ☐	D4 ☐	D5 ☐	
			P ☐	D1 ☐	D2 ☐	D3 ☐	D4 ☐	D5 ☐	
			P ☐	D1 ☐	D2 ☐	D3 ☐	D4 ☐	D5 ☐	
			P ☐	D1 ☐	D2 ☐	D3 ☐	D4 ☐	D5 ☐	
			P ☐	D1 ☐	D2 ☐	D3 ☐	D4 ☐	D5 ☐	
			P ☐	D1 ☐	D2 ☐	D3 ☐	D4 ☐	D5 ☐	
			P ☐	D1 ☐	D2 ☐	D3 ☐	D4 ☐	D5 ☐	
			P ☐	D1 ☐	D2 ☐	D3 ☐	D4 ☐	D5 ☐	
			P ☐	D1 ☐	D2 ☐	D3 ☐	D4 ☐	D5 ☐	

ANNEX B
Exhibits which the prosecution intends to make available to the jury at the start of the trial

Exhibit reference	Page No	Exhibit reference	Page No.	Exhibit reference	Page No.

Use continuation sheets as necessary

INDICTMENT   No. T0155/06

THE CROWN COURT AT OXTON

THE QUEEN –v– NICHOLAS SPRING, JOHN HANSON, MARTIN THOMPSON, SEAN BAKER, LOUIS BUCKNELL, SIMON BRATT and ANTHONY MEAD

are charged as follows:

Count 1

STATEMENT OF OFFENCE

VIOLENT DISORDER, Contrary to Section 2(1) of the Public Order Act 1986.

PARTICULARS OF OFFENCE

NICHOLAS SPRING, JOHN HANSON, MARTIN THOMPSON, SEAN BAKER, LOUIS BUCKNELL, SIMON BRATT and ANTHONY MEAD on the 11th day of July 2006, being present together with each other and with other persons unknown used or threatened unlawful violence and their conduct (taken together) was such as would cause a person of reasonable firmness present at the scene to fear for his personal safety.

Count 2

STATEMENT OF OFFENCE

CAUSING GRIEVOUS BODILY HARM WITH INTENT, Contrary to Section 18 of the Offences Against the Person Act 1861.

PARTICULARS OF OFFENCE

NICHOLAS SPRING, JOHN HANSON, MARTIN THOMPSON, SEAN BAKER, LOUIS BUCKNELL, SIMON BRATT and ANTHONY MEAD on the 11th day of July 2006 unlawfully caused grievous bodily harm to Martin Kemp with intent to resist or prevent the lawful apprehension or detainer of the said Nicholas Spring.

Count 3

STATEMENT OF OFFENCE

ATTEMPTED ROBBERY, Contrary to Section 1(1) of the Criminal Attempts Act 1981.

PARTICULARS OF OFFENCE

JOHN HANSON, on the 11th day of July 2006 at Kelly's Off-Licence, Crewkerne Street, Upton attempted to rob Michael Kelly of the contents of a cash till.

OFFENCES ADDED UNDER SECTION 40 of the CRIMINAL JUSTICE ACT 1988

STATEMENT OF OFFENCE

DRIVING WHILST UNFIT THROUGH DRINK OR DRUGS, Contrary to Section 4(1) of the Road Traffic Act 1988.

PARTICULARS OF OFFENCE

JOHN HANSON, on 11th day of July 2006 at Upton in the county of Downshire drove a motor vehicle on a road or other public place, namely the junction of Upton Road and Lymehurst Road, whilst unfit through drink or drugs.

<u>WITNESS STATEMENT</u>

Statement of   Stephen Jordan PC 303 ....

Age if under 21   ....

This statement (consisting of **1** pages each signed by me) is true to the best of my knowledge and belief and I make it knowing that, if it is tendered in evidence, I shall be liable to prosecution if I have wilfully stated in it anything which I know to be false or do not believe to be true.

Dated the 13th day of July 2006

Signature: ....S. Jordan..

I am a PC in the Downshire Constabulary currently stationed at Upton. I am currently assigned to 'Homebeat' duties on the Abbey Estate. On the 11th July 2006 I went with other officers to an incident on the Abbey Estate.

We arrived at about 3.35 pm. On arrival I saw that PC 37 was being led to a vehicle by PC 211. Both of them appeared to be dishevilled and PC 37 was bleeding profusely from the nose area. A number of youths appeared to be dispersing from the area, some of them were being chased by other officers. As I am familiar with the estate and the people living there I was able to identify 2 men, who got into a blue Vauxhall parked at the rear of Fountains House, as Tony Mead and Simon Bratt. Tony Mead was wearing blue jeans and a yellow shirt. I was able to identify him easily as he has a shaved head and is 6 3. I only saw the back of Simon Bratt but I have arrested him on a number of occasions and he is well known to me. He was wearing a denim jacket and jeans. There were other people in the car but I was unable to identify any of them. I am unable to say who was driving the car. I then assisted other officers in dispersing the crowd and removing prisoners to Upton police station.

On the 12th July at 6.15 am with other officers I went to 27 Fountains House where I arrested Simon Bratt for an offence of violent disorder. He was cautioned at 6.20 am and made no reply. Also at 27 Fountains House were Kieran Bratt, Tony Mead and Louis Bucknell. They were also arrested for Violent Disorder and taken to Upton police station.

Signed: S. Jordan

Signature witnessed by: R. Parry.

WITNESS STATEMENT

Statement of   Raymond Parry PC 211 ....

Age if under 21   ....

This statement (consisting of 1 pages each signed by me) is true to the best of my knowledge and belief and I make it knowing that, if it is tendered in evidence, I shall be liable to
prosecution if I have wilfully stated in it anything which I know to be false or do not
believe to be true.

Dated the 13th day of July 2006

Signature: .... R. Parry ....

I am a PC in the Downshire Constabulary currently stationed at Upton. On the 11th July
2006 I was operating a single manned mobile unit when I was called to an incident on the
Abbey Estate at about 3.20 pm.

When I arrived I saw PC 37 struggling with a youth I now know to be Nick Spring. Spring
was behaving in a very aggressive and violent manner and PC 37 was acting merely to
restrain him. Gathered around them was a group of about 15 youths. There were also a
number of bystanders, some with children. The children, in particular, appeared to be
scared about what was going on. I parked my vehicle some 30 yards away and immediately
radioed for back-up and then got out of my vehicle to assist PC 37. When I got to the edge
of the group I shouted out for them to stop and attempted to force my way through to
assist PC 37. At this I was immediately set on by a number of youths including one whom
I know as Sean Baker. These youths started to punch and kick me. I resisted and attempted
to arrest the group but as I was about to tell them they were under arrest I was pulled to the
ground and pinioned. One of them, who I now know to be Kieran Bratt spat at me and said
'shut up copper or we'll kick the shit out of you'. At that stage the largest of the youths who
were attacking me sat on my legs and groin whilst Bratt with another youth called Louis
Bucknell knelt on my shoulders and pinioned my arms. I was extremely frightened at this
stage and fearful for my life and safety.

I had been on the ground for a minute or two and was attempting to get up when I heard
the sound of police sirens. The youths then let go. I got to my feet and went to see if PC 37
was alright. He was covered with blood which seemed to come from his nose area.
I assisted him to his feet and to waiting police transport.

Of the youths I remember Bucknell was wearing a purple tie-dye T shirt with white
trousers and black trainers. Baker was wearing a brown bomber type jacket with black
jeans and trainers and a baseball cap. Bratt, who was about 5' 9" with collar length hair
and bad acne was wearing a denim jacket and jeans with white trainers and a white T shirt.

Signed: R. Parry .

Signature witnessed by: S. Jordan

WITNESS STATEMENT

Statement of   Martin Kemp PC 37 . . . .

Age if under 21   . . . .

This statement (consisting of   2   pages each signed by me) is true to the best of my know-ledge and belief and I make it knowing that, if it is tendered in evidence, I shall be liable to prosecution if I have wilfully stated in it anything which I know to be false or do not believe to be true.

Dated the   14th   day of   July   2006

Signature: . . . . M Kemp . . . .

I am a Police Officer. On 11th July 2006 I commenced duty at 8 am as a car response driver. At about 3.20 pm. I was called to a domestic incident at Augustinian Close on the Abbey Estate, Upton. I was single manned at this time. On arriving at Augustinian Close a member of the public directed me to the rear of Fountains House where I saw a man I know to be Nicholas Spring. He was speaking to a girl with long fair hair who he identified as his girlfriend. He was shouting at her that she was not having her car keys because she had been drinking. It was obvious to me that they had both been drinking. I asked where she had to go and she said that she lived in Lymehurst. I stated that was not a problem and if she went to my police car I would ensure that she got home and could collect her car and keys when she was sober.

During this conversation Spring was joined by 3 other males, one of whom I knew as Sean Baker. The other two were not known to me. All 4 men were white. Of the 2 others the first who I shall call (1) was about 6 foot tall with a blue denim jacket, blue shirt, blue jeans and white trainers. He had dark cropped hair and tattoos on his wrists. The other man (2) was 5 10, also with dark cropped hair. He was wearing a brown jacket with black jeans and white trainers. He had a light coloured shirt on but I do not recall if it was white or grey. Both men appeared to be in their early twenties.

Spring didn't say much at this stage and after I had arranged transport for the girl everyone seemed happy. I then walked the girl across to my police car. The four men had walked in the direction of the phone box at the far end of the Close. I reached the police vehicle and as I did I heard a loud bang. I turned to see Spring and the others and could clearly hear Spring shouting that his girl was 'going off with a fucking pig'. I walked towards them and they walked towards me. As I got close to them Spring raised his fists and pushed them towards my face in a 'boxer like' pose. I pushed his hands away and he called me a 'fucking wanker'. I then decided to arrest him for an offence under section 4 of the Public Order Act 1986. I put my left hand on his right shoulder and said 'you are under arrest'. At this point Spring threw a punch at my head with his left fist. The punch missed but he then threw further punches at me which connected with my upper body. I then grabbed hold of him and wrestled him to the ground. In doing so I lost the grip on my radio which fell a few feet away. Whilst I was wrestling with Spring I attempted to reach my radio to call for assistance but he shouted out 'don't let him get it' and man 2 kicked it away so that I could not possibly reach it. We continued to struggle with Spring throwing punches. By this stage the original group had been joined by a number of others from Fountains House who formed a ring about me. At this stage I was on top of Spring. Man 1 then came up and with his right foot and kicked me on the left thigh. Spring shouted 'get the bastard off me'. I shouted back 'anyone who tries will get nicked'.

Spring continued to struggle and shout. My watch had come off my wrist and there was some money on the floor. The money was not mine. Male 2 then picked up the money whilst another youth took the watch. I was restraining Spring and had my hands on his shoulders whilst I was attempting to restrain him from kicking me by holding his legs with my knees. At this stage Spring shouted at the group and in particular at man 2 'Get him off me, kick the bastard in the face or you're out of my house and back on the fucking street'. Man 2 appeared to do nothing and Spring shouted out again 'you're a fucking wanker'. Spring then managed to get his arms free again and punched out hitting me in the chest, body, back and head. I pinned his arms with my hands and told him he was lucky that I wasn't going to hit him back. At this point I looked up and man 2 was standing right in front of me and kicked me in the face. It was a quite a deliberate kick as I am sure that he paused before doing it. I lost my grip on Spring and felt a rain of kicks from a number of quarters. One of those kicking me was Sean Baker and man 1. I was pushed off Spring by the force of the blows.

At this point Spring managed to get free and I then heard a police siren and the group began to scatter. Other officers then arrived. I saw Spring, Baker and man 1, who I now know as Martin Thompson, being arrested as were a number of others. However I did not see man 2.

I sustained injuries to my face and body and was admitted to Upton District Hospital where they diagnosed a broken nose and fairly extensive bruising.

Signed: *M Kemp*

Signature witnessed by: *G.G. Hartley*

WITNESS STATEMENT

Statement of   Charlotte Robinson WPC 7 ....

Age if under 21   ....

This statement (consisting of   1   pages each signed by me) is true to the best of my knowledge and belief and I make it knowing that, if it is tendered in evidence, I shall be liable to prosecution if I have wilfully stated in it anything which I know to be false or do not believe to be true.

Dated the   14th   day of   July   2006

Signature: *C Robinson* ....

I am WPC 7 of the Downshire Constabulary currently stationed at Upton. At 15.43 hrs on 11th July 2006 I was on duty in full police uniform in a marked police vehicle in company with police sergeant Church when as a result of information received we attended Augustinian Close on the Abbey Estate.

On arrival I saw a number of youths dispersing from outside Fountains House with PC 37 Kemp lying in the road. About 20 feet away from him PC 211 was getting up from the ground. I stopped the vehicle and ran up to PC Kemp. As I did so he shouted 'get the one in the brown jacket he's just kicked me'. I saw a male running up the slope by the side of Fountains House about 30 yards away. He was with but slightly ahead of a youth I know as Sean Baker. At this stage PC Kemp shouted out 'Get Baker as well he kicked me too'. I gave chase and managed to catch Baker but the man in the brown jacket had run to a blue Cavalier parked at the rear of Fountains House. He got into the driver's door and 2 others got in the car and it drove away. I was able to see the number plate and remember the first part of the registration as CLP but as I was in the process of arresting Sean Baker I was unable to make a full mental note of the number of the car.

I managed to restrain Baker who was struggling and then arrested him for assault on PC Kemp. I handcuffed him and cautioned him and he replied 'I can't hear you'. I then placed him in the rear of a marked police van and he was subsequently conveyed to Upton police station arriving at 16.07 hours when he was taken in front of the custody sergeant.

Signed: *C Robinson*

Signature witnessed by: *G.G. Hartley*

WITNESS STATEMENT

Statement of   Ronald Keith PC 375 ....

Age if under 21   ....

This statement (consisting of **1** pages each signed by me) is true to the best of my knowledge and belief and I make it knowing that, if it is tendered in evidence, I shall be liable to prosecution if I have wilfully stated in it anything which I know to be false or do not believe to be true.

Dated the   12th   day of   July   2006

Signature: ...... *RKeith* ....

On the 11th July 2006 I was on duty with PC 63 Raymond Tarry in a marked police vehicle. At about 19.30 hours we were outside Tesco's on the Upton Road when I noticed a metallic blue Vauxhall Cavalier registration number CLY 853X. This vehicle was being driven by a single white male and was driving very slowly and in an erratic manner. As a result of information that we had received earlier and because of the way that the vehicle was being driven I decided to stop the vehicle. This we did about 300 yards past Tesco's at the junction of the Upton and Lymehurst roads.

I approached the vehicle and spoke to the driver who I know as John Hanson. I leant in to the open window of the car, seized the keys and asked him to get out. He was very unsteady on his feet and disorientated. After he got out he collapsed on to the ground. I then arrested him on suspicion of driving a motor vehicle whilst under the influence of drugs and on suspicion of attempted robbery and cautioned him. I do not think that he understood the caution. Together with PC Tarry I then handcuffed him and called for police transport. He was then conveyed to Upton police station where the facts were related to the custody sergeant.

At the time of his arrest he was wearing a brown sports coat, black trousers and trainers.

Signed: *RKeith*

Signature witnessed by: *BBlake*.

WITNESS STATEMENT

Statement of   P. Waller PS 8 . . . .

Age if under 21   . . . .

This statement (consisting of 1 pages each signed by me) is true to the best of my knowledge and belief and I make it knowing that, if it is tendered in evidence, I shall be liable to prosecution if I have wilfully stated in it anything which I know to be false or do not believe to be true.

Dated the 12th day of July 2006

Signature: *P Waller* . . . .

On the 11th July 2006 at 19.45 hours I was the custody sergeant at Upton Police Station. At that time PC 375 and PC 63 brought a John Hanson into the custody area. I then opened a custody record on the CJS computer and the number 5OBC/00317/06 was allocated to the record.

Mr Hanson was unable to stand properly and was obviously disorientated. His eyes were glazed and his breath smelt of intoxicating liquor. I formed the view that he was intoxicated. PC 375 related the facts to me and as a result of what had happened during the the afternoon on the 11th July, the facts of which were known to me, I then arrested him on suspicion of an offence of violent disorder and told him that he was being detained for the breathalyser procedure to be conducted and that in addition he was under arrest on suspicion of robbery. I cautioned him to which he then replied 'I only tried to rob the place'. This was contemporaneously recorded on form 439M and 441N and attached to the custody record.

I then commenced the breathalyser procedure but after a short period it was apparent that Mr Hanson was unable to understand what was going on and I then had him placed in cell 11 and the FME was called. At this stage I was unable to give him his rights as he was intoxicated. On her arrival at 21.13 a specimen of blood was taken from Mr Hanson. The FME, Dr Craig also carried out a number of tests on Mr Hanson in my presence in the detention room. I then arrested Mr Hanson for an offence of driving a motor vehicle on a road whilst unfit to drive through drink or drugs and further cautioned him to which he made no reply.

I produce the custody record, marked as exhibit PW/1.

Signed: *P Waller*

Signature witnessed by: *R Keith*

<u>WITNESS STATEMENT</u>

Statement of   Nuala Carroll ....

Age if under 21   19 ....

This statement (consisting of **1** pages each signed by me) is true to the best of my know-ledge and belief and I make it knowing that, if it is tendered in evidence, I shall be liable to prosecution if I have wilfully stated in it anything which I know to be false or do not believe to be true.

Dated the   **14th** day of   **July**   2006

Signature: ....**Nuala Carroll**...

I am the above named. I live with my sister, Michelle Davison in Jervaulx House on the Abbey Estate in Upton. I have just finished studying for my 'A' levels at Upton College and hope to go on to a degree course in Portsmouth in September.

On 11th July 2006 I was at home when my sister came in and asked me to telephone the police. Before I did this I looked out of the window of the flat and saw Nick Spring and his girlfriend arguing, it looked to me as if Nick had hit her as she was clutching her face and crying hysterically. I telephoned the police and a car arrived about 5 minutes later with one police officer in it. I could see that Nick was with a number of other men. I didn't recognise any of them except that I remember one was wearing a brown type bomber jacket. When the policeman arrived there was a bit of noise and then it seemed to go quiet and I went to make some tea in the kitchen which overlooks the other side of Jervaulx House.

A few minutes after I heard a loud bang. I carried on making the tea but then after a few more minutes I heard shouting and screaming. I went to the window and saw 2 police officers being set on by a number of men. Some of them I recognised as coming from Fountains House opposite. The first police officer to arrive, who was a very large man appeared to be sitting on Nick, I heard him shouting out 'get the fuck off me' and 'you're strangling me'. The second officer to arrive, who was much smaller than the first officer and was quite slight, was being held back and hit by 3 men from Fountains House, includ-ing one I recognised as Sean Baker. I also think I recognised John Hanson in the crowd that had gathered around. I can't remember what he was wearing. He just seemed to be on the edge of the fight. I know John from the pub in Upton where I used to work as a part-time bar maid, he has only just come out of prison.

The fight seemed to go on for ages and while it was going on a number of people seemed to get involved and there were a number of people watching. I kept on watching but it was difficult to see all the time although I could hear a lot of threats and swearing. Towards the end of the incident, just before more police officers arrived I saw a man come out of the crowd and deliberately kick the first officer in the face. It made a sickening dull thud and must have been very painful. Then others started to kick and push him and Nick got free, stood up and went to talk with his girlfriend who was standing close by. At this stage a number of other policemen arrived and everybody scattered. I saw Sean Baker being arrested and Martin Thompson and Nick Spring. I don't really recall what clothes were worn by whom or what their footwear was.

I am willing to attend court and give evidence.

Signed: Nuala Carroll

Signature witnessed by: C Robinson

WITNESS STATEMENT

Statement of   Paula Anne Ryan . . . .

Age if under 21   . . . .

This statement (consisting of   pages each signed by me) is true to the best of my knowledge and belief and I make it knowing that, if it is tendered in evidence, I shall be liable to prosecution if I have wilfully stated in it anything which I know to be false or do not believe to be true.

Dated the   14th   day of   July   2006

Signature: P A Ryan . . . .

I am Paula Anne Ryan and I live on the Abbey Estate, Upton at an address known to police.

At about 3.40 pm on the 11th July 2006 I was walking along Augustian Close coming from Bishop Montford School. I had my 5-year-old son, Thomas, with me and I was pushing my daughter Siobhan in a push chair.

As I came round the corner from the road which leads to the school I heard loud shouts from several male voices. I could see 2 men lying on the road just outside Fountains House. I immediately saw that one of the men was a police officer who was restraining a man on the tarmac. The man was lying on his back and the police officer was holding his arms and lying half across the man's chest.

I recognised the man as Nick Spring who I have known for 4 years or so, but only on a casual basis. He was shouting very loudly things like 'get off me', 'bastard, get off you bastard' and a barrage of foul language like that. I did not hear the police officer say anything. Nick was kicking violently with his legs and struggling to escape from the officer.

At that time I saw a number of men immediately next to the policeman and Nick. A handful of onlookers had gathered, including a number of youths from Fountains House. There were 2 men in particular close to the policeman, one was Sean Baker, the other was a man I have seen before but not recently. He was wearing a short jacket, I can't remember the colour. He had his hair short cropped and had dark trousers and white trainers on. I'm not sure that I would recognise the man again. Sean was wearing white trainers as well.

Nick was struggling very violently. I saw him break free a couple of times and the officer would grab him. Each time Nick would lash out at him, punching out with clenched fists and kicking out in a crazed and determined manner, trying with all his effort to punch the policeman in the head and face as hard as he could. The police officer's face was red where he had been punched, although I could see no blood. As Nick was flailing away the police officer bent forward to duck the punches and at the same time grabbed Nick around the waist and pushed him to the ground. Nick landed on his back and the policeman landed squarely on Nick's front. Sean and the other man carried on standing next to the policeman. They were swearing and saying things like 'get off him or you're dead' and other threats. The crowd was also noisy. During the fight another officer arrived. I don't know where he came from but some of the youths were struggling with him to prevent him from assisting his colleague. I then saw a girl come up to where Nick and the policeman were and tried to pull Nick off the policeman. Nick shrugged the girl off and continued to kick and punch in a violent manner. It was obvious nothing was going to stop him.

At that stage a whole load of other police officers arrived and a number of the crowd, including Nick and Sean were arrested. I did not see the man in the dark jacket again but I lost sight of a lot of what was going on because of the number of police and onlookers although I did have a clear and uninterrupted view of the incident which lasted for at least 5 to 10 minutes. I have a clear recollection of how red the police officer's face had turned from being repeatedly punched by Nick Spring.

I am willing to attend court and give evidence.

Signed: *D A Ryan*

Signature witnessed by: *C Robinson*

WITNESS STATEMENT

Statement of   Michele Martine Davison . . . .

Age if under 21   . . . .

This statement (consisting of **1** pages each signed by me) is true to the best of my know-ledge and belief and I make it knowing that, if it is tendered in evidence, I shall be liable to prosecution if I have wilfully stated in it anything which I know to be false or do not believe to be true.

Dated the   *14th*   day of   *July*   2006

Signature: . . .*Michele Davison*. . . . .

I live with my husband, 11-month-old son and sister Nuala in Jervaulx House on Abbey Estate in Upton.

At about 3.15 pm on 11th July 2006 I noticed an incident outside Fountains House, which is opposite Jervaulx House, involving Nick Spring and his girlfriend. Because I was con-cerned I asked Nuala to telephone the police when I got back to my flat. After a while a police car arrived and later I saw Nick's girlfriend go with the police officer to his car. At the same time Nick and a number of other men walked down to the phone kiosk at the bottom of the close. Nick was with Sean Baker and Martin Thompson and another man who I don't know. I can't really remember what they were wearing but Martin had a dark jacket on and the other man was wearing white trainers. As they got to the kiosk I saw Nick kick the glass in the kiosk and there was a loud bang as if it had smashed.

The policeman left Nick's girlfriend and walked towards the kiosk. Nick walked towards him with his friends just behind. I then heard Nick say 'he pushed me' pointing behind him with his thumb. At that stage Nick began to turn as if to walk away and the policeman took hold of his right arm. At that they began to struggle and were having a scuffle in the middle of the road. They both fell to the ground, the officer managing to sit on top of Nick and pinning his arms to the ground. After a while a number of other youths came out of Fountains House and joined Nick's friends who were gathered round the officer. Nick was struggling violently and kicking and lashing out at the officer. At one stage I saw one of the group kick the officer's radio away and there was a lot of shouting and swearing and abuse but I couldn't understand what was being said.

After a while another police officer arrived and he was set on by some of the youths from Fountains House. They were trying to stop him interfering with Nick Spring. I saw the girl get out of the car and go up to the group. I then saw one of the group, I think it was the male with the white trainers, approach the policeman who was restraining Nick and with great force kicked the officer directly in the face. The blow was with such force that the policeman's head went back and he lost his grip on Nick. Then a number of the group started to punch and kick the officer. At that time the other officer was being restrained near the edge of the group. I can't be sure but I think he was on the ground, my main atten-tion was directed towards the first officer who had arrived.

I had already phoned the police during the fight but I became so incensed at their beha-viour that I left and phoned again. When I came back I saw that a number of other officers had arrived and the group had dispersed and were being chased by the police. A number of people were arrested and taken away by the police.

I am willing to attend court and give evidence.

Signed: *Michele Davison*

Signature witnessed by: *C Robinson*

WITNESS STATEMENT

Statement of   Robert Lloyd-Jones . . . .
Age if under 21   . . . . .Occupation: Dental Practitioner

This statement (consisting of **1** pages each signed by me) is true to the best of my knowledge and belief and I make it knowing that, if it is tendered in evidence, I shall be liable to prosecution if I have wilfully stated in it anything which I know to be false or do not believe to be true.

Dated the   17th day of   July   2006

Signature: . . . .

I am a registered Dental Practitioner and my qualifications are: BDS 1977.

On the 17th July 2006 I examined Martin Kemp and found him to be suffering from psychological trauma associated with dental trauma.

On examination the upper right first central incisor was fractured at its distar incisal edge. This has been repaired by an incisal alisecthed restoration but in the long term may become non vital and need further treatment.

There was a fractured filling at the lower right first permanent premolar which was repaired with a routine filling.

There was extensive bruising to the sockets of the upper right molar teeth which was eased and improved by reshaping the occular fillings.

1. The injury to the upper right first central incisor was probably caused by minor trauma (physical force).

2. The fractured filling and the bruising of the sockets of the upper molar teeth may have been caused by stress related to a traumatic incident.

Signed: *Lloyd-Jones*

Signature witnessed by: *G Jordan*

WITNESS STATEMENT

Statement of   Richard Purkiss BSc . . . .

Age if under 21   . . . .

This statement (consisting of 1 pages each signed by me) is true to the best of my knowledge and belief and I make it knowing that, if it is tendered in evidence, I shall be liable to prosecution if I have wilfully stated in it anything which I know to be false or do not believe to be true.

Dated the   10th   day of   August   2006

Signature: . . . . . APurkiss . . . .

I am a forensic scientist employed by the Downshire Constabulary. On the 2nd August 2006 I took receipt of exhibit CC/1 a blood specimen labelled John Hanson. I tested the specimen and found it to contain not less than 103 milligrams of alcohol per 100 millilitres of blood.

Signed: APurkiss

Signature witnessed by: S.T. Harcourt

WITNESS STATEMENT

Statement of   Charlotte Craig. Forensic Medical Examiner . . . .

Age if under 21   . . . .

This statement (consisting of **1** pages each signed by me) is true to the best of my knowledge and belief and I make it knowing that, if it is tendered in evidence, I shall be liable to prosecution if I have wilfully stated in it anything which I know to be false or do not believe to be true.

Dated the   11th   day of   July   2006

Signature: . . . *Charlotte Craig* . . . .

On the 11th July 2006 I was called to Upton Police Station arriving at 21.09 hours. I then examined a man identified to me as John Hanson. I conducted a number of tests on Mr Hanson and as a result of my examination I formed the view that he was drunk and unfit to drive a motor vehicle. He was then asked to provide a specimen of blood which I took from him. I then divided the specimen into two parts labelled CC/JH/1 (container no. 01765) and CC/JH/2 (01766). In my presence Mr Hanson was offered the second container which he refused.

Signed: *Charlotte Craig.*

Signature witnessed by: P C H Mansell

<u>WITNESS STATEMENT</u>

Statement of　　　　　Michael Kelly . . . .

Age if under 21　　　　. . . . .

This statement (consisting of **1** pages each signed by me) is true to the best of my knowledge and belief and I make it knowing that, if it is tendered in evidence, I shall be liable to prosecution if I have wilfully stated in it anything which I know to be false or do not believe to be true.

Dated the　**12th** day of　**July**　　2006

Signature:　. . . . . **Michael Kelly** . . . .

I am the owner of Kelly's off-licence in Crewkerne Street, I live in a flat over the shop with my family. On 11th July 2006 at about 6.25 pm. I was at the till when a man burst into the shop. He was white, about 25, 5' 10" and had close cropped dark hair. He was wearing a brown jacket, blue shirt, jeans and white trainers. When he came into the shop he was waving his arms around and shouting. As he came up to the till he pulled his jacket over his face and rushed around the side of the counter shouting 'This is a stick up. Get on the floor'. He didn't have any weapon. The shop is well lit having a large front window and the lights were on. I am certain I would be able to recognise him again.

I started to go down on the floor and he pushed me on the neck. As I got to the floor he shouted at me again to open the till. As I turned to open the till I intended to grab him around the waist or the legs but Francis came running across and pushed him over me and into a display by the front window. I got up and as Francis appeared to be dealing with matters I decided the best thing was to ring the police. The male was shouting all the time this was going on and thrashing around. I tried to keep an eye on what was going on. I saw the male strike Francis on the nose and he then got up charged at me and shouted 'Ring the fucking police and you're dead'. He pushed me over again and ran out of the shop. Francis chased after him and I carried on contacting the police.

I am willing to attend court.

Signed:　**Michael Kelly**

Signature witnessed by:　**RKeith**

WITNESS STATEMENT

Statement of   Francis Kelly ....

Age if under 21   ....

This statement (consisting of 1 pages each signed by me) is true to the best of my knowledge and belief and I make it knowing that, if it is tendered in evidence, I shall be liable to prosecution if I have wilfully stated in it anything which I know to be false or do not believe to be true.

Dated the   12th   day of   July   2006

Signature: *Francis Kelly* ....

I am the above named and live at the address overleaf. I am employed by my brother Michael at his off-licence in Crewkerne Street. On 11th July 2006 I was in the shop in the store room at the back of the shop when at about 6.25 pm. I heard a man shouting at Michael to get on the floor. I went to the door of the stock room and saw a man about 25–30, 6' tall with a blue jacket, black jeans and trainers pushing Michael by the neck. The shop is well lit and the lights were on. I would recognise him again. As he was pushing Michael he also started to hit him and he was screaming at him to open the till. I couldn't see if he was armed or had a weapon but as he had his back to me I ran at him and pushed him over Michael into a display near the window.

After he had fallen into the display I leaped on him and we started to fight. He was obviously drunk and struggled very violently. The next thing I knew he had punched me in the face and caused me to loosen my grip on him. With that he got up and ran over to Michael who was at the telephone. He shouted out 'Call the police and you're fucking dead' and then ran out of the shop colliding with a customer who was coming through the door.

I was dazed but managed to run after him and chased him part of the way down the street to the junction with Crown Street. As I got to the corner I saw him getting into a metallic blue Vauxhall Cavalier which drove down Crown Street in the direction of the Old Market Place. I did not see any one else in the vehicle and I did not manage to take the registration number of the car although I think it was 'Y' registered.

I would be willing to attend court.

Signed: *Francis Kelly*

Signature witnessed by: *RKeith*

DOWNSHIRE CONSTABULARY   Form MG15(T)
RECORD OF TAPE RECORDED INTERVIEW

Person interviewed	Nicholas SPRING	Police Exhibit No TH1
Place of interview	UPTON POLICE STATION	Number of pages 3
Date of interview	11.07.06	
Time commenced	20.03	Time concluded 20.24
Duration of interview	21 MINS	Tape Reference no's 101124
Interviewing Officer(s)	WPC 7 ROBINSON	
Other persons present	DC 431 COLE, Mr J ARCHER (SOLICITOR)	

Tape counter times	Person speaking	Text
001		INTRODUCTION TO INTERVIEW. CAUTIONED
054		WPC ROBINSON explained that SPRING had been arrested at 3.30 pm following an incident at the Abbey Estate involving SPRING and others.
0410		General discussion about the estate and who lived with SPRING including SEAN BAKER, MARTIN THOMPSON, ANTHONY MEAD AND JOHN HANSON.
0715	ROBINSON	Nick, why did you assault PC KEMP?
	SPRING	I didn't, he assaulted me. I went to speak to him after he shouted out to me, when Charlie was about to get in his car. We met in the road and he put his hand up and grabbed my arm . . .
	COLE	Which arm?
	SPRING	My right one. I pushed him away and he grabbed me round the neck and pulled me to the ground. WPC Robinson then reads the first half of PC Kemp's statement.
	ROBINSON	You were clearly told you were under arrest but you were looking for a fight as your girlfriend was going off with PC Kemp.
	SPRING	No. KEMP is enormous you'd have to be fucking mad to fight him . . .
1020	COLE	But you did Nick, didn't you.
	SPRING	No, I defended myself, he was strangling me.
	ROBINSON	Who else was there?
	SPRING	The BAKERS, LOUIS BUCKNALL, TONY, JOHN, . . .
	ROBINSON	JOHN who?
	SPRING	HANSON.
	ROBINSON	You said earlier that he was living with you
	SPRING	Yes
	ROBINSON	In the fight PC KEMP was kicked in the face. He is seriously injured. Who kicked him?
	SPRING	JOHN.
	ROBINSON	But you told him to.

	SPRING	Never. I'm asthmatic, KEMP was strangling me, I couldn't breath and I just shouted to get off, to get him off . . .
1215	ROBINSON	Reads remainder of PC KEMP'S statement. You told HANSON to kick him in the face.
	SPRING	I didn't. HANSON kicked him in the face. He hates KEMP because he got him sent down last time. I just wanted KEMP to stop throttling me so I asked for help.
	ROBINSON	You threatened to put him out on the street.
1500	SPRING	That's rubbish, HANSON could always go and live in another squat or with his Mum or girlfriend, he didn't have to stay with me.

Further questions and discussion about the fight. SPRING Stated that he was too pre-occupied with what was going on with PC KEMP to notice anything else. He agreed that HANSON had kicked the radio away. He also stated that a number of the others appeared to have kicked or punched PC KEMP but denied that he encouraged them in any way.

INTERVIEW CONCLUDES 20.24 HOURS.

DOWNSHIRE CONSTABULARY   Form MG 15(T)
RECORD OF TAPE RECORDED INTERVIEW

Person interviewed	John HANSON	Police Exhibit No TH1
Place of interview	UPTON POLICE STATION	Number of pages 3
Date of interview	12.07.06	
Time commenced	12.07	Time concluded 12.45
Duration of interview	38 MINS	Tape Reference no's 101137
Interviewing Officer(s)	WPC 7 ROBINSON	
Other persons present	DC 431 COLE, Mr J ARCHER (SOLICITOR)	

Tape counter times	Person speaking	Text
001		INTRODUCTION TO INTERVIEW. CAUTIONED
024		WPC ROBINSON explained that HANSON had been arrested at 19.30 hours by police on suspicion of an assault at Kelly's off-licence.
0350		Discussion regarding what HANSON had been doing prior to the incident. He stated that he had been drinking throughout the day. He'd been to 3 pubs, the last being the Ratcatcher. He cannot remember anything after the Ratcatcher. He was drinking cider and might have had some lager and whisky. He cannot remember going into Kelly's and was not aware until told by an Inspector during his detention.
0900		WPC Robinson read excerpts from Mr F Kelly's statement but HANSON could still not remember. Discussion of injuries received, he stated he had a cut wrist and a sore neck and shoulder.
1100		Discussion regarding statement by Mr Kelly.
1415	WPC 7	So you can't remember any of that?
	HANSON	No, not at all, no.
1530		WPC Robinson showed HANSON the custody record where the Custody Sergeant had written his reply when being booked in. HANSON could not remember saying 'All I tried to do was rob the place'.
1640		Discussion regarding possession of cannabis.
		HANSON accepts the tin is his and the 2 pieces of greeny brown substance is cannabis belonging to him and that possession of cannabis is illegal.
1850		DC Cole asked HANSON to describe his clothing and self.
	HANSON	About 5' 11", dark hair.
	COLE	Brown wouldn't you say.
	HANSON	Brown, darkish anyway, I'm wearing a brown sports coat, blue denim shirt, black denim jeans, white trainers. Green brown eyes.
	COLE	Darkish skinned?
	HANSON	No.

	COLE	With cropped hair.
	HANSON	Close cut, not cropped.
	COLE	Well I'd say cropped.
	HANSON	That's for you.
2000	SOLICITOR	That can be determined, you've taken his photo.
	COLE	Yes. You know Nick Spring?
	HANSON	Yes.
	COLE	And you've been staying with him at Fountains House?
	HANSON	Yes, for about the last week.
	COLE	Since you were released from prison.
		Yesterday afternoon there was an incident on the Abbey Estate involving Spring. Where were you at 3.30 yesterday?
	HANSON	I think I was in the 'Coach' with VICKY BRYANT. Discussion regarding Vicky Bryant and where she lives.
2215	COLE	What about the car you were driving. Is that yours?
	HANSON	What car?
	COLE	Come off it John, the one you were driving when you were nicked.
	HANSON	I can't drive.
	COLE	That's what the arresting officer said.
	HANSON	No need to get snidey. I've had enough of this. Reminded of the caution/given special caution.
	ROBINSON	Whose car is it CLP 853Y a blue Cavalier.
	HANSON	It's not mine, I don't have a car.
	ROBINSON	You were driving it, whose is it?
	HANSON	I've had enough, I don't feel well.
	ROBINSON	You look fine to me. Whose is it?
	HANSON	No comment. I want to speak to Mr Archer.
	Tape off.	
2500	SOLICITOR	My client finds your manner aggressive. He is unwell and is currently being treated by his GP. On legal advice he does not wish to answer any further questions at this stage.
2515		Further matters put to HANSON who declines to comment.
2900		Interview terminated.

DOWNSHIRE CONSTABULARY

C.R. No.　7651/02

Division　A　**Date**　14th July 2006

Antecedents of: (full name)　John Hanson

Committed from　Upton　**Magistrates' Court on**　17th July 2006

For trial/sentence at　Upton Crown　Court

for offence(s) of　Grievous Bodily Harm with intent, Violent Disorder, Robbery

---

Date and place of birth: 12.04.82, Temple Newsome　　**Age:** 24 years

Date of first entry into U.K.: n/a　　**Nationality:** British

Date of arrest: 11.07.06, Remanded in custody　　**In custody/on bail:** In custody

Education: 1993–1998 Bishop Cross School, Disbury Bridge.
　　　　　　1998–1999 Upton Technical College

Main employments since leaving school

1999–2002	Royal Artillery	Bombadier	
2002–2004	Unemployed		
2005	Sherratts Furniture	Labourer	Dismissed for theft
2006	Unemployed		

Present employment: (Show date of commencement, capacity in which employed, net salary/wage and employer's assessment.)

Hanson is unemployed and in receipt of income support. Amount not disclosed.

At the time of his arrest he was a single man living with friends at 27 Fountains House, Abbot's Down, Abbey Estate, Upton, Downshire.

Hanson does not hold a firearms/shotgun certificate.

At time of the offence Hanson was on licence from Portsmouth Prison. He was released on 28.06.06 having served 2 months of a 4 month sentence for ABH, theft and kindred offences.

List of previous convictions attached:

Offences against the person:	1	**Theft and kindred offences:**	11
Offences against property:	3	**Public Order offences:**	2
Fraud and kindred offences:	0	**Others:**	0

If recently fined state whether paid or not: None traced

Date of last release from custodial sentence: 28.06.06

Names of co-prisoners (if dealt with elsewhere, give details):

DOWNSHIRE CONSTABULARY

PREVIOUS CONVICTIONS

Convictions recorded against: John Hanson   CRO No: 7651/02

Charged in name of: John Hanson   * Denotes spent conviction

Date	Court	Offence(s) (with details of any offence)	Sentence	Date of Release
12.05.02	Driffield Mags	Theft × 3 Taking without consent Criminal Damage	CSO 100 hours CSO 100 hours £135.00 compensation	
18.10.02	Alderley Mags	Theft × 2 S. 4 Public Order Act Breach CSO	6 months Young Offenders Institution 2 months Y.O. 6 months Y.O. concurrent	18.01.03
11.6.03		Deception × 3	Probation 2 years	
31.08.04	Upton Crown Court	Aggravated vehicle taking Affary Making off without payment	6 months' Imprisonment L/E Disqualified 1 year 4 months' imp concurrent 2 months' imp Concurrent	30.11.05
29.06.06	Driffield Mags	Actual Bodily Harm	4 months' imprisonment	28.06.06

DOWNSHIRE CONSTABULARY

C.R. No. _____3741/03_____

Division _____A_____ **Date** _____14th July 2006_____

Antecedents of: (full name) _____Nicholas Spring_____

Committed from _____Upton_____ **Magistrates' Court on** _____17th July 2006_____

For trial/sentence at _____Upton Crown_____ **Court**

for offence(s) of _____Grievous Bodily Harm with intent, Violent Disorder_____

Date and place of birth: 21.06.85, Driffield   **Age:** 21 years

Date of first entry into U.K.: n/a   **Nationality:** British

Date of arrest: 11.07.06, Remanded on bail   **In custody/on bail:** on bail

Education: 1996–2001 Upton Comprehensive
                  2001–2002 Upton Technical College

Main employments since leaving school

2002–2005   Various periods of unemployment with casual labouring jobs
2005–2006   Floral Garden Centre.

Present employment: (Show date of commencement, capacity in which employed, net salary/wage and employer's assessment.)

Spring works as a labourer at the Floral Garden Centre, Driffield, earning £160 a week gross, £133.95 net.

At the time of his arrest he was a single man living at 27 Fountains House, Abbot's Down, Abbey Estate, Upton, Downshire.

Spring does not hold a firearms/shotgun certificate.

List of previous convictions attached:

Offences against the person: 0	**Theft and kindred offences:** 2	
Offences against property: 1	**Public Order offences:** 1	
Fraud and kindred offences: 0	**Others:** 0	

If recently fined state whether paid or not: None traced

Date of last release from custodial sentence: n/a

Names of co-prisoners (if dealt with elsewhere, give details):

DOWNSHIRE CONSTABULARY

PREVIOUS CONVICTIONS

Convictions recorded against: Nicholas Spring   CRO No: 3741/03

Charged in name of: Nicholas Spring   * Denotes spent conviction

Date	Court	Offence(s) (with details of any offence)	Sentence	Date of Release
15.06.03	Upton Mags	Theft	Conditional Discharge 12 months	
17.12.03		Taking vehicle without consent	CSO 60 hours	
		Criminal Damage	CSO 60 hours concurrent	
		Breach of Conditional Discharge	CSO 60 hours Concurrent	
31.08.05	Upton Crown Court	Affray	Probation 12 months	

STATEMENT OF JOHN HANSON

I, John Hanson, of HMP Ardington, will say as follows:

I am currently on remand at HMP Ardington and have been since the 11th July. I left full time education in 1995 when I was 17. I had 6 GCSE's and I decided because things were not good at home to join the army. I served in the army for 3 years including a period in Northern Ireland where I witnessed a number of very traumatic incidents. As a result I have felt far from well since then and I believe this has led to my offending. In particular I had been prescribed Prozac from about May by the prison doctors. I am not sure if this led to my loss of memory on the 11th July. It may also explain why I behaved as I am alleged to have behaved in the off-licence. When I woke up in the police station I discovered that the bottle of Prozac which I had contained 4 less tablets than it should. I have never been warned against taking Prozac and alcohol together although I now understand that mixing the 2 can be dangerous.

On the 11th July I was living at 27 Fountains House on the Abbey estate in Upton. I had only been released from prison the week before from a sentence of 4 months' imprisonment imposed by Driffield Magistrates on the 29th April. I was living with Nick Spring at Fountains House but my girlfriend, Vicky Bryant had offered me a place at her house and I was due to move there on the 12th. I was also able to live with my Mother in Driffield but because of the events which led to my imprisonment in April I was not anxious to move there. I have known Nick since 2004 and we were co-defendants in the charge that led to me being imprisoned in August of 2004. I was at that time working for Sherratts furniture as a labourer but lost my job, not because of theft, but because I was imprisoned.

On the 11th July I received some money (£850) from an inheritance and I decided to celebrate. The Cavalier is Vicky Bryant's I had borrowed it the day before to get back from Vicky's place. I left Fountains House about 10 am and collected the cheque from Chapmans (the solicitors in Upton) and then arranged to get some money from the bank. I had left the car and the keys at Fountains House. After I had got some money from the bank I went drinking. I was in the 3 Bells, then the Coach and Horses where I met Vicky and some other friends and later I went to the Ratcatcher. When I got to the Ratcatcher it was about 4 pm Tony a bloke who was also staying with Nick came in with Louis Bucknell, Simon Bratt, Kieran Bratt and a load of others. I could see that he had the keys to the Cavalier. They were all drunk or stoned. We had a row about him driving it and I took the keys back. They all then left. I was pretty drunk by this time and until I woke in the Police Station that is about all I can remember.

I have no recollection of going back to the Abbey Estate. I have spoken to Vicky and she is sure that I was with her at about 3 o'clock. I left her and went to the 'Rat' to meet a friend of mine called Frank. I owed him £50 and had arranged to pay him back. As far as I know I did but I haven't seen him since and although Vicky and some of my friends have been trying to find him it may not be easy as he is a 'Traveller'.

I do not dispute that I was in Kelly's off-licence and I understand that I am on the in-store video. I would like advice on my plea as I have, once again, no recollection of what took place there and no recollection of what I am alleged to have said to the custody sergeant at Upton Police station.

CUSTODY RECORD Police & Criminal Evidence Act 1984

Police Station   Force/Station reference

ARREST	DETAINEE

Comments made: YES/~~NO~~
 Where arrested: Upton Road jn Lymehurst Road
 Arrested by:
   Name: Keith
   Rank/No: 375   Station: Upton
      Time of arrest: 1932 Date: 11.7.06
 Time of arrival at Station: 1943 Date: 11.7.06
	Surname: Hanson
	 Forenames: John
	 Address: 27 Fountains House
	      Abbey Estate
	      Upton
	
	 Occupation: Unemployed
	 Age: 24 Date of Birth: 12.4.82
	 Place of Birth: Newton Abbot
	 Height: 5'11' Sex: M
	 Ethnic Appearance: Caucasian
	 Nationality: British

DETENTION AUTHORISED

Attempted robbery

To obtain evidence by questioning

Comments made: YES/~~NO~~
Name: P Waller   Rank/No: P58

Signature: P Waller   Time: Date: 11.7.06

Officer in case
    Name: Cole
    Rank/No: DC

Officer opening record
    Name: Waller
    Rank/No: P58
    Signature: P Waller

PRISONERS RIGHTS

1. A notice setting out my rights has been read to me and I have also been provided with a written notice setting out my entitlements whilst in custody.

    [Signature: John Hanson]   Time: 1945 Date: 11.7.06

Notices of the detained persons rights and entitlements have been read to me and I have received a copy of each. I have been informed of the Grounds for the detention of the detained person.

Appropriate Adult   n/a   Signature   Time: Date:

2. I DO require somebody to be informed of my arrest.

    [Signature: John Hanson]   Time: 1945 Date: 11.7.06

Nominated Person: V Bryant
Address/Contact no:

3. I DO require a solicitor as soon as practicable.

    [Signature: John Hanson]   Time: 1945 Date: 11.7.06

Nominated Solicitor: D.Sol.

Appropriate Adult: n/a   Signature: Time: Date:

MEDICAL DETAILS

Are you currently:– Receiving medication   Remarks:–
              Suffering any illness/injury   Intoxicated
              Suffering any infirmity

(FormCustody) 04/04/1995

CUSTODY RECORD (Property) Police & Criminal Evidence Act 1984

Police Station   Upton

Force/Stn ref   SOBE/00319/06   Date: 11·7·06

Detained Person Surname: Hanson

Forenames: John

Property retained by Police: re value, prevent harm/damage, interfere with evidence or effect an escape			
Description: Bottle Prozac tablets	Qty: 1	Value: N/K	Seal: 00356113
Description: Lighter	Qty: 1	Value:	Seal: ,,
Description: Belt	Qty:	Value:	Seal: ,,
Description: Wallet + various corresp	Qty:	Value:	Seal: ,,
Description: £75 (7×10, 1×5) notes	Qty:	Value:	Seal: ,,
Description: £4·36 (3×1, 2×50 + change)	Qty:	Value:	Seal: ,,

Property retained by Person at own risk

Description: Qty: Value:

1   Packet B+H cigs

1   comb (plastic)

The above is a true record. Property retained by me is at my own risk.

Signature of detainee	Signature of Custody Officer *PWaller*	Name: WALLER P / Rank/No: 585
Refused to sign	Signature of Witness *KSimp*	Name: SIMPSON K / Rank/No: PC 171

I have received all property listed above, subject to any variation shown in the custody record log.

Signature of person receiving	Signature of witness	Name: / Rank/No:

Detainee searched by

Signature *KSimpsn.*   Name: SIMPSON K   Rank/No: PC 171

(FrmPtyCus1) Ver 1 Feb 95

RECORD OF PERSONAL PROPERTY

Sub-Divisional Custody No. SOBE/00317/02

RECORD OF PERSONAL PROPERTY			RECORD OF PERSONAL PROPERTY CONTINUED	
Denominations of Notes	Cash Totals			
10 × 7 : 5 × 1	Notes £ 75			
	£ Coin £ 4			
	Silver £ 20			
	Bronze .16			
	TOTAL £ 79-36			
Item	Other Property			
1	Prozac tablets		Searched by (sign) Klinger.	
2	Lighter		Items 3 + 6	
3	Cigarettes		I wish to retain the above items at my own risk	
4	Wallet + coins		Signature Refused	
5	Belt		Seal No. 0035611B	
6	Comb (plastic)		Officer Sealing (sign) Klinger.	
			Witness (sign) P Walker	
			Property Locker No. 7	
			PROPERTY SUBJECT OF CHARGE	
			None	
			Property Seal No.	
			Officer Sealing (Sign)	
			Witness (Sign)	
			Special Property Reg. No.	

DOWNSHIRE CONSTABULARY

Detainee's Name: John Hanson

Any comments made after reasons for arrest given:

> ' I only tried to rob the place'

Any comments made after grounds for detention explained:

Any reasons given for not requiring legal advice:

Signed: *P Ulculler*   Rank/No: P 58

DOWNSHIRE CONSTABULARY

CONTINUATION OF CUSTODY RECORD

| Page No. | 5 |

Last review of detention conducted at .....1945.....

Sub-Divisional Custody No. ...SOBC/..00317/..06.........

Name .....HANSON.........................

Date	Time	Full details of any action/occurrence involving detained person (include full particulars of all visitors/officers) Individual entries need not be restricted to one line All entries to be signed by the writer	Signature
11.7.06	1945	Fit + well. Detention authorised.	PS8
	1955	To cell (8). Check every 15 mins due to state of dp.	۱۱
	2010	Checked in cell; asleep.	۱۱
	2025	ditto	۱۱
	2040	ditto	۱۱
	2055	ditto	۱۱
	2110	Checked in cell; asleep. Waken for ex by RMF. Blood with consent. Concluded 2119. On arrest suspect stated in response to caution 'I only tried to rob the place'. Pillaller	۱۱ PS8
	2125	Awake. In cell. Refreshment + tea provided.	۱۱
	2140	Awake drinking tea.	۱۱
	2155	Asleep	۱۱
	2210	ditto	۱۱
	2225	Wakened to check alright	۱۱
	2240	Asleep	
	2255	Asleep.	
	23:10	Asleep:- To be checked every 30 mins.	PS34
	23:40	"	"
12/7/06	00:10	Asleep	"
	00:40	"	"
	01:10	"	'
	01:45	Further detention authorised to obtain evidence by questioning. Review at 07:45. Check every hour.	"

DOWNSHIRE CONSTABULARY

CONTINUATION OF CUSTODY RECORD

| | | Page No. | 6 |

| Last review of detention conducted at ....O.I.4.5.... | Sub-Divisional Custody No. ....SOBE./.OO.3I7./.06.......... |
| .... | Name ....HANSON...................................... |

Date	Time	Full details of any action/occurrence involving detained person (include full particulars of all visitors/officers) Individual entries need not be restricted to one line All entries to be signed by the writer	Signature
12/7/06	02:45	Asleep	PS34
	03:45	Awake. Provided with tea + light.	PS34
	04·45	Asleep.	"
	05:45	Asleep.	"
	06:45	Asleep.	"
	0730	Review. Further detention authorised. Breakfast provided and light for cigs	PS15
	0845	Awake, wishes to see D/solicitor	PS15
	0915	Duty Sol unavailable	PS15
	0935	D. Sol phoned. Unavailable until 11oo am	PS15
	0947	Phone enquiry from V Bryant. Access to DIP refused.	PS15
	1133	D/Sol (Mr Archer) arrives in custody area. DIP to solicitors for consultation.	PS15
	1145	Back to Cell 5 pending interview	PS15
	1200	Out of cell for interview.	PS15
	1257	Interview concluded, back to cell 7	PS15
	1310	Out of cell. Charged. Bail refused. To MC for 2 pm hearing	PS15

Custody Record No: SOBE/00317/06

Station: Upton

**DOWNSHIRE POLICE
CHARGE SHEET**

CUSTODY RECORD

PERSON CHARGED: John Hanson

ADDRESS 22 Fountain's House, Abbey Estate, Upton

PLACE/DATE OF BIRTH Newton Abbot/12.4.06   OCCUPATION Unemployed

You are charged with the offence shown below.
You do not have to say anything. But it may harm your defence if you do not mention <u>now</u> something which you later rely on in court. Anything you do say may be given in evidence.

OF61019

1) On the 11th July being present with Nicholas Spring Martin Thompson, Sean Baker, Louis Bucknell, Simon Bratt and Anthony Mead used unlawful violence and this conduct (taken together) was such as would cause a person of reasonable firmness present at the scene to fear for his personal safety, contrary to section 2(1) of the Public Order Act 1986.

Reply: None

Officer in case: D.C. Cole
Station: Upton   Date Charged: 12th July 2006

Signature of person charging: Richard Cole

Signature of Officer accepting charge: Peter Maxwell.

Legal Aid forms served by:
Notices served:

Bail: Refused

DOWNSHIRE CONSTABULARY

Full Name John Hanson	Custody No SO3E / 00317 / 06

CONTINUATION OF CHARGES

You are charged with the offence(s) shown below. You do not have to say anything. But it may harm your defence if you do not mention now something which you later rely on in court. Anything you do say may be given in evidence.

2) On 11th July 2006 at Augustian Grove, Abbey Estate, Upton, unlawfully and maliciously caused grievous bodily harm to PC37 Martin Kemp with intent to cause grievous bodily harm, contrary to s. 18 of the Offences Against the Person Act 1861.

3) On the 11th July, attempted to rob Kelly's off-licence, contrary to s. 1(1) of the Criminal Attempts Act 1981.

4) On the 11th July 2006 at Upton Road junction with Lymehurst Road, drove a motor vehicle whist unfit through drink and drugs, contrary to s. 4(1) of the Road Traffic Act 1988.

Continuation Sheet   Yes   No

Reply (if any) ....

.... Time/Date....13 : 10/12 : 7 : 06...

Signed (Person reading charge) ...Richard Cole........... Rank/No....DC 341............

Signed (Custody Officer) ...Peter Maxwell........... Rank/No....DS15............

Officer in Case: Name ...R Cole... Rank/No ...DC431......... Station ...Upton...............

Custody Record copy

DOWNSHIRE CONSTABULARY
CRIME COMPLAINT/REPORT

Upton

M. F. No. ...1263.........

Area ..(Abbey Estate) Sub. Div ...6................. Div...F8................ C. R. No. ..1054.......
(Where Committed)

SEE NOTES FOR GUIDANCE ON COVER

H.Q.'s USE ONLY		

CRIME COMPLAINT

H.Q. use only
H.Q. Classification ....

1. OFFENCE AS REPORTED ....G.B.H.........
2. REF. (TIME AND DATE REPORTED) ..1538........ TO WHOM REPORTED ....
3. NAME AND ADDRESS OF PERSON REPORTING ..Not given. Report... from telephone box on Abbey Estate... TEL. NO. —
4. ACTION TAKEN AND BY WHOM ...Vehicles despatched.......

CRIME REPORT

5. NAME/ADDRESS OF INJURED PERSON ..Martin Kemp PC37... c/o Upton Police Station........ TEL. NO. — AGE ..29.
6. PLACE, TIME, DAY, DATE OF OFFENCE ....1530 Abbey Estate.... ....Augustian Close........ 11 July 2006.....
.... MAP REF: ...C6....
7. INJURY TO VICTIM. FATAL ...... SERIOUS ..✓.. SLIGHT ...... THREATS .... NONE ......
TYPE OF WEAPON USED ......Foot......
8. TYPE OF PREMISES (NOTE 1) ....Abbey Estate......
9. METHOD (NOTE 2) ....
Police officer investigating report of fight (see CR1052) set upon by youths. Initial telephone report supplemented by officers who attended scene and victim who was attacked by N. Spring and then kicked in the face by suspect wearing blue jacket and jeans and white trainers.
10. OFFENCE DETECTED YES/NO ....
11. DESCRIPTION OF SUSPECT OR VEHICLE USED ...Suspect decamped.... ...in blue Vauxhall

STOLEN		RECOVERED	
£	p	£	p

12. PROPERTY STOLEN/DAMAGED (NOTE 3)

.....1 police radio. Value........
...not known..........

TOTAL

13. ENQUIRY TYPE

		NEIGH. WATCH AREA		PRIMARY INVESTIGATOR	
Child Abuse		Yes	✓	Uniform	✓
Domestic Violence		No		C.I.D.	
Other	✓				

<u>R v John Hanson</u>

Draft Defence Statement Issued Pursuant to Section 5 of the Criminal Procedure and Investigations Act 1996

John Hanson: alleged offences of assault and violent disorder

Mr Hanson was not present at the time of the alleged offences. He had drunk a considerable amount of alcohol and had taken Prozac tablets, but to the best of his recollection he was in either the Three Bells or the Coach and Horses public house at the time in question (both are in Bow Avenue, Upton). He was in the company of Miss Victoria Bryant of 13 Onyx Close, Upton.

John Hanson: alleged offence of attempted robbery

Mr Hanson has no recollection of the events constituting this alleged offence. Prior to the time in question he had drunk a considerable amount of alcohol, and had taken Prozac tablets. In the circumstances he was unable to form the intent necessary to commit the offence.

14

Sample advice in *R v Spring, Hanson and others*

IN THE OXTON CROWN COURT

THE QUEEN

v

NICHOLAS SPRING, JOHN HANSON and OTHERS

ADVICE ON EVIDENCE

Introduction

1. I am asked to advise John Hanson and (if there is no conflict of interest) Nicholas Spring on evidence, plea and possible sentence. Both are charged with violent disorder and causing grievous bodily harm with intent to resist the arrest of Mr Spring. Mr Hanson faces additional charges of attempted robbery and driving while unfit through drink or drugs.

The alleged offences

2. The charges of violent disorder and assault arise from an incident on the Abbey Estate, in which a police officer, PC Kemp, sustained a number of quite serious injuries. The prosecution case is that after the officer had attempted to mediate between Mr Spring and his girlfriend, he was punched by Mr Spring. While he was in the process of arresting Mr Spring, PC Kemp was set upon by a group of young men and was repeatedly kicked by his assailants. The crowd dispersed when a number of other officers arrived and arrested several of the participants, including Mr Spring.

3. As far as the charge of attempted robbery is concerned, this arises from an incident at an off-licence in which a man burst in, pulled his jacket over his face and demanded that the owner open the till and give him money. The would-be robber was frustrated by the entry of the owner's brother, whom he punched before escaping. No weapon was involved. Mr Hanson was arrested while he was in a car about an hour later, apparently on the basis that he and the car answered the description given by the witnesses at the off-licence.

Separate representation

4. Those instructing me have asked whether there is a conflict of interest between Mr Spring and Mr Hanson, such that two counsel may be required. My view is that there is such a conflict of interest. In his interview, Mr Spring states that Mr Hanson was present during the Abbey Estate incident and played an active part in kicking PC Kemp, whereas Mr Hanson has no recollection of being there, and may in fact have an alibi. Accordingly, my advice is that separate representation is required, and in accordance with the wishes of those instructing me, the remainder of this advice relates to Mr Hanson alone.

Severance of the indictment

5.   I turn next to the indictment. It would seem to be in Mr Hanson's interests for the charges of attempted robbery and driving while unfit to be separated from those arising from the attack on PC Kemp. The counts in question do not appear to arise from the same facts, nor are they part of a series of offences of the same or similar character. They do not, therefore, meet the requirement of the Indictment Rules 1971, r 9. I would advise that an application to sever Counts 3 and 4 from the indictment be made at the Plea and Directions Hearing.

The strength of the case: assault and violent disorder

6.   As far as the counts of violent disorder and causing grievous bodily harm are concerned, Mr Hanson's primary defence appears to be that of alibi. There is some doubt about this, in that his recollection of the events of the afternoon is unclear, and there is no statement as yet from Vicky Bryant or any of the others who may have been present in the various public houses in question that afternoon. It follows that those instructing me should as a matter of urgency take statements from these potential alibi witnesses. In doing so, of course, such times as the witnesses can recollect will be crucial, together with any reasons they might have for remembering dates and times. Those instructing me will no doubt be aware of the provisions of s 6A of the Criminal Procedure and Investigations Act 1996, which were inserted by s 33(2) of the Criminal Justice Act 2003, with effect from 4 April 2005. The defence statement must include any particular defences which the defendant relies on, the matters of fact upon which he takes issue with the prosecution, and any points of law and authorities relied upon. The date of birth of any alibi witnesses must be given. As has always been the case, where the name or address of the alibi witness in question is not known, information should be given to assist in identifying and finding the witness. Once the process of taking statements from the potential alibi witnesses has been completed, it will be necessary to update the defence statement. If so instructed, I would be prepared to undertake this task.

7.   Mr Hanson's possible defence of alibi throws into question the strength of the prosecution's identifying evidence. The evidence as to Mr Hanson's presence depends largely on what PC Kemp says about 'Man 2', and the consistency between the description of that man and Mr Hanson on arrest. When PC Kemp's statement of the man who assaulted him is compared with those of PC Keith of Mr Hanson on arrest and Mr Hanson's description of himself in interview, it is apparent that there are a number of similar features, but also a number of discrepancies. To this should be added the statement of Nuala Carroll that 'I also think I recognised John Hanson in the crowd that had gathered round'. There is also the fact that the man in the brown jacket (who is apparently, on the prosecution's case, Mr Hanson) drove off in a blue Cavalier — the same colour and make of car as Mr Hanson was driving when he was arrested (see PC Keith's statement).

8.   Clearly a schedule of the various descriptions would be a useful working document for trial, but for the present suffice it to say that the identification of Mr Hanson as a participant in the assault is weak. In the light of this, it is astonishing that no identification procedure in accordance with PACE Code D was held, and the police failure to hold one can clearly be raised at trial in order to underline the weakness of the evidence of Mr Hanson's presence. Incidentally, it appears from Mr Spring's interview that PC Kemp knew Mr Hanson, and was responsible for his conviction on an earlier offence. The facts surrounding this allegation need to be ascertained from Mr Hanson. If it is true, it means that PC Kemp's failure to mention that he recognised 'Man 2' means that it is very unlikely that it was Mr Hanson.

9.   The effect of Mr Hanson's interview also needs to be considered. The fact that he refused to answer questions relating to the assault could potentially lead to inferences which might strengthen the case against him. In order to confirm this, it is necessary to know whether he was cautioned prior to interview about the effect of the refusal to mention matters which he might later wish to make use of in his defence. For this and other reasons, I need to listen to the tape of interview.

10.   As those instructing are aware, under the Criminal Justice Act 2003, s 101(1)(d) a defendant's character may be admitted as part of the prosecution case where it is relevant to an important matter in issue between the prosecution and the defence. I note that Mr Hanson has a number of previous convictions for offences involving violence and deception which may be capable of establishing a propensity to commit offences of violence and/or a propensity to be untruthful respectively. Any occasions on which Mr Hanson has been disbelieved at trial by a court or a jury may also be taken into account in determining whether he has a propensity for untruthfulness. The prosecution have not applied to adduce Mr Hanson's character at this stage. However, if I am provided with the details of his previous convictions, I will be able to give Mr Hanson some preliminary advice about the likely outcome and of any such application and the effect that the introduction of such evidence would have on the trial. With regard to the attempted robbery and the driving charge Mr Hanson has no previous convictions for such offences but the prosecution may still wish to adduce evidence of his bad character to the extent that it is capable of showing a propensity to be untruthful.

The strength of the case: attempted robbery

11.   As far as the attempted robbery is concerned, there are substantial gaps in the evidence which need to be filled before Mr Hanson can be properly advised. In particular, according to Mr Hanson's proof of evidence, there appears to be an in-store video on which he is alleged to have appeared. His further instructions on this point need to be obtained, so that I can assess its likely evidential weight. Again, there is the failure to hold an identification procedure, which means that, in the absence of an admissible video, the prosecution will find it difficult to prove that it was Mr Hanson who attempted the robbery.

12.   In addition, there is the question of the words which Mr Hanson is alleged to have uttered when arrested: 'I only tried to rob the place'. Its admissibility ought to be challenged, both under s 76 of the Police and Criminal Evidence Act 1984 (reliability) and s 78 (fairness). It is also remarkable that the custody record entry for 2110 hours states that these words were uttered on arrest. Yet Mr Hanson had been arrested shortly after 1930 hours by PC Keith; and was booked in by PS Waller at 1945 hours. This anomaly needs explanation at the least, and is likely to undermine the admission it contains, even if the judge rules that it is admissible.

13.   Leaving aside the question of whether Mr Hanson was involved in the incident at the off-licence, there is the question of whether he had the capacity to form the necessary intent. In his proof of evidence, he raises points relating to his state of mind. In my view it is necessary to obtain expert evidence on the likely effect of the combination of Prozac and alcohol upon his mental state.

The driving charge

14.   The driving charge is stated to have been added to the indictment under s 40 of the Criminal Justice Act 1988. In fact, it cannot have been added under that provision, since 'driving while unfit through drink or drugs' is not one of the charges which appears in s 40. That means that the charge can only have been dealt with at the Crown Court if it was

sent under s 51(5) of the Crime and Disorder Act 1998. Sight of the notice listing the offences for which Mr Hanson and Mr Spring were sent for trial will settle this question definitively. If the charge was committed by the magistrates under that provision, then it can only be dealt with if Mr Hanson is convicted of one of the indictable offences presently on the indictment, the court is satisfied that the summary offence is related to that offence and he pleads guilty to the driving whilst unfit charge. If it was not sent to the Crown Court under s 51 by the magistrates, then it cannot in any event be dealt with.

Sentence

15.   As far as sentence is concerned, if convicted Mr Hanson faces a custodial sentence on each of the violent disorder, assault and attempted robbery charges. It is likely that the first two would together attract a sentence of two to three years' imprisonment, given that serious injuries were caused to a policeman by kicking him while he was on the ground, and while the assailant was acting as part of a group. In coming to this conclusion, I have taken into account Mr Hanson's substantial record, which includes several offences of violence. As far as the attempted robbery is concerned, there is likely to be a consecutive sentence since the offence was entirely separate. Given the embryonic and disorganised nature of the offence, however, and the fact that no weapon was involved, the sentence may be no more than 18 months, despite the fact that one of the victims was punched. These estimates are based on conviction after trial. A substantial discount of perhaps as much as a third would be likely in the event of an early plea of guilty.

Action to be taken

16.   It will be apparent from the points made above that there are a number of actions which I advise my instructing solicitors to take. In particular, I would ask that:

(a) statements be taken from Vicky Bryant and anyone else who may be able to establish Mr Hanson's presence in the various public houses in question on the afternoon in question;

(b) the defence statement be updated to deal with the additional matters set out in paragraph 6, once these have been clarified;

(c) an early conference be arranged in order to obtain Mr Hanson's instructions on various of the matters canvassed above, and advise him more fully;

(d) the CPS be asked for the schedule of unused material, a copy of Mr Hanson's tape of interview, summaries of the interviews of the co-accused, copies of the criminal records of the co-accused and any witnesses, the crime report sheets and any relevant radio/telephone messages;

(e) a map of the estate be agreed;

(f) a schedule of the descriptions of the co-accused put forward by the various witnesses be prepared for use as a working document by the defence at trial;

(g) expert evidence be sought as to the effect of combining Prozac and alcohol in the way in which Mr Hanson did.

17.   The case is not yet in a state where the Plea and Case Management Hearing Questionnaire can be completed, but that position should be reached once a conference with Mr Hanson has been held. The arrangement of a conference is therefore a matter of urgency, given that the CPS must be notified of the prosecution witnesses whose presence will be required within the next few days. At the PCMH, it will also be necessary for the defence to notify the points of law and admissibility canvassed above, and those relating to the defendant's state of mind.

Summary

18. In summary, my advice is that there is a conflict of interest between Mr Hanson and Mr Spring, such that they should be represented by separate counsel at trial. As far as Mr Hanson is concerned, his instructions suggest a plea of not guilty on all counts. There are defects and discrepancies in the evidence against him, such that his chances of an acquittal on the violent disorder and assault charges are good. Until more information has been received regarding the attempted robbery, it is difficult to evaluate his chances on that count. There are a number of steps which need to be taken by instructing solicitors in the next few days to prepare for trial, and these are set out in paragraph 16.

CHARLES STRYVER

2 Atkin Building
London WC1

INDEX

A

abuse of process 21
  burden and standard of proof 22, 25
  delay 21–2
  destroying evidence 23–4
  entrapment 23
  failing to obtain evidence 23–4
  failure to honour undertaking 22–3
  going back on promise 22–3
  losing evidence 23–4
  magistrates' court 25
  manipulation of procedure 24
  Practice Direction 25–6
  procedure 25–6
  staying proceedings 21–2
  time of application 25
accused
  sample statement 153
advice on evidence 115–16, 164–7
affray 59–60
aggravated trespass 71–2
alarm 61–2
  intentional 61
  to person in dwelling 75–6
antecedents 149–52
appreciation
  margin of 34
assemblies
  demonstrating in designated area 77
  failure to comply with conditions 68
  trespassory 72–3
Assets Recovery Agency 54

B

banning orders 67
bomb hoaxes 69

C

campers
  unauthorised 73–4
careless driving 88–90
  causing death when under influence 101
  charging standard and 89
  procedure 90
  punishment 90
case listing arrangements 125
case preparation
  advice on evidence 115–16, 164–7
  closing speech 117
  comparing notes 118

  cross-examination 117
  examination in chief 118
  preparing for conference 116–17
  preparing for trial 117–18
  sample brief 119–63
  submissions 117
charge sheet
  sample 160–1
collective trespass 69–74
computer material
  seizure 18
confiscation orders
  amount of order 51–2
  appeals by prosecution 56
  asset dissipation 54–5
  criminal conduct 49, 50
  criminal lifestyle 49, 52–3
  enforcement 54–5
  other sentences and 54
  postponement 55
  procedure 48–50
  proceeds of crime 48–57
  prosecutor's statement 53–4
  reconsideration 55–6
  recoverable amount 51–2
  restraint orders and 54–5
  statements of information 53–4
  statutory assumptions 52–3
  time for payment 54
  valuation of property 51
Criminal Damage Act (1971)
  search with warrant 12
custody record
  sample 154–9
cycling under influence 102

D

dangerous driving 82–8
  aggravating features 87–8
  alternative verdict 86
  evidence 83–4
  mitigating features 88
  notice of intended prosecution 84–6
  punishment 87
  sentencing guidelines 87–8
dangerous drugs
  being concerned in supply 41
  confiscation orders *see* **confiscation orders**
  controlled drugs 39
  defences 44–5
  Drugs Act (2005) 43, 48
  enforcement 46–8

expert evidence 42, 44
export 39–40
forfeiture 48
import 39–40
Misuse of Drugs Act (1971) 39–45, 46
occupiers of premises 45
offences 39–44
offer to supply 40, 41
permitted use 46
possession 41–2
possession with intent to supply 41
'prescribed amount' 43
production 40
search and seizure 46
sentencing guidelines 46–8
supply 40–1
    being concerned in 41
    offer to supply 40, 41
    possession with intent to 41
dangerous weapons
other offences 81
defence statement
sample 163
delay
abuse of process 21–2
childhood sexual abuse 22
**demonstrating in designation area without
    authorisation** 77
discrimination
European Convention on Human Rights 31
disorder
violent 59
see also **public order offences**
disqualification from driving
discretionary 110
ending 110
obligatory 109
    exceptional hardship 110
penalty points 109–10
retest order 111
distress 61–2
intentional 61
to person in dwelling 75–6
drink driving offences
above prescribed limit 94–5
breath tests 96–7
causing death when under influence 101
cycling under influence 102
failure to give permission for test 100–1
failure to provide specimen
    breath tests 96–7
    failure 99
    hospital patients 100
    reasonable excuse 99–100
    specimens 97–8
hip-flask defence 95
laced drinks 96, 111
no likelihood of driving 95
prescribed limits 92–3
procedure 102
sentence 102
specimen tests 92–3
when unfit 93–4
driving *see* **drink driving offences; road traffic offences**
drugs
causing death when under influence 101
cycling under influence 102
see also **dangerous drugs**

E
emergency driving 111
entrapment 23
European Convention on Human Rights
admissibility requirements 32
approach of court 33–4
Court 33–4
discrimination 31
equality of arms 30
exhausting domestic remedies 32
fair and public hearing 29–30
freedom of expression 31
hearing 33
Human Rights Act (1998) 27
individual petition 28
inhuman treatments 28
jury bias 30
liberty and security of person 28–9
margin of appreciation 34
procedure 32–3
proportionality 34
reporting cases 34
settlement 33
time limit 32–3
torture 28
UK law status 27–8
war or public emergencies 31–2
evidence
abuse of process 23–4
advice on 115–16, 164–7
expert 42, 44
sample records of taped interviews 145–8
expert evidence 42, 44

F
failure to give permission for test 100–1
failure to provide specimen
breath tests 96–7
failure 99
hospital patients 100
reasonable excuse 99–100
specimens 97–8
failure to stop/failure to report 91
football offences 66–7
banning orders 67
forfeiture
dangerous drugs 48
freedom of expression
European Convention on Human Rights 31

H
harassment 61–2, 74–6
intentional 61
to person in dwelling 75–6
hip-flask defence 95
human rights
delay as abuse of process 21–2
see also **European Convention on Human Rights**
Human Rights Act (1998) 27

I
indictment
sample 126
instructions to counsel 120–1

J

jury
    bias 30

L

laced drinks 96, 111
land *see* trespass
law reports 6
legal advice
    right to 30–1
legal privilege
    protected material 15

M

margin of appreciation 34
Misuse of Drugs Act (1971) 39–45
    search and seizure 46
    search with warrant 12
    search without warrant 10

N

nuisance on land 69–74

O

offences *see individual offence eg* Road traffic
        offences
offensive weapons
    Criminal Justice Act (1988) 80–1
    dangerous weapons 81
    has with him 78
    lawful authority 79–80
    national dress defence 80, 81
    offensive weapon 79
    Prevention of Crime Act (1953) 78–80
    public place 78, 80
    reasonable excuse 79–80
    religious reasons defence 80, 81
    school premises 81
    use at work defence 81

P

periodicals 6–7
    specialist journals 7
    updating 7
practitioner works 6
privilege
    protected material *see* protected material
proceeds of crime
    case law 56
    confiscation orders *see* confiscation orders
    criminal lifestyle 49, 52–3
    seizure 17
    useful websites 56
processions
    contravening prohibition 68
    failure to comply with conditions 68
    failure to give notice 67–8
proportionality 34
protected material
    excluded material 11, 15–16
    legal privilege 15
    special procedure material 11, 16, 17

special warrants 16–17
    see also seizure
public assemblies
    failure to comply with conditions 68
public order offences
    affray 59–60
    aggravated trespass 71–2
    alarm 61–2, 75–6
        intentional 61
    assemblies 68
    bomb hoaxes 69
    demonstrating in designated area 77
    distress 61–2, 75–6
    fear or provocation of violence 60–1
    football 66–7
    harassment 61–2, 74–6
        intentional 61
    harassment, alarm or distress to person in dwelling 75–6
    processions 67–8
    racial hatred
        broadcasting 65
        cable programmes 65
        possession of inflammatory material 65–6
        public performance 64
        publishing or distributing written material 63–4
        recordings 64–5
        stirring up 63–6
        use of words, behaviour or display of written material 63
    racially aggravated 62–3
    raves 70–1
    religiously aggravated 62–3
    riot 58–9
    sports 66–7
    trespass 69–70
    trespassing on designated site 76
    trespassory assemblies 72–3
    unauthorised campers 73–4
    violent disorder 59

R

racial hatred
    broadcasting 65
    cable programmes 65
    possession of inflammatory material 65–6
    public performance 64
    publishing or distributing written material 63–4
    recordings 64–5
    stirring up 63–6
    use of words, behaviour or display of written material 63
racially aggravated public order offences 62–3
raves 70–1
religiously aggravated public order offences 62–3
riot 58–9
road traffic offences
    careless driving 88–90
        procedure 90
        punishment 90
    charging standard 83–4, 89
    dangerous driving 82–8
        aggravating features 87–8
        alternative verdict 86
        evidence 83–4
        mitigating features 88
        notice of intended prosecution 84–6
        punishment 87
        sentencing guidelines 87–8
    disqualification

discretionary 110
ending 110
exceptional hardship 110
obligatory 109
penalty points 109–10
probationary period 110
retest order 111
drink driving *see* **drink driving offences**
endorsement
expiry 103
penalty points 104–8, 109–10
production of licence 103
failing to stop/failing to report 91
penalty points
disqualification 109–10
endorsement 104–8
probationary period 110
retest order 111
special reasons
emergency driving 111
laced drinks 111

S

sample brief 119–63
accused's statement 153
antecedents 149–52
case listing arrangements 125
charge sheet 160–1
crime report 162
custody record 154–9
indictment 126
instructions to counsel 120–1
pleas and directions hearing 122–4
records of taped interviews 145–8
witness statements 127–44
search
breach of rules consequences 20
Misuse of Drugs Act (1971) 10, 12, 46
with warrant
Criminal Damage Act (1971) 12
Misuse of Drugs Act (1971) 12
other statutory powers 12
PACE 10–12
powers 10–12
Theft Act (1968) 12
without warrant
arrest warrant and 8–9
Misuse of Drugs Act (1971) 10
other statutory powers 10
PACE 8–10
powers 8–10
premises of arrested person 9–10
search warrants
All Premises Warrant 11
procedure 13–15
protected material
excluded material 11, 15–16

legal privilege 15
special procedure material 11, 16, 17
special warrants 11, 16–17
Specified Premises Warrant 11
seizure
computer material 18
copies 18
Criminal Justice and Police Act
(2001) 18–20
Misuse of Drugs Act (1971) 46
PACE 18, 20
Proceeds of Crime Act (2002) 17
sources
electronic source 5
law reports 6
paper sources 5
periodicals 6–7
practitioner works 6
primary 5–6
secondary sources 6–7
specialist journals 7
statutory materials 5–6
special procedure material 11, 16, 17
sporting offences
alcohol 66–7
football 66–7
statutory materials 5–6
stirring up racial hatred *see* **racial hatred**

T

Theft Act (1968)
search with warrant 12
trespass
aggravated 71–2
collective 69–74
on designated site 76
nuisance on land 69–74
powers regarding 69–70
raves 70–1
trespassory assemblies 72–3
unauthorised campers 73–4
trespassory assemblies 72–3

V

violence
fear or provocation of 60–1
intentional harassment, alarm or distress 61
violent disorder 59

W

weapons
offensive *see* **offensive weapons**
witnesses
experts 42, 44
sample witness statements 127–4

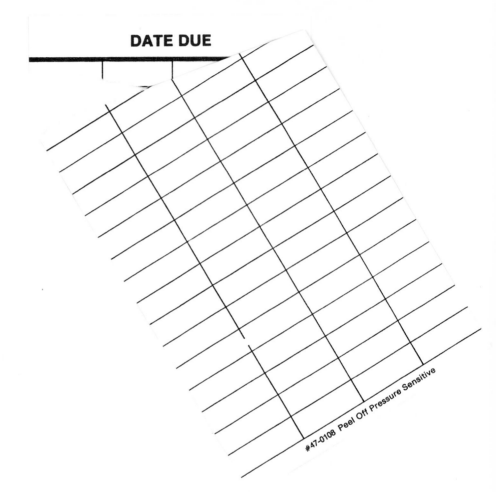

DATE DUE

#47-0108 Peel Off Pressure Sensitive